"For anyone teaching online—novice or seasoned—*Small Teaching Online* is a must-read! Darby expertly combines educational research and her expertise as an instructional designer to suggest practical solutions to challenges faced in the online environment in bite-sized chunks that don't overwhelm."

—Mel Young, Teaching and Learning Innovation Hub, Cambrian College, Blogger, disruptivepedagogy.ca

"Darby and Lang extend the powerful *Small Teaching* paradigm successfully to the online teaching and learning environment. Faculty who are new to online teaching are especially well-served with this superb introduction to research-based incremental strategies."

—Victoria Mondelli, Founding Director, Teaching for Learning Center, University of Missouri

An unexpected delight! Flower brightens the literature she cites with her experiences and experiments in her own online classes—what she tried, what worked well and what didn't, and how she improved on less-than-perfect results. You feel like you're getting to know her and finding a new friend and mentor.

—Linda B. Nilson, Director Emeritus, Office of Teaching Effectiveness and Innovation, Clemson University

Any professor would find this book useful, whether you teach entirely online, in a flipped classroom, or just want your course website to be more than a folder of readings. Flower Darby mixes her rich experience as a teacher and learner with a careful review of the most current literature to bring us a work that's deep with context and immediately applicable.

— Joseph M. Murphy, Director of the Center for Innovative Pedagogy, Kenyon College.

In his book *Small Teaching: Everyday Lessons from the Science of Learning*, Jim Lang provided instructors with practical, simple, and easy strategies for maximizing student learning and success. Flower Darby and Lang now offer *Small Teaching Online: Applying Learning Science in Online Classes*, an equally important book for those who strive to create engaged learning experiences for students in an online environment. This will be really helpful to many instructors, whether teaching online or face-to-face or in a hybrid format. Indeed, anyone who cares about student learning and student success in the 21st century would benefit from implementing the lessons presented in this book.

—Dr. Jerry Daday, Executive Associate Dean, Institute for Engaged Learning, Professor of Sociology, IUPUI

The work of teaching is hard. Coupled with the often-uncharted paths involved in teaching online, it can feel downright discouraging. Enter *Small Teaching Online*. It is a practical guide to help us design our online classes to support learning, be more experimental in our pedagogy, give effective feedback, help students persist, and create more authentic connections. This book helps us see how we can continue to iterate one small step at a time toward excellence in online teaching.

—Bonni Stachowiak, director, Institute for Faculty Development, Vanguard University; host, Teaching in Higher Ed podcast

"What faculty members teaching online need most of all are research-based, but very practical, strategies they can use in their online learning environments tomorrow. Darby and Lang's book, chocked full of great ideas that faculty can use right away, is just the resource we have all been looking for."

—Larry Gallagher, former Director of Faculty Professional Development at Northern Arizona University

Small Teaching Online

Small Teaching Online

Applying Learning Science in Online Classes

Flower Darby
James M. Lang

JB JOSSEY-BASS™
A Wiley Brand

For Emerald, Piccadilly, and Britannia, for whom I learned to teach online so I could be home when they were small.

Contents

About the Authors   xi

Acknowledgments   xiii

Introduction: Small Teaching Online   xv

Part I   Designing for Learning

1   Surfacing Backward Design   5

2   Guiding Learning Through Engagement   27

3   Using Media and Technology Tools   47

Part II   Teaching Humans

4   Building Community   75

5   Giving Feedback   107

6   Fostering Student Persistence and Success   131

Part III   Motivating Online Students (and Instructors)

7   Creating Autonomy   157

8   Making Connections   179

9   Developing as an Online Instructor   199

Conclusion: Finding Inspiration   **221**

References   **227**

Index   **237**

About the Authors

Flower Darby is a senior instructional designer and adjunct faculty member at Northern Arizona University, where she has taught for over 22 years. She is also adjunct online faculty for Estrella Mountain Community College. She's taught over 75 online classes to more than 2,000 online students. Darby also teaches in-person and blended courses in a range of subjects: English literature, composition, technology, education, dance, and fitness. She regularly writes and presents nationally and internationally on excellence in teaching and learning design. She is zealous in her promotion of student success through effective classroom practice, whether the classroom is physical or online. Her bachelor's and master's degrees are from Northern Arizona University in English literature.

James M. Lang is a professor of English and the director of the D'Amour Center for Teaching Excellence at Assumption College in Worcester, Massachusetts. He is the author of five books, the most recent of which are *Small Teaching: Everyday Lessons from the Science of Learning* (Jossey-Bass, 2016), *Cheating Lessons: Learning from Academic Dishonesty* (Harvard University Press, 2013), and *On Course: A Week-by-Week Guide to Your First Semester of College Teaching* (Harvard UP, 2008). Lang writes a monthly column on teaching and learning for *The Chronicle of Higher Education*; his work has been appearing in the *Chronicle* since 1999. His book reviews and public scholarship on higher education have appeared in a wide variety of newspapers and magazines, including the *Boston Globe, Chicago Tribune*, and *Time*.

Lang edits a new series of books on teaching and learning in higher education for West Virginia University Press; he co-edited the second book in the series, *Teaching the Literature Survey Course: New Strategies for College Faculty* (2018). He has conducted workshops on teaching for faculty at more than a hundred colleges or universities in the United States and abroad, and consulted for the United Nations on the development of teaching materials in ethics and integrity for college faculty. In September 2016 he received a Fulbright Specialist grant to work with three universities in Colombia on the creation of a MOOC (massive open online course) on teaching and learning in STEM (science, technology, engineering, and math) education. He has a BA in English and Philosophy from the University of Notre Dame, an MA in English from St. Louis University, and a PhD in English from Northwestern University.

Acknowledgments

To say that I'm grateful to Jim Lang is an understatement of epic proportions. This book would literally not exist if it weren't for his original book, *Small Teaching*. Further, you would not be reading this book if not for Jim's willingness to take a chance on a complete stranger, his openness to working with me, an unknown. Jim has been unfailingly patient as he guided me, a new author, through this process. Through the journey, Jim has modeled courage, wisdom, generosity, grace, and kindness. Thank you, Jim, for the opportunity to work with and learn from you. Sincerely.

My colleague and friend Wally Nolan is next on my list of people who were essential to the creation of this book. All of my colleagues at the Northern Arizona University e-Learning Center have helped me develop as a passionate advocate of excellent online course design and teaching practice, but Wally Angel, as he is affectionately known around here, has had a special, selfless influence on who I am as a professional and what came to be in this book. Thanks, Wall, and happy trails to you.

Many other friends and colleagues contributed in countless ways to the knowledge and approaches represented in this book, or have otherwise supported me personally and professionally. Sirscha Nicholl, Melissa Schoeffel, K. Laurie Dickson, Stephanie McCarthy, Larry MacPhee, Peggy Gregory, Jim Nichols, Amy Nichols, Sharon Gorman, John Doherty, Wayne Field, Erin Shelley, Betsy Buford, Jerry Gile, Michelle Miller, Larry Gallagher, Anne Scott, Sharon Crawford … too many to name. For all of these (and others), I'm thankful.

Pete Gaughan provided invaluable editorial advice; Amy Fandrei and Roger Hunt on the Wiley team were of immense practical assistance; our reader reviewers provided numerous helpful suggestions. Thank you all.

Two more very special people deserve recognition: my parents, Patrick and Lesley Hesselmann, who have always only ever supported me, encouraged me to take on whatever goal, whatever challenge was before me, who have always known, and have always told me so, that I could do whatever I set my mind on doing. Thanks, truly. I so very much appreciate your ongoing support.

I would be remiss if I neglected to give a quick shout-out to my kind and generous mother-in-law, Janis Flynn, for doing so much to enable my chaos. You know I couldn't do what I do without your help. I appreciate you!

And of course, finally, Tim, my husband, to whom you will see multiple references in this book because of how involved he has been in the process. Tim, who tirelessly engaged in hours and hours of discussion of the concepts in this book, who helped to generate the most insightful ideas you will find here, who is the best instructional designer I know, who's the wisest and most patient faculty support professional, and who's an ideal case study of what today's online students are experiencing since he himself is halfway through an online graduate program. Not to mention Tim's incredible support at home, taking on the vast majority of parenting and domestic duties while I wrote, never complaining, just quietly serving the needs of the family and home, freeing me up to do this work. Though it's a cliché, it rings true: Words can't express my gratitude. So I'll conclude with a simple, yet inadequate, thank you. For everything.

Flower Darby
Flagstaff, AZ

Introduction: Small Teaching Online

T hink back to when you were a brand-new college student. Imagine it's the first day of the fall term. You are excited, nervous, maybe even a bit overwhelmed at the thought of your class schedule. You're not sure what to expect or whether you have what it takes to succeed.

Your printed schedule lists the building number, but since you are new to this college, you don't know which buildings are where. You consult your creased campus map, looking for landmarks, building names – anything to help you determine whether you are still going the right way. You consider asking someone for directions, but everyone around you seems sure of themselves and of where they are going. Clearly you're the only person on this campus who doesn't know how to get to class.

Suddenly, your building appears as you round the next corner. Relieved, with little time to spare, you stride up to the door and give it a good, strong pull. The door doesn't budge. Now you're frustrated as well as stressed. Is this college preventing students from getting to class? In a last ditch effort, you walk around the perimeter of the building looking for other ways to enter. Almost predictably, the last door you try opens. At last you're inside.

You find the classroom listed on the schedule, but what you see inside only adds to your mounting despair. Almost predictably, the lights are out and no one is in the room. The desks are tumbled crazily on top of each other with no rhyme or reason. It's not clear where you're supposed to sit or what you're supposed to do. Now you're getting annoyed. Having been so keyed up about the first day of class, this is more than anticlimactic. It's defeating. Demotivating. Downright obstructive.

You muster up a renewed sense of determination, flip the light switch, and spot a pile of papers on a table in one corner of the room. Thinking maybe there are instructions, or some notice of a room change, you walk over and take a small packet. It's the class syllabus, just left there for students to find and read on their own.

Skimming through the pages, you glimpse information about the textbook, assignments, and testing dates, but not much else. You'd like to get a better sense of what this class will be like, what your instructor will be like, but there's not much to go on. Disheartened, you trudge out the door. Is this class even happening? If so, how are you supposed to learn anything when so many barriers have been raised, when there is so little support from anyone?

THE CHALLENGE OF ONLINE COURSES

The scene we've painted here seems so unlikely that it might be difficult to imagine it actually happening in the real world. We all know from experience that the first day of a college semester buzzes with excitement, energy, and nervous tension. Instructors and students gather in classrooms to conduct a ritualized first-day dance of putting faces to names, reviewing the syllabus and class expectations, forming impressions of each other, and making initial connections.

But the bleak scenario we've presented here represents an all-too-common version of what our online students experience. If anything, students in online classes can be even more keyed up than they are in our onsite classes, especially since so many of them are returning to school after an absence. And that's not the only cause of anxiety: Today's students face additional challenges based solely on their circumstances. What we've typically thought of as being a 'non-traditional' student is quickly becoming the new normal, according to Alexandria Walton Radford, head of RTI International, a think tank in North Carolina. In a September 2018 interview with Elissa Nadworny of National Public Radio, Radford stated that almost three-quarters of today's college students have one of the following characteristics: they've delayed enrollment in higher education, they have a child or other dependent, they're enrolled in school part-time, they work full-time, or they are a single caregiver. About a third of today's students have two or three of these challenging circumstances to manage (Nadworny and Depenbrock, 2018).

These factors are the very reason many of our online students choose to take college classes online. They need a flexible option that accommodates their work and family obligations. But juggling so many concerns adds to the uncertainty of taking an online class. It's easy to become overwhelmed.

For example, many new online students struggle even to find the log-in page for the Learning Management System (LMS). If they find the site, they might not know their user ID and password. If they find and call the help desk number, they may be greeted by an overworked, stressed-out employee who might not provide patient and friendly support. All of this effort is required just to get in the door of an online program. Even after they successfully log in to the LMS, newer students may not know how to get into the virtual classroom. It is not necessarily self-evident that students should click the link or the tile with the often-abbreviated class name and confusing session code.

Once online students finally get into their class, it is frequently unclear what they should do first. When college students walk into a physical classroom, they know the norms and routines. Sociologist Jay Howard, the author of *Discussion in the College Classroom*, points out that students in physical classrooms follow basic behavioral norms that they have internalized from many years of classroom education. They sit in a student desk, face front, and wait for the instructor to come in and begin the class session. "On the first day of class," he writes, "have you ever arrived in your assigned room to find a student seated at the professor's desk or standing behind the podium ready to lead the class session?" (Howard, 2015, p. 9). If you haven't, it's because your students are well familiarized to the norms of classroom education. They govern where students sit, how they interact with you and one another, and many other aspects of the learning experience.

Many of these familiar educational norms do not operate in an online class. Instructors and other students are not physically present to help guide or shape an online student's behavior. They're being guided by words on a screen instead of by the fully embodied humans they're used to seeing in their courses. They might not be aware of how to start engaging with the course content. If they're new to taking online classes, they might stumble over seemingly simple tasks like posting to a discussion board or taking an online quiz or checking their status in the gradebook – and there's no one there in real-time to ask for help.

Because online courses do not provide these kinds of basic social supports, we can hardly blame our online students for what might look to us like poor, disengaged performance. We do little to set them up for success even from the very first point of access. Just as in our imaginary first-day scenario, the system barriers and the lack of social support frustrates, demotivates, and discourages our online learners. Many students are tempted to give up altogether.

And, quite frankly, so are many faculty.

THE GROWTH OF ONLINE LEARNING

Online courses are not going away. *Grade Increase: Tracking Distance Education in the United States* reported that distance enrollments increased for the fourteenth year in a row, with 6.3 million students taking at least one online course, at a rate higher than enrollments have grown for the past several years (Seaman, Allen, and Seaman, 2018). The authors further indicate that "there are now fewer students studying on campus than at any point since 2012" (p. 26). Our students are moving away from traditional on-campus classes and moving toward online classes.

This growth of online courses poses a new challenge for higher education: preparing faculty to teach effectively in this format. A quick Google search on this topic reveals a wealth of resources to help faculty learn to teach online. This highlights the *newness* of online teaching. Many online instructors have not taken many online classes as students. This is certain to change over time. But at this point, most faculty teaching online have not experienced "the apprenticeship of observation," a phrase first coined in 1975 by Dan Lortie. The 2002 second edition of his book *Schoolteacher* describes the unique experience found in the teaching profession (Lortie, 2002, p. 61). Lortie argues that new teachers entering physical classrooms have had decades of experience observing professionals on the job. These observations typically form the basis of our approach to teaching, especially considering the dearth of faculty preparation programs for teaching in general.

But most of us don't bring any prior experience with online classes. We can't fall back on the apprenticeship of observation. "Distance educators lack a model or benchmark for online teaching because many of them have not taken online courses as students," note a team of researchers in a recent article on how faculty learn to teach online (Schmidt, Tschida, and Hodge, 2016). If faculty have had experience as online students, it's limited, not like the years of experience they've typically had as students in a physical classroom. This is one reason why we urgently need programs to prepare faculty to be successful in their online teaching.

An October 2018 report from Hanover Research, *Best Practices in Online Faculty Development*, states that institutions should have a focused approach for professional development for online faculty. Just such a concentrated effort is underway at Northern Arizona University (NAU). Over the past several months we have engaged in an extensive review of institutional expectations of online faculty and corresponding support models as we seek to equip our faculty to teach online. Our leadership recognizes that providing this additional support would help many faculty to be more successful in online classes – but online faculty at other institutions might not find themselves in such a supportive environment, and might feel unprepared for their work as online teachers.

One way to address this lack of preparation is to think critically about how we define effective teaching and what makes a good class. In her 2019 book *Thrive Online: A New Approach for College Educators*, Shannon Riggs observes that the format in which a class takes place does not, by default, determine its quality:

> [G]ood teaching does not spring naturally from a particular modality. A good course on campus is not good because of the location or traditional brick-and-mortar ambiance. Likewise, a weak online course is not weak because it is delivered via the internet. Good teaching in any learning environment requires careful attention to course design and facilitation. (Riggs, 2019, p. 4)

Helping faculty prepare to design and teach effective – no, excellent – online courses can and should be a primary goal of educational developers and institutional leadership. If we want to successfully grow our online programs, and many colleges and universities do, to meet the growing demand for rigorous and engaging online education, we must attend to the all-important foundational step of developing our faculty and helping them thrive in this relatively new learning environment.

If faculty don't feel prepared to thrive in online classes, the same can be said of our students. Online classes are not always the best fit for the diverse range of learners in higher education today. To succeed in online classes, learners must take more responsibility for their learning. This requires self-regulation skills that enable students to motivate themselves, stay on schedule, ensure assignments are completed on time, and more. For many of today's students, these abilities are still developing (Nilson, 2013, p. 1). Our students may enroll in our online class for the flexibility and convenience, but these advantages of online learning can cause problems for students who may not have the self-discipline to enable them to succeed. Too much flexibility can turn out to be not such a good thing.

So what characterizes successful online learners? In a 2015 review of learner characteristics that lead to success in and satisfaction with online classes, Heather Kauffman identified several qualities that may contribute to a student's ability to thrive online. Kauffman's synthesis showed that students who are organized, good at planning, good at managing their time, disciplined, aware of the need to seek help when appropriate, and resilient will fare better in asynchronous online classes (p. 7). No surprise there. Such students are likely to succeed in face-to-face classes, too.

But what about our online students who don't display these attributes? What, if anything, can we do to help them succeed?

THE SMALL TEACHING APPROACH

This book has been written to promote success for both faculty and students by following the premise and principles outlined in the book *Small Teaching: Everyday Lessons from the Science of Learning* (Lang, 2016), and applying them specifically to the context of online teaching and learning. The genesis of this book occurred, in fact, when Flower saw Jim give a presentation on *Small Teaching* at NAU, and approached him immediately afterward with a proposal: "I want to work with you to write a version of this book for online faculty." Jim immediately agreed, because at the conclusion of almost every lecture or workshop he gave, someone always asked: "How can I apply small teaching techniques in my online courses?"

The first and primary premise of *Small Teaching* is an extraordinarily simple one: Paying attention to the small, everyday decisions we make in teaching represents our best route to successful learning for our students, in almost any learning environment we can imagine. Jim developed this theory as a result of observing his children play sports, and noticing that, when small bodies were not really capable of extraordinary feats of physical prowess on the field, successful coaches worked with them on small, fundamental skills that had powerful effects.

This argument has resonated with many faculty, who have reported to Jim in workshops that they have been overwhelmed by pressure from their administration to revamp their teaching and their courses according to whatever the latest new educational fad might be. Making these kinds of significant, wholescale changes to your teaching is a time-consuming and intimidating process and can lead to two unhappy outcomes. First, faculty often find that their first effort to make large changes to their teaching does not go well. This might cause them to retreat immediately to their previous habits and stifle the possibility of future innovation. Second, the prospect of making large changes can seem so intimidating that faculty never bother to start, and instead just continue to default to their current practice. The small teaching approach seeks to effect change by giving faculty small, actionable modifications that they can make without having to overhaul their teaching from the ground up.

Many faculty around the world have seen the wisdom of this approach, but the premise is hardly a new one. To the contrary, you can find variations of this kind of "small" approach to effecting change in the work of many other thinkers and contexts. Aristotle famously argued, for example, that one grandiose virtuous action does not make a person virtuous; we become virtuous by practicing virtue on an everyday basis. A biologist pointed out to Jim, after the book had been published, that evolution creates massive changes to life on this planet through tiny, incremental changes. The popularity of books like Stephen Covey's *The 7 Habits of Highly Effective People*, which point us toward habits rather than grand gestures, demonstrates the appeal of effecting change through small decisions and actions, instead of focusing on major overhauls of behaviors and attitudes that can be difficult to sustain.

But a second important premise underpinned the work of the original *Small Teaching*, and underpins this one as well: We should make our small decisions about teaching based on the best research we have about how humans learn. We have seen an extraordinary growth in that research in recent years. Initially, that work was confined to the laboratories and journals of specialists in the field, but more and more of those learning scientists are translating their findings for higher education faculty. You can find that research in books like *Make It Stick: The Science of Successful Learning* (2014) or *How Humans Learn: The Science and Stories Behind Effective College Teaching* (2018), as well as in websites like http://RetrievalPractice.org or http://LearningScientists.org, both excellent collections of resources and ideas for faculty.

You'll find that kind of research in the original *Small Teaching* as well. In that book, Jim culled nine key learning principles from the research and used them to guide instructors in their work. The principles were divided into three parts. To help students obtain and retain foundational knowledge and skills, he argued for the importance of *prediction, retrieval,* and *interleaving.* To deepen their understanding and foster more highly developed thinking skills, the principles were *connection, self-explanation,* and *practice.*

Motivation and *mindset* were the keys to inspiring students, and were covered in the third section of the book, which finished (as this book does) with a chapter aimed at faculty, designed to help them *expand* their pedagogical knowledge and skill base.

APPLYING *SMALL TEACHING ONLINE* IN MULTIPLE CONTEXTS

Readers will gain the most from their encounter with the small teaching philosophy if they read the original *Small Teaching* and acquaint themselves with these core learning principles, which can help support effective learning in any kind of environment, face-to-face or online. But if you have already read *Small Teaching* (or if you pause here and go read it now), you'll notice a major difference between that book and this one. The chapter topics here do not align precisely with those in the original. You will find all the same learning science principles interwoven throughout this work, but because online teaching has its own special opportunities and challenges, we developed a separate set of principles to guide effective change in online teaching and learning.

Another difference between this book and the original is our reference throughout this text to Universal Design for Learning (UDL) principles. Although many higher education professionals associate UDL with accessibility for students who have documented disabilities, this is a too-limiting view of the reach of this framework, according to Thomas Tobin and Kirsten Behling, authors of *Reach Everyone, Teach Everyone: Universal Design for Learning in Higher Education* (2018). Still, many people think about making online content accessible more often than they think about alternative formats and experiences when teaching in person, so we would be remiss if we neglected this important topic.

As we examine small teaching strategies in multiple areas of online classes, we'll seek to expand our understanding of how UDL principles can benefit a diverse student population. "In addition to respecting the ethnic, gender, socioeconomic, and ability-based diversity on our campuses, we can design courses ... that expand the reach and efficacy of higher education" (Tobin and Behling, 2018, p. 1).

And there are many good reasons for doing so, notably that UDL increases all of our learners' ability to engage with our content and demonstrate their knowledge in ways that they might prefer:

> UDL is a way of thinking about creating the interactions we have with our learners so that they do not have to ask for special treatment, regardless of the types of barriers they may face – time, connectivity, or disability. (Tobin and Behling, 2018, p. 130)

When we reframe our thinking about how UDL can help all our learners engage and succeed, we see the value of the approach in every course design decision we make, whether teaching online or in person. Thankfully, the Plus-One design model presented by these authors aligns perfectly with the *Small Teaching* approach of making small changes in order to enhance student learning and engagement.

With UDL principles undergirding all of our small teaching suggestions, we divided the learning science principles in this book into three sections, just as you will find in the original *Small Teaching*. Part I of the book focuses on designing online courses. Chapter 1, on backward design, presents an approach to course development that applies in both traditional and online courses. But we still encounter new and experienced faculty who have not come across this idea, so we wanted to begin the book with a thorough grounding in a fundamentally sound approach to course design. Even if you are an experienced instructor, we hope that you will find it helpful to walk your way through the course design process in this comprehensive way, using small teaching principles to guide you through what can seem like a very intimidating task. From there, Chapters 2 and 3 move into two core challenges that every online instructor will face, both in the design process and throughout the semester: How will I invite my students into the course and get them engaged so they are ready to learn, and what materials and tools will I provide to help my students learn? For both of these challenges, we've provided research and techniques to help you and your students succeed.

In Part II, we consider the human element in online courses. In recent years, an increasing amount of attention has been paid to this aspect of online education; however, it is still the case that many online learning environments could benefit from more effort to welcome and support the people who are in them—including us. A primary strategy to address this concern is to make a deliberate, research-based effort to create a sense of community in our online classes, the topic of Chapter 4. Chapter 5 looks at ways of providing effective feedback, a necessary ingredient for people to learn and grow. In Chapter 6, we acknowledge that a significant concern in online classes is the attrition rate, and we give you theory and strategies to help your students stay present and engaged so they may successfully complete your class. Each of these chapters helps us to nurture and support our students such that they want to be in class and they want to learn.

Part III of the book tackles the complex matter of motivation. Creating and maintaining motivation can be a constant challenge for online faculty. Not only do many students struggle to inspire themselves to work consistently on their online courses, many faculty might face a similar struggle. Lots of people prefer to teach and learn in person, but for various reasons, they're engaged in online education. Some of the simple supports that naturally occur in onsite classes don't exist in asynchronous online classes. For example, online courses lack a predictable class meeting schedule and the built-in accountability that such a schedule provides. As such, Chapters 7 and 8 focus on helping students sustain their own motivation by developing learner autonomy and by making connections with the material and discovering how course content relates to their future academic and career goals. Both of these approaches have been shown to increase learner motivation; we'll share research and small changes you can make to address this concern. Finally, in Chapter 9 we turn our attention to finding ways of motivating ourselves to continue learning and improving as online faculty.

As you might imagine, we deliberately selected and organized chapter topics with a view to addressing some of the unique challenges presented by online education. No one single book can cover all of the issues and opportunities we face in our online teaching, at least not in any depth. What follows reflects our considered judgment on the topics and strategies that are most likely to have an outsized impact on online student engagement and learning.

Our primary audience for this book is one that grows larger with each passing year: instructors who have experience with face-to-face teaching and are now being asked to develop the knowledge and skills they need to teach online. In other words, we presume some basic familiarity here with teaching at the college level; what we hope to offer in the pages that follow are knowledge and skills that will enable an experienced teacher – even if that experience consists of a few courses taught as a graduate student – to teach their first online courses successfully.

While we have written this book with a special eye toward instructors who are new to online teaching, we hope and expect that the research and small changes we present will find an equally welcome audience with experienced online faculty as well. Newer instructors will benefit most from reading both the original *Small Teaching* and this volume in their entirety; experienced online faculty or experienced faculty who are shifting to online teaching might find themselves gravitating toward particular chapters in one book or the other, and that's just fine. We believe that each chapter in this book stands on its own, just as the chapters in the original *Small Teaching* do. If time is limited (and isn't it always?) you can skip from here to the chapter that addresses the problem you have, or the teaching task immediately in front of you. You'll find a myriad of solutions, tailored for online classes, which you can implement immediately. In short, this book can be read as a standalone introduction to online teaching, or paired productively with the core principles from the original book for a more comprehensive view.

Please note, we're aware that not all online classes are the same. Some have smaller enrollments, perhaps fewer than 30 students; some are larger, with 50 or more students in a class. Some online courses rely heavily on publisher content and activities that students complete in the vendor's platform instead of in the institution's LMS. Increasingly, publisher content may consist of sophisticated adaptive courseware that adjusts to individual student's learning preferences and needs – commonly known as personalized learning – but even here, human interventions and interactions are important to maximize the impact of the adaptive system. Sometimes instructors teach highly coordinated courses that require (or allow) little customization on the part of the individual faculty member. All of these factors undoubtedly impact your ability to implement changes in your online teaching. But we believe every instructor of asynchronous online classes, regardless of these kinds of variables, will find approaches in this book to be more effective.

Further, the suggestions we present here can be applied in blended or hybrid courses, that is, classes in which some percentage of seat time has been reduced and replaced with online content and activities. According to a 2017 Educause Center for Analysis and Research (ECAR) study, many definitions of "blend-edness" exist (Pomerantz and Brooks, 2017, p. 23). If at least part of your course takes place in an LMS, you'll likely find ideas here to improve the impact of those activities and interactions.

Even if you teach all your classes in person, chances are good that you may have access to your institution's LMS. At NAU, for example, all class sections automatically come with a course shell. The ECAR study found that "the most common faculty uses of the LMS are all operational, course management functions. These are functions that require little or no interaction between the instructor and the students" (Pomerantz and Brooks, 2017, p. 20). In other words, many faculty use their course site, presumably for their in-person classes, to provide the syllabus and static materials such as readings and handouts. Many also use the gradebook to notify students of their current grades. Notice these are one-directional uses of the LMS; they communicate information to students without requiring students to engage in any learning activities online. These platforms are quite robust; they can facilitate interactions with your students that will no doubt help them – and you – be more prepared to use in-class time strategically. Read on to discover small ways of adjusting your communication and creating online assessments and activities to make the most of in-person class time.

THE STRUCTURE OF SMALL TEACHING ONLINE

In the chapters that follow, we replicate both the structure of each chapter and the general guidelines for activities and techniques that were used in *Small Teaching*. The small teaching online approaches presented here will fall into one of three categories:

· *Brief teaching and learning activities.* Asynchronous online classes are unique in that typically, students may be active 24 hours a day, 7 days a week, while the class is in session. This most certainly does not mean that *you* have to be online 24/7. But as you will see, making frequent appearances in class, or designing quick learning activities for students, can be hugely beneficial to your students. We will look at several ways of interacting with students and being present that generally take not more than 10 minutes at a time. You'll find outsized potential benefits from these small investments of time.

· *Small course design modifications.* Good teachers always seek to improve their classes. We note what works well and what does not, and we tweak our courses and/or our class sessions in order to keep making our classes better. This approach carries over into online classes as well. It is not necessary, indeed not even desirable, to make radical changes to your online courses from session to session. But it is absolutely possible to make minor design improvements each time you teach a course, or to apply slight improvements to new online courses that you develop. The result will be increasingly effective online classes in which your students learn more deeply and you teach more authentically.

· *Minor adjustments to the way you communicate with online students.* Communication strategies may not be top of your mind when teaching online, but they should be. We experience significant barriers in online classes that we don't find in the face-to-face classroom. First, there is virtually no real-time feedback, either for us or for our students. Also, we are almost entirely stripped of nonverbal communication cues, unless we strategically employ audio and video in our courses (more on that later). For now, suffice to say that it's important to be intentional in our communication with online students. We'll explore many strategies to improve this class element without excessively overloading your time commitment.

Our guiding principle for this book is that these changes to the way we design and teach online classes must not feel too daunting. We trust that you will find approaches that you can employ tomorrow, next week, or next term that will positively impact student learning. Expect your outlook on online teaching to be positively impacted, too. You'll find that making some of these small adjustments will enhance your enjoyment of online teaching, further adding to your motivation to continue to improve your online teaching to enable all our diverse learners to succeed.

As in *Small Teaching*, you'll see the same structure in each of the chapters in this book. Each chapter includes the following elements:

· *Introduction*. We begin with examples of how the particular learning phenomenon described in that chapter might appear in everyday life or educational contexts.
· *In Theory*. This section delves very quickly into the research that supports the recommendations of the chapter.
· *Models*. Four or five detailed models are described in each chapter – fully fleshed-out examples of how instructors could incorporate a small teaching approach into their course design, teaching practice, or communication with students.
· *Principles*. The models can't possibly cover every context in which readers might be teaching, so the principles provide guidance for creating your own small teaching strategies.
· *Small Teaching Online Quick Tips*. These are brief reminders of the simplest means of putting the small teaching strategy of that

chapter into practice; flip through or return to these when you need a quick tip for an engaged learning activity.

· *Conclusion*. A final reflection on the main theory or strategy of the chapter.

This structure is designed to provide a range of ways to consume this content. If you have time, if you truly want to revolutionize your online teaching, small step by small step, read each chapter in full. This will provide you the context to ensure that your implementation of small online teaching strategies will be as successful as possible. On the other hand, if you are looking for a quick fix, read the Quick Tips part of your selected chapter for practical things you can do now.

A NOTE ON OUR COLLABORATION

The authors of this book have very different levels of experience with online teaching and learning. Jim's has been quite limited; he has helped to create two massive open online courses (MOOCs). Flower, on the other hand, has taught dozens of online courses in multiple contexts and has supported hundreds of online faculty in the design and teaching of their courses. These different levels of experience conditioned how we collaborated on the authorship of the book. Flower drafted the majority of the book, drawing on both her extensive experience and her familiarity with the research in teaching and learning online. Jim's contributions were limited to this Introduction, the "In Theory" sections of each chapter, and to revising and editing throughout. All of the personal stories and examples come from Flower, which is why the remainder of the book has been written in first-person singular. We wanted to keep the personal, intimate voice that characterized *Small Teaching*, and ensure that the book's voice reflects the fact that Flower is the primary author of what follows.

FINAL THOUGHT

Small Teaching encourages us to "give new activities time to flower" (Lang, 2016, p. 11). Give yourself time to flower, too. Class activities rarely go perfectly the first time you try them. And your transformation into a more effective online teacher, one who communicates and designs for both empathy and significant learning, will not resemble the emergence of a butterfly from its cocoon. Pick something small. Try it. Note what worked and what didn't. Refine your approach. Try it again. Stay the course and, over time, you'll be teaching exemplary online courses that exceed the standard for the best in distance education.

But, as Jim points out in the original *Small Teaching*, it can be overwhelming to imagine the big picture all at once. Instead, focus on today. Are you teaching online now? Or does your online class start in a few days or weeks? If you're reading this, you're likely looking for strategies to be more effective in your online teaching. This book can help.

We'll take it one small online step at a time.

Part I

Designing for Learning

Consider your entry into teaching, no matter your discipline. With the possible exception of education or teacher training programs, almost all disciplines fail to provide robust training opportunities for new and future faculty. Many research universities now *offer* opportunities for their graduate students to take courses in pedagogy or participate in teaching development programs, for example, but very few require it (Haras, Ginsberg, Férnandez, and Magruder, 2017, p. 56). We can hardly blame overburdened PhD students for prioritizing their research over their development as teachers, especially when faculty at research universities might not see teaching as priority in their own professional lives.

Likewise, professionals in the field entering the teaching force for the first time might be working full-time and coming to campus in the evening out of a desire to share their knowledge with the next generation, and have to balance teaching work with full-time jobs. Given the low rate of pay that institutions often provide to these adjunct instructors, schools might be reluctant to require teaching development activities as a prerequisite for the job.

As a consequence, most new teachers fall back on what we experienced as students, and what we observe our colleagues doing in the classroom (*if* we observe our colleagues in the classroom – teaching is a notoriously isolating business), as we develop our own classroom persona and methods.

So how do we learn to teach? We might have been given a syllabus from someone who has previously taught the class. Perhaps we then chose a textbook either based on what the previous instructor(s) used, or maybe based on our experience as students. Having selected the textbook, we proceeded to comb through any syllabi that we were given. We co-opted several elements, made adjustments according to our preferences, and established due dates for major assignments and exams. That may have been the extent of our big-picture planning. When preparing to teach my first literature survey course, I remember thinking to myself: *Well, all 200-level lit classes have two papers due, a midterm exam, and a final exam. So I guess that's what I'll do.* Looking back, it doesn't seem like a very intentional way to plan a course.

To be fair, once we've selected a textbook and roughed in the main assessments of the class, most of us then do everything we can to plan a cohesive course that equips students to succeed on those assessments. In all the years I've spent working with, mentoring, and developing college faculty, I've never met anyone who set out to create a random class with no sequential logic, no connection between readings and tests, no central organizing principle. We assign readings, videos, and other content that will prepare students to do well on tests, papers, and projects. We plan class sessions and homework assignments in a way that we hope will help students understand class concepts. We may even provide study guides, rubrics, and other materials to help students do well on our assessments. But while we have good intentions, there is frequently a lack of deliberate thought about exactly *why* we are asking students to do what we are asking them to do.

Because thinking about the purpose of classwork is so foundational to our teaching, in the next chapter we will take a closer look at backward design. This framework helps us bring intentionality to our teaching. Backward design may be new to you, you may have unconsciously been doing it all along, or you may be well acquainted with the approach. Whatever your familiarity with backward design, we'll consider how we can be more deliberate in the design – or planning – of our online courses, and how, using small teaching strategies, we can reinforce and make explicit our online course design for our students.

Chapter 2 explores how we guide and support students through our carefully designed online courses, ensuring that they have a clear view of the purpose of each course component. In a face-to-face environment, we have frequent, informal opportunities to remind students about the big picture of the course, and about how a piece of content or an assessment contributes to that big picture. We can intervene on a regular basis to check student understanding, respond to spontaneous concerns and questions, and support students through the learning process. Students in online courses can feel isolated from these essential learning supports. Chapter 2 provides small teaching approaches that will help students keep the purpose of the course, and all of its components, clearly in view. It also offers models that will help you monitor the progress of your students and provide you opportunities to intervene with support and guidance when they most need it.

After considering how to intentionally design the course, and how to create structures that support student learning, in Chapter 3 we'll examine how to intentionally select technology and media tools for our online classes. The tools and media that we use comprise a huge part of the course experience, yet it's easy to fall into the same kind of default thinking that we were susceptible to when we first began teaching in person. Maybe your department chair gave you someone else's online content to use, so you just stuck with that content and the tools that were already in the course. Maybe you weren't so lucky; maybe you had no example to follow and little guidance, so you created an online course based on your best guess of what it should contain. Maybe you've taught online for a while but have fallen into a rut of using the same technologies that you've always used. Whatever your situation, we'll examine a series of small teaching questions that will help us think through what tools and technology we're using, and why.

Learning doesn't happen by accident. Successful and engaging online classes don't, either. Designing an online course is a large endeavor, but even large endeavors have to start small.

Chapter 1

Surfacing Backward Design

INTRODUCTION

I yanked open the door of the English building, only moments to spare before class was due to begin. Along with several students who were cutting it equally close, I hurried up the stairs to my First-Year Composition classroom on the second floor. Reaching the open doorway mere seconds before 8:00 a.m., I rushed into the room, gown flying behind me (well, not literally, but you get the idea) like *Harry Potter*'s Snape bursting into his dungeon Potions classroom.

I slung my professorial-looking leather school bag onto the table in the front of the room and pulled out my green "Modern Class Record" attendance book, the one supplied by the English department to every graduate teaching assistant (GTA). I took my place behind the lectern, opened my authority-bestowing book, and proceeded to call roll. My sleepy (or bored) students – it was difficult to distinguish between the two – took turns responding with a mumbled "here," or occasionally (for variety) "present."

Having completed the housekeeping, I opened my college-ruled spiral notebook, the one in which I jotted down my lesson plan for each day. As I skimmed over my hasty and underdeveloped agenda, I drawled, "Let me seeee heeeeeere ...." while I tried to remember what we would do that day and why.

Every. Single. Day. Every single day of my very first semester teaching college, I began class with those not-so-inspiring words—or so my students told me at the end of the semester (I didn't realize I was doing this). The class met at 8:00 a.m., four days per week. And every day I would race into class, take roll, and say, "Let me see here," while trying to figure out what the plan was. Not exactly a great start to my teaching career.

I've thought a lot about that semester. At only 22, I faced a sullen bunch of 18- and 19-year-olds every morning across the podium. That their sullenness might be related to my teaching only occurred to me later. It came as a shock to me that not everyone loved writing papers. Didn't everyone find joy and satisfaction in expressing themselves in the written word?

Somehow or other, I made it through that first semester. Prior to the first day of class, I and the other new GTAs had sat through a few days of training. After the semester started, we met every week to continue learning how to teach First-Year Composition. We'd discuss the content, the writing assignments, and sometimes even teaching methods. What we never discussed was the overall *purpose* of the course. What were the objectives of the course? Certainly we wanted students to become better writers. But *better* in what sense? For what purpose? To get jobs? Become novelists? Write better memos in their business careers?

Since I didn't have a clear view of the specific purpose of the course, I didn't have a clear sense of how all of its elements came together. The course seemed like a collection of different parts and practices - assignments, classroom activities, grading - that were each their own thing. But what connected them all? Why, for example, were the papers assigned and structured the way they were? What was the purpose of peer review? Why had the course readings been selected? None of this was apparent to me.

I suspect that many of us learned to teach college courses in the same way that I did: by the seat of our pants. Of course, flexibility and agility are virtues in our teaching, and every successful teacher must learn to improvise in the classroom. But that doesn't mean we should not also begin with a robust, systematic, and purposeful overall plan for the course. Having such a plan allows us to flex within the boundaries of our well-designed class, one that has developed answers to the kinds of questions articulated above.

Cue backward design.

IN THEORY

Imagine you are planning a road trip for your summer vacation. Do you hop in the car one day and mindlessly drive wherever the road leads? The more free-spirited among you might well try something like that. But most of us decide on a destination first. Where do we want to go?

Having settled on the destination, we make other plans to help us get there. We consider various routes for the trip. We research and select incremental milestones: Where might be a good place to break the journey for meals or exercise? Where should we stay overnight? We also have to make decisions about supplies we might need, the tools to make a successful journey. What do we need to pack? Do we need beach chairs and sunscreen for a trip to the ocean? Or are hiking boots and trekking poles needed for a mountain adventure?

Very few of us begin journeys without thinking about where we are going, how we will get there, and what we will need on the way.

In their seminal book *Understanding by Design*, Grant Wiggins and Jay McTighe propose taking a similar approach to the design of educational experiences. They suggest beginning the process of teaching a course by thinking about the end first. If you're not familiar with this book, I highly recommend reading it before you teach your next class, as it provides many useful strategies for putting their theory into practice. You might also look at

Dee Fink's *Creating Significant Learning Experiences: An Integrated Approach to Designing College Courses* (2013), which takes a parallel – and equally thorough – approach to the process of creating a meaningful learning experience for your students.

The very short version of the arguments that both books make is that we should begin the course-planning process by focusing first on the most essential goals that we have for our students. Wiggins and McTighe refer to those goals as the "enduring understanding" that we want students to take away from the course. They explain that in order for an understanding to qualify as enduring, it should have "endured over time and across cultures because it has proved so important and useful," and also that it should "endure in the mind of the student … it should be learned in such a way that it does not fly away from memory once the unit is over or the test is completed" (Wiggins and McTighe, 2005, p. 136). Only after we have identified those deep goals should we worry about the content of the course, or the methods of instruction, or the kinds of assessments we will invite students to undertake. Everything must be anchored in the goals for enduring understanding; everything stems from those goals. New faculty members often begin the course-planning process by selecting the content: the textbooks and lecture materials. The backward-design process forces them to forget about the content until they decide what they really want students to learn.

When you backward design a college course, you might consider how you would answer three large questions, drawn from the road-trip analogy:

· *Where do we want to go?* What are our primary goals for the course? What do we want students to know and be able to do by the end of the term? This should form the basis of our thinking around course learning objectives or outcomes. Early in your career you might have taught courses without a clear sense of what the learning objectives listed on the syllabus actually say or really mean. Maybe you inherited a syllabus or a course shell from someone else, or maybe you just whipped up some objectives in order to fill a spot on a required course template. When we take a backward approach to designing our course, we think carefully about our destination. Where do we want students to end up? This helps us to slow down and consider both the substance and the wording of our objectives.

- *How will we know if we have arrived?* Once we are clear about the course learning objectives, it's essential to measure students' achievement of those objectives to determine whether they attained them. We do this by way of both summative and formative assessments. Summative assessments such as final exams, papers, and projects allow students to demonstrate their mastery of our course learning objectives. Formative assessments such as low-stakes quizzes or weekly reflections help us to know whether students are making good progress. Planning intentional measures designed to reveal whether students are achieving the course outcomes forms a critical part of deliberate course design.

- *What will we need to help us get there?* After deciding on the destination and effective ways of measuring whether or how well we arrived there, the final core step in backward design is to consider what students will need in order to succeed on our assessments. Here is where we (finally) select course materials such as textbooks and other content. We design activities that help students engage with and process new information and concepts. We devise a course schedule with milestones, often in the form of incremental deadlines or formative assessments that keep students accountable and allow us to give feedback on their work along the way. In doing so, we help our students make steady progress toward the destination – that is, achieving the course learning objectives.

We've provided here only the barest sketch of backward design, because the core concept of it is relatively simple to understand. You can find a much more thorough explanation of the idea from either Fink or Wiggins and McTighe, as well as plenty of overviews through some simple online searching.

The goal of this chapter is to help you make sure that the work you put into backward design has the desired impact on your students. When you have lots of time to spend with your students in a face-to-face environment, you have frequent, informal opportunities to remind them about the larger purpose of the course, connect classroom activities to the course learning objectives, and provide the reasoning behind your assessments. You can write all of those same things to your online students, but when students are viewing everything through a screen, such text can become white noise that they filter out while they are getting to the requirements. So online teachers need to work a little harder to ensure that students see the purposes that underlie the activities they are undertaking. They need to ensure that their backward design floats a little closer to the surface, visible in multiple ways throughout the semester.

The small teaching strategies in this chapter will ensure that your carefully designed course demonstrates to students that you have created meaningful goals for them, reveals to them how the assessments will help them achieve those goals, and ensures – both for you and for them – that all of the course content has been created with the end in mind.

MODELS

The concept of alignment underpins the theory of backward design. Course materials, learning activities, assessments, and objectives should all align. In other words, every element of a course should line up with and support the achievement of the learning objectives. You have worked hard to create that alignment in your well-designed course, but it's important to make it transparent to your students, who otherwise might view some aspects of the course as busy work. Helping your students understand what they are to do and why it's valuable is especially important in online classes, because you don't have the opportunity to detect confusion and answer assignment-related questions in real time the way you would in the physical classroom. The small teaching strategies described will help to clarify course learning and assessment activities as well as the purpose of each. This will help your backward-designed online course to have the greatest positive impact on the learning of your students.

Begin Work on the Final Assessment in Week 1

One of the challenges of online classes is that major assignments can get buried in endlessly nested content folders or learning modules. I've known many students who were caught by surprise toward the end of an online class. Somehow they overlooked the part of the syllabus or the course site that describes the final paper or project or exam. Suddenly, after navigating and completing the majority of the course, students stumble across a major assessment they were not expecting.

Of course, students should take responsibility to thoroughly review the syllabus, familiarize themselves with the entire course site, even review assignments that are not due until the last week of class. We can even help them do this. For example, we may require a syllabus quiz to obtain cursory agreement that students read and understood the course requirements. But it can still be hard for students to "see" everything in an online class, especially once they are deep into the semester, and taking other courses as well. There can be a lot of material to sift through, and we lack the advantage of getting together in the classroom to review important details. We can send emails, make announcements, and otherwise beg our students to pay attention to course requirements, but these methods may not be enough.

Instead of policing student compliance, we can encourage their meaningful engagement with the end-of-term assessment (which might carry more weight than any other assessment) right from the very start. If you've taught online for any length of time, you know that busy online students tend to skip any task for which they are not held accountable. If there are no points attached, for example, students may not read your helpful announcements, watch your videos that provide additional guidance, or even read your assignment feedback.

Knowing this, create an online activity in the first week that requires students to familiarize themselves with the final assessment and – more importantly – to do something with it. Maybe they share initial ideas for the final project in an online discussion forum. Maybe they ask at least one question about what to expect on the final exam in the discussion board – this way, others benefit from answers that emerge from the posts. Perhaps they take a low-stakes quiz that presents questions in the same format as they will find on the cumulative final exam. Or students can read the instructions for the final paper and submit a brief written assignment in which they describe the assignment purpose and requirements in their own words.

This model aligns well with one of the principles articulated in *Small Teaching*. In that book, Jim reviewed evidence that suggested that students receive significant cognitive benefits from trying learning tasks *before they are ready*. In other words, we often think we must teach content and skills to students, and then give them tasks that will put that knowledge or those skills to use. But research from the learning sciences tells us that when we ask people to complete tasks before they learn something new, they will learn it more effectively (Lang, 2016, pp. 41–62). The authors of *Make It Stick: The Science of Successful Learning* explain that "unsuccessful attempts to solve a problem encourage deep processing of the answer when it is later supplied" (Brown, Roediger, and McDaniel, 2014, p. 88). In other words, when we give students a cognitive task at the beginning of the semester, before they have learned the skills they will need to complete it, we are creating that "fertile ground" for their learning throughout the semester.

So this first model has both cognitive and metacognitive benefits. It helps students learn, and it helps them become more aware of the major assessment of the course, which will allow them to plan their learning and study more effectively.

Consider, then, creating a (low-stakes) graded assignment in the first week that gives students a preview of the final product, provides a little taste of what to expect, and requires them to begin thinking about and working on it. Start with the end in mind, and require interaction with that final assessment. Tell your students why, too. They'll appreciate your transparency and will be more motivated to engage meaningfully when they see the relevance of class activities beginning in the first week.

Make the Purpose of Class Activities Explicit

When you develop your online course using backward design, you have good reasons for every design decision you make. With specific and measurable course learning objectives in mind, you create assessments that allow students to demonstrate mastery of the objectives. You select readings, videos, and learning activities that enable students to gain new knowledge and practice using and applying it before they are assessed on that new information. You write instructions that provide clear guidance on what students should do to succeed on learning activities, assignments, and assessments.

All of the logical and carefully considered reasons for these decisions are crystal clear to you. You thought it all through. Everything makes sense in your own head. But your students aren't in your head. It's possible, even quite likely, that your students don't know why you are asking them to do what you're asking them to do.

You should therefore make it a regular part of your online teaching practice to keep the rationale for your decisions in full view of your students. This principle lends itself especially well to small teaching applications that you can make throughout the semester in regular bursts.

For example, at the beginning of each online module or unit, provide a short, written description that introduces that module's content, describes what students are doing, and explains why they are doing it. I like to open each module with a two- to three-sentence overview of the module, an explanation of how module content and activities will help students succeed in the class (or help them achieve academic and career goals, become better employees, better citizens – think big!), and a list of four to six learning goals or objectives for that module that align with the course learning objectives.

You can begin your list of learning goals with something like, "After successfully completing this module, you will be able to … " and then provide a bulleted or numbered list of specific demonstrable skills students will acquire as they complete the module work. Provide this guidance in a short, written element at the beginning or top of each module in order to clearly establish why they are doing what they are doing in that module. Alternatively, or in addition to your text-based overview, you may want to give a quick video introduction to each module, in line with the principles of Universal Design for Learning (UDL).

Reinforce the reasoning behind class activities using announcements at intentionally timed intervals throughout the course. Video announcements are perfect for this. Written announcements are also an option, but in my experience students are more likely to click on and view a (brief!) video thumbnail than to read yet another wall of text.

Most Learning Management Systems (LMSs) include native or third-party integrated tools that allow you to capture a quick webcam video of yourself talking to the camera. The YouTube app on your smartphone also makes it relatively easy to record and upload these kind of casual videos. Studies show that students appreciate informal class videos that reveal your personality (Guo, 2013; Cavanagh, 2016). Don't stress too much about creating professional-looking videos that require editing skills you may not have. Prepare a few talking points to further explain the purpose and the reasons for engaging in that week's classwork. Share some examples, tell a story that illustrates your pedagogical thinking, or describe a video or blog post that you just came across that reminded you of the relevance of that week's work. Remember to provide captions, a text transcript, or a text-based outline for any videos in your online class (Tobin and Behling, 2018). And then provide a link to the media or news item that caught your attention, and might likewise catch the attention of your students.

... and Do the Same for Assignments

Everything I've said above about the clarity of classroom activities in your head, and the potential lack of such clarity to your students, applies to your assignments as well. Create assignment instructions that provide a clear rationale for the work your students will do, as well as clear directions for how they can accomplish it successfully. You can also relate the task to the current module and to the course learning objectives.

John Warner, the author of two excellent books on the teaching of writing, provides one great model for how to do this in his book *The Writer's Practice* (2019), which contains multiple samples of assignments you can give to students to improve their writing. Each of those assignments – which he calls "experiences" – comes with a written explanation that contains four core components: audience, process, reflect, and remix. As he walks students through these core aspects of the assignment, he has plenty of opportunity to help them understand what that particular writing experience will help them accomplish. They might be learning to tailor their prose to different audiences, for example, or learning to become a more careful evaluator of sources. Whatever the purpose, they learn about it from the way Warner has structured the assignment and instructions.

Mary-Ann Winkelmes has researched the impact of the kind of transparent assignment design we're talking about. Her work has led to the creation of the Transparency in Learning and Teaching in Higher Ed project, with extensive data on how this approach helps students and many examples and support materials to help you begin to incorporate this into your own teaching. You can find a great deal more information at https://tilthighered .com.

I've had a lot of success with a method similar to those proposed by Warner and Winkelmes. My husband, who has been my personal sounding board and instructional designer since Day 1 of that First-Year Composition class over two decades ago, helped me develop an approach that I've been using for a long time now, one that I find particularly helpful in online classes, where busy students want concise yet thorough information about what they have to do. I offer it here as another variation so you can expand your thinking about what your assignment prompt might contain. My husband's advice was to follow a simple template when creating instructions for an online assignment, discussion forum, or project. I now use these headings in the instructions I give to my students:

Here's what I want you to do: I explain the task.

Here's why I want you to do it: I explain the reason this task will contribute to the student's success in class and beyond.

Here's how to do it: I provide detailed instructions, rubrics, checklists, and exemplars to help students clearly see and understand my expectations.

You would verbally provide this guidance and explanation in your in-person class, but somehow this often gets neglected online. Create assignment instructions that clearly convey the *what, why,* and *how* of each assignment. Your effort will pay off in two important ways: You'll get fewer student questions about what they should do, and better-quality work that demonstrates student learning and achievement of outcomes.

Have Students Reflect on and Respond to Learning Objectives

Reflection on our learning is a significant part of making learning durable. Turning again to *Make It Stick: The Science of Successful Learning*, we find multiple cognitive benefits of reflection:

> Reflection can involve several cognitive activities ... that lead to stronger learning. These include retrieval (recalling recently learned knowledge to mind), elaboration (for example, connecting new knowledge to what you already know), and generation (for example, rephrasing key ideas

in your own words or visualizing and mentally rehearsing what you might do differently next time. (Brown, Roediger, and McDaniel, 2014, p. 89)

Additionally, reflection is a key part of learning to regulate our own learning – a crucial skill for our students to develop (Nilson, 2013). A perfect way to structure this reflection while also reinforcing the intentional design of our classes is to require students to review learning objectives at various points of the class.

For example, in the first week of class, have students reflect on and respond to course learning objectives as stated in the syllabus. We typically default to written assignments in higher education, but you can just as easily invite reflection through audio or video, which aligns with UDL principles and might provide a welcome alternative for some of your students. Hesston College faculty members Karen Sheriff LeVan and Marissa E. King argue:

[B]ecause we often rely on writing as the primary mode of metacognitive reflection, some students, especially those who struggle with college-level writing, may not experience the full cognitive benefits of reflection. For such students, the stress of writing can compromise their focus on reflection. (2016)

They advocate for the use of quick audio reflection assignments to encourage a more informal and reduced-stress response.

Many LMSs and widely used third-party tools facilitate the recording of such media. On the flip side, there will always be students who prefer writing over audio. You could accommodate both preferences by allowing students to choose whether to submit their reflection in writing or as a recording. The point is to get students to think carefully about what they are about to learn in this course.

Asking students to respond to the learning objectives also ensures that they know what the objectives say and mean, or alerts you to the need to clarify the objectives if students struggle to articulate their response. But students might feel overwhelmed by the requirement to respond to all of the objectives. You could ask them to select a few objectives that they are most interested in, or think are most valuable for them personally, or that they are the most concerned about. Many students don't even read the course learning objectives, so requiring a written or recorded response to some or all of the objectives facilitates their engagement with these goals right from the start.

You can also build in a regular opportunity to review and reflect on module learning objectives. In my graduate online class on technology fluency, students answer a series of questions at the end of each module. One of the questions on each of these assignments asks them to list each module learning objective and to write about how they made progress that week, why the learning goal is significant or important, and what they need to do to continue their learning in this area. Students write a sentence or two about each objective. It's not an overwhelming activity in terms of the time it takes to write or to grade, but it pays off in significant learning dividends. Students actually have to read, pay attention to, and think about what we said we would do in that module and how it helps them achieve the objectives for the course. I've received some initial pushback on this activity, but once my students get used to the idea, they like the opportunity to actively think about what we're doing and why.

With a little thought, you can find many ways to continually draw students' attention to the learning goals. Doing so pays off in important ways in developing self-aware, productive students who will likely become more successful learners in both their online and face-to-face courses.

Look Back, Look Ahead

Magnify the impact of your course alignment by building in one final opportunity to think about what students have accomplished in the course. As a concluding activity in the class, zoom out from the weekly or module learning goals. Take a high-level look at where students have come from, at how much they've achieved. Reinforce their learning, solidify important concepts, and further motivate your students to become lifelong learners.

One way to do this is to revisit an activity from Week 1 (Lang, 2019). If you asked your students to reflect on and write or talk about the course learning objectives in a syllabus review assignment, have them review what they said then. Ask them where we said we were going. Did we get there? Why or why not? What was particularly helpful in reaching the destination? What might have helped them make even better progress along the way? It's amazing how far students can come even in the four- to eight-week condensed online classes we often teach. Point this out to them, or better yet, guide their discovery of their growth. Depending on what you ask in your prompt, you may also get constructive feedback to help you refine and improve the course. Either way, you will help your students develop important reflection skills that will benefit them in any new learning context, be it personal, academic, or professional.

One of my favorite ways to get at this, while also helping students see for themselves the personal value and relevance of the course, is to include a Three Takeaways assignment. Ask students to think about the three most important things they have learned in your course. Ask how they will continue to develop that learning and apply it in a future academic, workplace, volunteer, or family life setting. Their submission could be in the form of a journal entry, blog post, written assignment, or audio or video recording posted to the class discussion board.

You'll want to think carefully about whether individual, private reflection is best for this task, or whether you want students to learn from each other's insights in a more public way. If you were teaching in the classroom, would you ask students to write this down and turn it in as they leave the room? Or would you structure a Think-Pair-Share activity, which becomes a discussion that the whole class engages in? The differences between public and private reflection are important to consider. Think about your purpose for this activity and decide whether that's best achieved by having students submit privately or asking them to submit something for public consumption and discussion.

I use the Three Takeaways in my Technology Fluency and Leadership class, offered as part of a master's degree leadership program at Northern Arizona University (NAU). The students are almost always working professionals who balance family obligations with school; to a person, they seek career advancement and personal betterment of their situation. But I get a wide range of tech savviness in the course. I've had IT professionals who could be teaching the class, administrative professionals who are nervous about trying new tech, and people in service or retail industries who, for example, aren't required to create PowerPoint presentations in their work, but know that in order to make a career move, they need new skills. Every student arrives at a different place in the journey. The Three Takeaways assignment allows each individual to think carefully about their own learning and growth and to consider how they plan to apply what they have learned to their personal and professional context. They can choose to write or talk about class concepts or more metatopics, like what they learned by being a first-time online student. Whatever their three takeaways are, there are always insightful revelations that help them develop as an individual and reinforce the learning we experienced in the class.

PRINCIPLES

Helping your students see and benefit from the intentional design of your course pays off in important ways: They'll be more engaged when they know why they are doing what they're doing, and how it will benefit them in the course – and in other contexts, too. Better engagement leads to more meaningful learning. A few principles can help guide your approach.

Design with the End in Mind

This is just basic backward design: Keep your final destination squarely before you in every phase of your planning process. Articulate where you want your students to arrive. Plan a final assessment that will measure whether they got there. Then think critically about what they need along the way: readings and media content to provide information and knowledge they need to get where they are going; incremental tasks and assessments to act as signposts and to let students know whether they are making good progress; and learning activities and tasks to help them practice using and applying the new knowledge before being tested on their mastery of it. Equip your students with the necessary tools and supplies to help them reach the final destination.

Provide Frequent Reminders of the Purpose of Content and Activities

Using written instructions, video announcements, and weekly reminders, help students clearly see the purpose behind course activities and assessments. These reminders accomplish two goals.

First, they help *you* think through the purpose of classwork. You'll have lots of opportunities to remind yourself that there's a reason you've assigned various readings and tasks. Keeping your purpose in view will help you avoid giving students busy work, an accusation commonly made about online classes.

These reminders will also help your students stay engaged. Tell your students – often – that you deliberately designed tasks to help them learn and succeed in the class. When they see the relevance of coursework, the thread that ties everything together, students are more willing to complete activities and assessments in a way that promotes meaningful learning.

Point Students Back to the Core Objectives

You put a lot of careful design work into the creation of your class. Make the design overt for students to maximize the impact of your efforts. Create tasks that draw students' attention to course and module learning objectives. In many college classes, students don't even know what the objectives are. Have students read, think about, and respond to objectives as part of a syllabus review or orientation to the course. Provide module learning objectives that detail how module work supports course goals. Require an end-of-module or post-assessment reflection in which students evaluate how well they achieved module objectives, or what they might do differently next time. In your announcements, emails, even in individual feedback, reinforce the core objectives again and again. We all perform better when we know what the goal is. Encourage your students to achieve their best learning by repeatedly pointing out the learning goals for the class.

Connect the Beginning and Ending

Bookend your class with activities that help students see the end at the beginning, and conversely, see the beginning at the end. In Week 1, get students working toward the final assessment. In the final week of the class, have them reflect back on where they started. Doing this enables your students to see the direct connections between the beginning and the end of class. They'll see, and value, the straight path that led them from where they were on Day One to where they got to by the end.

SMALL TEACHING ONLINE QUICK TIPS: SURFACING BACKWARD DESIGN ONLINE

Learning activities, content, assessments, and core objectives must all align to ensure successful arrival at the final destination. Help your students recognize the intentional design of your course in order to maximize their learning.

- *Get students working on the final assessment in Week 1.* Is there a piece they can tackle right up front? Create a (low-stakes) graded task that requires students to read and think about the final project instructions or begin to plan the topic of their final paper. Or assign a quiz that mirrors the format of the final exam and gives them practice with that format. Explain that because you want students to succeed on the final, they'll begin preparing for it in the first few days of the class. Set them up for success by starting with the end.
- *Clarify the purpose of classwork and assessments.* What might seem clear to you could be mystifying to your students. Throughout the term, tell them why they're doing any given task so students see the connections between activities and core objectives for themselves.
- *Assign tasks that foster self-reflection on learning as it relates to course objectives.* At the beginning or middle of class, ask students to read, think about, and respond to learning goals and their progress toward or achievement of them.

· *At the close of the semester, have students reflect on where they've come so far and what they intend to do to continue their learning.* Create opportunities to think about learning objectives to reinforce and maximize the design of the course.

CONCLUSION

When the wheels of your car are in alignment, travel proceeds in the intended direction. The wheels respond correctly to the input you provide through the steering wheel. You arrive at your destination smoothly, almost effortlessly. When you have proper alignment, you don't even notice. All works harmoniously as it should to get you where you want to go.

Contrast that to what happens when a wheel is out of alignment. The vehicle keeps veering slightly to one side, requiring constant pulling on the steering wheel to stay on track. More effort is required to drag the car along its intended path. Misalignment creates additional wear and tear on the tires, too, which can become costly and dangerous.

When we have effectively applied backward design, all course components are aligned. We arrive at our destination more smoothly, with less effort, less wear and tear, and less frustration and confusion than we (and our students) experience when intentional design has not been part of the course-creation process.

The value of starting with the end in mind is clear. The small teaching approaches outlined here ensure that we are getting the most out of our backward design. In so doing, we can significantly increase the quality and effectiveness of our online classes without significantly increasing the time and effort required from us.

Chapter 2

Guiding Learning Through Engagement

INTRODUCTION

I've discovered a lot about the science of learning in the dance studio.

I began teaching beginning and intermediate jazz dance at the local community college after having been a dancer for more than 20 years. But nobody actually gave me any instruction in terms of how I should help students become dancers. Instead, I learned how to teach dance through the twin methods of emulating my favorite teachers of the past and by trial and error.

I learned, for example, that when introducing a new step, it helps beginners to get the feet down first before learning what the arms will do. Otherwise (though I didn't know it was called this then), there's too much cognitive load. Beginning dance students can't process the footwork and the arm movement at the same time. They learn more successfully if they tackle one, then add the other, with me guiding them along every step of the way.

I learned that beginning dancers get frustrated and demotivated if I constantly throw new things at them. Better to practice one new step for a while, get feedback from me on their progress, and build confidence and self-efficacy before introducing a slightly more complex step or one that requires greater skill.

I learned, most generally, to pay close attention to process: Teach the simple stuff before you move on the more advanced steps. I had to ensure that dancers had strong basic technique before I asked them to execute advanced turns or leaps. Otherwise, if a dancer wasn't prepared to hurl their body through space in a double stag or switch leap, I'd be helping them limp or hop or sometimes crawl out of the studio with a dislocated knee, bad sprain, or broken bone.

What I learned in the world of dance holds true in sports as well. You don't see soccer coaches asking their players to perform scorpion kicks before they've had countless hours of drills and feedback on their work. Young gymnasts don't begin with death-defying aerials; they spend countless hours on the ground, working with their coaches to master basic skills.

But we often do the academic version of this with our students. We don't break down difficult tasks into more manageable steps. We don't provide process-oriented feedback while they are working; we wait until they have completed a major assignment to let them know how they performed. We don't help students build confidence as they complete segments. We put them on the bicycle with no training wheels and expect them to spin away with no falls, no scraped knees or elbows. Sometimes we even defend our approach in the name of rigor.

The first online class I taught, and the one I've taught the most, is a junior-level English composition class. As has happened to many of you, I was given online content for my class. When I first started teaching it, I'd made none of the decisions about the class except to adjust the due dates for the current semester. It was an accelerated writing intensive course. Students read lots of material in a short space of time, wrote the ubiquitous online discussion posts, submitted short- to medium-length papers. And then, out of the blue, came a major research paper. Little in the online course prepared students for this complex task.

Indeed, I hardly understood the requirements the first time I taught the class. My students were certainly not prepared to succeed.

I'll give them credit: They tried their best. But without any guidance and support from me throughout the process, their papers turned out badly. Topics were poorly selected. Arguments were nonexistent. Sources were neither credible nor scholarly. The writing itself was abysmal.

I learned something else that semester: Grading poor student work takes a long time. It's also painful and unrewarding, especially when you're fairly certain that students won't seriously consider your feedback and improve their work. In this case, the research paper was the last assignment of the course. Students submitted their papers and then likely put the whole experience out of their minds.

Looking back, it's clear that they would have benefited tremendously from consistent engagement with me, and even with each other, throughout the process of producing that final, high-stakes assignment – something that forms a more regular part of my teaching in face-to-face environments. The online classroom presents special challenges when it comes to creating those kinds of regular opportunities for engagement with our students, but small teaching strategies can make a difference.

IN THEORY

The theoretical justification for scaffolding the learning of your students could come from multiple directions. For example, we could review the importance of formative assessment, and the many studies that show how multiple, low-stakes assignments support learning more effectively than a single summative one. Or we could point to the connection between scaffolding and metacognition, and how scaffolding provides students with more opportunities to pause and reflect on their learning.

But consider instead the findings of *The Meaningful Writing Project: Learning, Teaching, and Writing in Higher Education*, an intriguing book published in 2016 by three researchers in the field of composition studies. Michele Eodice, Anne Ellen Geller, and Neal Lerner spent years trying to understand the kinds of writing assignments, from courses of any kind, that students found meaningful in their college courses. They surveyed more than 700 undergraduates at three different institutions, all of whom were given two core prompts:

1. Describe a writing project from your undergraduate education that was meaningful to you.
2. Explain why it was meaningful.

The authors spent several years interpreting and categorizing the responses to those two questions. Working with a team (which included undergraduates), they supplemented their survey data by interviews with two groups: (a) a subset of the survey respondents and (b) faculty members who had created meaningful writing assignments. The results of their analysis are fascinating reading, and – in our estimation – generalizable beyond writing assignments. The results, in other words, can help us understand what students find meaningful as they complete the work of their college-level courses.

Among the top three elements that they heard from students over and over again was that meaningful work allowed students multiple opportunities for engagement *throughout the completion of their assessments.* In other words, the faculty member did not simply hand out an assignment sheet and then send students away to complete it. Instead, the faculty member built into the assessment many small steps along the way.

Those small steps took many different forms, which means we have lots of flexibility to adapt the findings of their research into our courses. The specific forms of engagement the students reported in their surveys – including multistage feedback from the instructor, peer review sessions with their fellow students, and short assignments building to a larger one – were less important than the fact that regular engagement formed a fundamental part of the learning process.

Previous research, including a large-scale study conducted by the National Survey of Student Engagement (NSSE), had found that "interactive writing processes" – similar to engagement – proved especially effective in the teaching of student writing. *The Meaningful Writing Project* found an even stronger effect of such engagement: "Instructors in classes in which the meaningful writing project occurred," they write, "were more likely to use informal, nongraded writing … and to have students engage in peer review compared to NSSE respondents" (Eodice, Geller, and Lerner, 2016, p. 55). Both of these large-scale surveys of student writing thus report the power of multistep engagement throughout an assessment in helping students find it meaningful.

It might go without saying, but we'll say it anyway: Students who find an assessment meaningful are more likely to work hard on that assessment, learn from it, and complete it successfully. That link appears again and again in the student responses documented in *The Meaningful Writing Project*. "While I was writing I was given great feedback on my paper," one student wrote, "that helped me end up with a great finished product and a good grade." Another student pointed to the extent to which the learning from the writing project transferred to other contexts: "This assignment has affected all of my other writing projects because I am constantly mindful of audience, voice, tone, format, style, and other writing principles" (Eodice, Geller, and Lerner, 2016, p. 66). These are the kinds of responses we want from our assessments, and frequent engagement is the tool that can help us get there.

Students in online courses, just like students in face-to-face courses, can have trouble both understanding the purpose of their assignments and course activities and managing them successfully. Complex assignments might require a dozen or more cognitive steps that can be difficult for a student to organize and complete in a logical, timely manner. When we build in plenty of engagement along the way, as we will argue in the models that follow, we provide the opportunity both for students to complete our assignments successfully, and for them to see the deep value and meaning of the work we are asking them to do.

MODELS

The models in this chapter begin by drawing directly from the kind of research reported in *The Meaningful Writing Project* – in other words, by providing lots of small signposts and opportunities for feedback as students complete assessments. But from there we'll move on to ways in which we can provide frequent opportunities for engagement throughout the course, and not just on our assessments. Engagement can prove especially challenging in online courses, when students can feel isolated from both you and from one another (Bolliger and Inan, 2012). These models, and the principles that follow, will help break down the barriers between you and the students, between the students themselves, and between the students and the course content.

Break Down Complex Tasks

The Meaningful Writing Project helps explain why my online junior-level composition class research paper assignment was such a disaster. I had built in no engagement or scaffolding along the way. I taught the assignment a couple of times as it was presented to me – namely, requiring students to submit the final paper without any milestones or feedback opportunities before submission. Then I realized that I could improve the quality of these research papers, and improve students' learning as well, by doing what I do in my in-person classes. I set up an incremental sequence of tasks and deadlines designed to pace out the work and help students know they were doing the right thing.

This essential focus on process, common in face-to-face classes, often gets overlooked online. To bring it into your online courses, create a checklist with the steps required to make progress toward a cumulative assignment and the deadlines for each. Have students submit a topic for the paper or presentation, for example. This needn't be an overwhelming production. Have them write or record two or three sentences describing what they want to do and submit this as an assignment.

After getting your feedback on their topic, students can then submit a basic outline with their main argument and supporting bullet points. Require them to turn in a list of sources, whether that be a formal annotated bibliography or a simple list of sources and bullet points about the content and value of each. Next, assign a first draft. Build in peer review, using your Learning Management System (LMS) group tool to assign pairs. You could require the pair to meet using videoconferencing tools, or even just by phone, to give substantive feedback to each other.

All of what I suggest here can be embedded in group projects as well (and if this hadn't already occurred to you, you can use it in your face-to-face and blended teaching, too). Provide a checklist and incremental deadlines for the group to turn in evidence of their progress at various points of their work together. This can have the additional benefit of facilitating healthy group functioning.

Of course, you must review the incremental work of your students and provide timely feedback about their progress. Are they on track to succeed? Tell them so, or give pointers for improvement.

A few years ago, students in my graduate online educational technology class were to execute what I'd designed to be a meaningful and authentic final assessment. Their project required them to identify a problem in a class that they teach, research and identify a technology tool that could help them solve the problem, design a lesson that implemented the tool, teach the lesson to real or volunteer students, and then report back on their experience. For whatever reason that semester, lots of my students got the wrong end of the stick. They submitted the first piece, a description of their problem and the technology solutions they were considering. I read these with growing dismay one Saturday morning around 6 a.m., one of my most productive online teaching times. At least two-thirds of my students had turned in ideas that would not work at all, plans that would cause them to fail miserably on the project. This would inevitably be reflected in their grade.

I soon realized that my instructions must not have been clear since so many of my students were going about it the wrong way. So I created a quick slideshow featuring some freely available images of literal train wrecks. At such an early hour, I was not presentable for a webcam recording, so instead I narrated the slides to clarify instructions, identify where lots of them were going wrong, and suggest how they could start again or make significant changes to get them back on track. Before 8 a.m., I'd sent an announcement urging students to watch the video. They were therefore able to use all day Saturday and Sunday, valuable time for online graduate students with full-time jobs, to reassess and re-engage in a productive way. Several later told me how grateful they were for this correction before they'd invested too much time into the project.

Two key points: First, I had to acknowledge that I was partly to blame. Teaching requires a certain humility. It was necessary to recognize my own shortfall, some gap in the initial instructions, in order to help my students succeed. Second, I had to act fast. Had I waited to review student submissions until the middle of the following week, my correction would have come too late. Carving out a bit of unanticipated time on that Saturday morning, a small sacrifice that mildly impacted family life, was necessary in order to get the information to students in time for them to benefit from it.

Break down your big assignments into manageable chunks, help students pace their work, and provide meaningful feedback along the way. The quality of student learning will improve without a doubt.

Release Content Strategically

An effective way to provide multiple opportunities for engagement with online class content is to use the conditional release (CR) function available in most LMSs. Using this feature, a piece of content does not become available until the student meets a condition. For example, before students can access math instruction and homework practice for a new topic, they must achieve a minimum passing score on a quiz that reviews the skills learned in the preceding topic. This kind of scaffolding requires students to demonstrate some level of mastery (you can set the conditions as to what level you require) before they can see or access the next piece of content. Using conditional release, or adaptive release as it is sometimes called, can provide helpful structure and another point of engagement in online classes where students must direct much of their own learning.

A team of researchers examined the effects of CR on student performance in a comparison of the impact of CR in undergraduate entry-level face-to-face and online math classes (Fisher et al., 2015). They drew on their earlier work in which they established best practices for using CR, as well as a subsequent study that identified student perceptions of the value of CR. In their 2015 experimental study, they predicted that CR would improve student performance (resulting in higher test scores and average final grades) and that CR would have greater impact in online courses compared to in-person courses, "given that many features of CR are easier to implement and control in an online ... format" (p. 4). Their results showed that students in the online math courses did indeed earn higher exam scores and final grades than in the control group of online classes with no CR. But this was not the case in the face-to-face classes; students in these classes were not helped by the use of CR compared to students in face-to-face classes with no CR. For our purposes, a key finding is that using conditional release helped online students earn better grades. I suspect that a primary cause for increased success rates in online classes is that online students can benefit from the more structured process that conditional release provides, since they lack the structure and support provided by regular in-class meetings.

You can use CR to guide students and provide early feedback on their performance in many different ways. In a psychology class, create a mastery vocabulary quiz that requires students to demonstrate knowledge of key terms before being able to proceed with new content. In a political science class, ask students to submit an end-of-module written or recorded summary of key concepts before they can access the next module. In a philosophy class, create an assignment that requires students to outline the argument being presented in the assigned text before they can access the subsequent analysis paper assignment instructions.

In a criminal justice class, have students take a quiz on your video mini-lecture before they can access the next segment of your mini-lecture series on the topic. You can use conditional release in almost every discipline to check for student understanding and provide feedback, whether that is machine-graded feedback provided by an LMS quiz, which might be more practical in large enrollment classes, or your manual review of student work before they proceed to the next step of a major project or assignment, which might be more meaningful for the content you're teaching.

Here's one way you can structure this process in your online class. Create an assignment at the beginning of each module, which is the only thing that students see in the module. Provide detailed instructions. You might ask students to write one paragraph (around 200 words) in which they summarize the key points of the preceding module and predict how it might relate to this module's topic. Explain that the purpose of this task is to help them practice retrieval and look for connections between the previous module and the current one (for more on the cognitive benefits of retrieval practice and making connections, see Chapters 1 and 4 of the original *Small Teaching*). Once students submit their response, which, in line with Universal Design for Learning (UDL) principles, can be by text entry, uploading a document, or submitting an audio or video response, the rest of the module content becomes available.

You can assign points for these conditional assignments and quizzes, or you can choose not to count them toward the grade. If they are set so that students must submit a task, these activities don't necessarily have to be graded. Noted educator and author José Bowen often makes the point that the tennis net doesn't grade your swing. I heard Bowen speak in November 2018 at the Professional and Organizational Development (POD) Network in Higher Education conference, and he discussed the importance of the kind of nonevaluative feedback that a tennis net provides. The net doesn't assign points based on your performance. It provides feedback. Either your ball sails over it or the ball hits the net and bounces back to you. But the net doesn't give you a grade (Bowen, 2018). You can use conditional release to achieve the same purpose: help students get feedback on their learning without necessarily assigning points.

Don't overdo this. You could create frustration if students have to jump through this hoop (as they might see it) too many times before being able to proceed with the course. Use this approach intentionally, strategically, and in a limited way. Help students to make steady progress and receive valuable input on their learning, whether it's confirmation that they understand the concept or feedback that indicates they need further review, by the selective use of conditional release.

Scour Class Interactions for Cues

When you're teaching in person, you can look out at your students, walk the room, and observe nonverbal cues that indicate students aren't getting it. Or they're bored. Or you've lost their attention entirely. Good teachers acknowledge these cues and change tack accordingly. They might provide more explanation, or an illustration, or another way to describe the concept. Or they might stop the current activity – lecture or small group work or individual problem-solving – and start doing something else.

Online, you don't have these visual cues quite so readily available. You can't see the quizzical facial expression of your online student, trying to make sense of your assignment instructions, by themselves, alone with their computer screen. It's not so easily observable when students have lost interest and drifted off. You usually don't have a chance, real-time, to correct a misunderstanding the way you could during class discussion or small group work.

But you can still monitor and support the engagement of your online students, and it's important to do so. The small teaching approach here is to check in frequently and keep an eye on student interactions, even if only for a few minutes two or three times a day.

Notice what questions you receive through the LMS message system. Are several students asking you the same thing? Instead of replying to each one, post a quick video or text announcement to further explain and clear up confusion. Even better, send a quick copy-and-paste reply to each student individually, saying to check the announcement. This way you acknowledge individuals and help the group as a whole at the same time.

Many online classes include a question-and-answer discussion forum for just this purpose. If your course doesn't have this element, make that small teaching strategy number one: Add it! Students can post general questions about the course and assignments so that everyone benefits from the answer. Be sure to check it and reply promptly or at least in a reasonable amount of time. I've observed online classes in which the questions for the instructor remain unanswered for days, leaving students feeling abandoned and discouraged.

When you do reply, again, consider how to scale up your response. Sometimes I duplicate the answer I put in the post as a class announcement that goes to students' email addresses, just to be sure they are getting the information. You can apologize for any duplication, but make it clear that you want to make sure all your students have what they need to succeed. Another way to scale up is to collect frequent questions and post as frequently asked questions (FAQs) the next time you teach the class.

In addition to monitoring questions, you can monitor discussion interactions. This doesn't have to be the time drain you might imagine. Interacting with your students in discussion is an important way to guide their learning. Are they confused about a concept? Misapplying it to their context? You can detect this and correct it through a quick reply.

Some faculty don't engage in online discussion forums with their students, but doing so fosters both cognition and student engagement. When you teach in person, you wouldn't launch a class discussion and then walk out of the room, leaving the students to conduct their own discussion. Yet many online faculty do just that – leave students alone to lead their own discussion online. Instead, consider the findings of a meta-analysis of 41 research studies of online discussion (Zhou, 2015). One clear theme that emerged is that students highly value faculty interaction in online forums, and that the quality of faculty interaction can have a positive impact on peer-to-peer interaction. In other words, instructors who interact regularly in the discussion board and model good online discussion practice can enhance the learning experience of their students. Further, certain faculty behaviors, such as summarizing a student's post, directly addressing the subject of the post, and responding to students' posts more than once per week can encourage critical thinking in online classes (Belcher et al., 2015).

Interacting with students in your online discussions is well worth doing. Indeed, I tell my students that if they see a reply from me in the discussion board, it's in their best interest to read it. My best online teaching takes place in the forums.

To accomplish this efficiently, set aside 30 minutes per day, four to six days a week. The shorter your class session, the more days per week you should log in. Teaching a 16-week class? Four days per week is fine. Teaching a four-week summer session?

Help your students by investing the additional time you expect them to. Log in six or maybe even seven days per week when class is so condensed.

Skim through that day's discussions and post quick replies where needed. These can take two to three minutes each but can have a big impact on student learning. Most importantly, students see you in the class, guiding their learning, providing instruction. They know that you support them and care about them, and are likely to more fully engage as a result. This return on your investment of a few minutes per day is significant.

Provide Module Discussion Highlights

Another way to provide small signposts and feedback for students throughout the course is to help them focus on important concepts that arise in online discussions. These forums, at their best, can be invigorating, highly engaging, and motivating. Online discussions can be the highlight, the pinnacle of learning, in a well-designed and intentionally taught class. But it's equally true that robust online discussions can become overwhelming for both students and instructors.

To address this concern, write or record a summary of important and interesting points that emerged in the module's discussion. Post this in the forum, perhaps pinning your post so that it stays at the top. Or send it as a concluding announcement for each module. Either way, reinforce the learning that happened within the module to help students discern what is most relevant and what they need to retain from the lively conversation that can take place online.

I recently facilitated the ACUE (Association of College and University Educators) Course in Effective Teaching Practices for 65 or so of our faculty. After the nine-month online professional development course had ended, several faculty learners told me how much they appreciated it when I quoted their discussion posts at the end of the module. People love to see their contributions publicly recognized and praised.

Caitrin Blake, a faculty member at Arapahoe Community College, makes a similar point in a recent blog post, "An Online Instructor's Guide to Better Discussion Boards." Blake argues that we should "reward good work on discussion boards." One way to do this is to "identify posts that went above and beyond expectations" (2017).

I managed this task by copying and pasting important snippets and insightful comments into a running document throughout the week. I would check in to the discussion forums most weekdays. I'd reply to people, commenting and asking questions where appropriate to further the conversation. But I also knew that not everyone would be able to closely follow the details of the week's discussion.

Our faculty learners truly were making valuable contributions to our collective understanding of new concepts, and I wanted to ensure that these contributions were not lost. So I saved short quotes along with details such as the learner's name and the context of the comment. I added to this document each time I went into the online discussion. By the end of the week, I had an at-a-glance summary of highlights, which meant that it took only a few minutes to write a concluding announcement to share some quotes from the week and to draw people's attention to the most relevant and interesting elements from the conversation.

Incidentally, online discussions need not be solely reserved for fully online classes. When purposefully integrated into the course design, they can add an important dimension to blended and in-person classes, too. Incorporate opportunities for students to engage with concepts, you, and each other in between class sessions. Apply this same strategy: Shortly before the next class meeting, maybe the evening before, send an announcement highlighting key points and questions to help students be most prepared for class the next day.

Again, this suggestion serves multiple purposes: to emphasize key points, to increase motivation by calling out individuals with exemplary posts, to serve as study guides, to ensure students don't miss something important. Done well, online discussions can be just as noisy as a lively conversation taking place in the classroom. Help students get key takeaways by summing up what they've learned, just as you do in person.

PRINCIPLES

Engagement doesn't happen as naturally in online classes as it does in person. Context isn't created effortlessly. Connections aren't always quite as clear. But it doesn't take much to help your students check in regularly to get a sense of how they're doing in the class. Provide multiple opportunities for engagement to monitor their progress, give them quick feedback and encouragement, and promote better learning.

Break Down Complex Tasks

Help your students pace their work and feel confident that they are performing to your expectations by chunking major assessments into manageable pieces. Provide a checklist or an overview of the entire process. Schedule deadlines such that you can give timely feedback so that students can benefit from it as they work on the next part of the task. Build confidence and self-efficacy as you guide and support student learning.

Notice and Respond to Cues

Where are there communications breakdowns? Are multiple students asking the same questions? Have online discussions gone astray – or worse, silent? Spend a few minutes in class every day, or if not every day, on several nonconsecutive days of the week. Post announcements to answer the questions you receive by email. Reply in the discussion forums to praise a strong post or correct a minor misunderstanding. Provide regular but not time-intensive signals to your class to ensure they stay engaged and productive.

Give Feedback – Frequently

Look for every opportunity to help students know how they are doing in the class. Think early and often. It's easy for online students to feel isolated and unsupported. Go out of your way to tell students they're on track, or what to change to get back on track. It truly needn't take long. A few minutes per day, multiple days per week. This small investment will frequently result in big learning gains.

SMALL TEACHING ONLINE QUICK TIPS: GUIDING LEARNING THROUGH ENGAGEMENT

Without intentional effort on your part, online students can easily disengage. Use the models and principles of this chapter to increase the number of interactions that students have with the course, and the opportunities that you have to check progress and provide feedback.

- *Create several mini-assignments that become the cumulative assessment in the class.* Set deadlines for each. Provide feedback on each. Help students pace themselves. Build self-efficacy as you reinforce student learning during each step of the process.
- *Create conditional release assignments that guide students' learning, let them know whether they've mastered course concepts, and help students discover connections between class activities.* Get students to think about why they are completing module tasks, and why they're doing so in that particular order.
- *Seek out cues that indicate students may be confused.* Notice patterns in the kinds of questions students ask you. Pay attention to trends in student submissions that show misunderstanding or miscommunication. Take quick action via an announcement, clarification video, or email to the class. Help students get back on track and stay there.
- *Post summaries of each module's discussion forums.* Point out what's important and what needs paying attention to, in order to proceed with class content.

CONCLUSION

Some people are really great at teaching themselves. They're motivated. They know where to go for the information they need. They read the user manual or find a tutorial video online or download an app to learn a new language. They are self-sufficient learners.

But many of us are not like that. Many of us prefer, even need, a guided learning experience. I will never learn Adobe Photoshop by trial and error. If I were to need to learn to use this program, which I've successfully avoided until now, I would enroll in a class, knowing I'd need the structure and the expert help of the instructor to keep me engaged and learning.

We can guide our students' progress by providing incremental feedback and engaging them frequently through multiple means, in just such a way. When you actively and intentionally engage your students, they will likely respond to that attention by working harder and by immersing themselves in class content and activities. Best of all, this needn't be an overwhelming task. Your students will learn more, and learn better, when you give those small signposts, early and often, throughout the course.

Chapter 3

Using Media and Technology Tools

INTRODUCTION

Most of us take our everyday technologies for granted. We expect them to work seamlessly. We do not even notice when they work well.

Every morning, we are awakened by an alarm, whether on our smartphone or a bedside clock. We make our way to the kitchen, flip on the light, and brew the perfect cup of coffee with the touch of a button. We reach into the refrigerator for our favorite creamer to flavor our coffee. We sit down with our mobile device and scan the day's news.

Without the technology solutions we all have in our own homes, how much longer would each of these activities take? Two hundred years ago, we'd wake up naturally or rise with the sun. If it were still dark, we would light a candle. Coffee drinkers would have to grind the beans, light the stove, boil water. If we wanted cream, we'd have to trek out to the ice house to get it. We might collapse at the end of the day, after the work was done, with the day's newspaper to get a view of the outside world.

Technology has made our lives easier in many ways. We default to the assumption that it will be there to support us, that it will solve the problems we do not even remember we had before we had electricity, cars, the internet. It's easy to forget that technology serves a purpose, that it solves problems. It's easy to get distracted by the shiny.

A couple of years ago, a faculty colleague of mine took an unsolicited call from a representative from a vendor for a classroom response system, commonly known as clickers. The salesperson convinced her that this tool would solve all her large-enrollment lecture class problems, so my colleague signed on the dotted line and came to us for training on the tool. Fortunately, one of my learning design colleagues called a time-out to ask her whether this was really the right tool for the job. She'd been distracted by the shiny, but came to see that clickers would not address her challenges without a purposeful design for their use.

Consider the current state of classroom technology. In the name of active learning, institutions spend hundreds of thousands of dollars on high-tech learning spaces featuring sophisticated technology and flexible furniture to facilitate collaboration. The classroom tech is controlled by a highly complex console at the front of the room. But very often the systems are so complex that they are not used to full effect. I have known many faculty, people without adequate preparation to teach in these spaces, who are intimidated by the sophisticated technology and do not really use it at all.

That's a lot of very expensive shiny technology that does not serve a clear purpose.

IN THEORY

Derek Bruff is the director of Vanderbilt's Center for Teaching and one of the leading voices in higher education today on the use of technology in teaching. An early adopter of the use of personal response systems in class, Bruff authored one of the first books on the subject, and maintains an active blog on teaching and learning in higher education, with special attention to the role that technology can and should play in our courses. Bruff's more recent book, *Intentional Tech: Principles to Guide the Use of Educational Technology in College Teaching* (in press), begins with him describing the technology that he finds most essential to his own teaching: chairs on wheels. "By that," he explains,

> I mean classroom furniture, including tables and chairs, that I can easily move around before and during class. When I walk into my classroom, I have typically planned a series of activities for my students focused on my learning objectives for the day. Sometimes that involves whole class discussion, other times small group work, or pair work or a class debate or a jigsaw activity. Moveable furniture helps me create the kind of classroom environment that supports the learning activities I have planned.

You'll hear a similar message about teaching and technology from almost every leading voice in this field. Eric Mazur, the Harvard physicist who popularized the use of personal response systems in higher education, gives workshops around the world about his conversion from a traditional lecturer to an advocate for active learning. He has become known especially for his writing on peer instruction, which pairs the use of a personal response system with collaborative learning. At a recent workshop that Jim attended, Mazur had participants engaging in sample peer instruction activities by using hand signals instead of clickers or phones or other electronic devices. A presentation following Mazur's, given by biologist Mindy Maris, had us using colored index cards to show our responses. All three of these proponents and practitioners of technology-enhanced teaching are perfectly willing to step away from the shiny tools when they are not required to accomplish their objectives.

Cognitive psychologist Michelle Miller has been another pioneer in research and writing about technology in education, and she brings the findings of her home discipline to bear on the field, exploring applications of research from the learning sciences to the intersection of education and technology. When it first became possible to incorporate multimedia components into college courses, she points out, many faculty members leapt to do so – and many still do, even when it might not seem like a good fit.

> The contemporary era of educational technology offers a wealth of multimedia bells-and-whistles we can add to our learning activities. Most of us have an intuitive sense that these media engage students beyond what we can do with plain text ... Intuitions, however, are not always right. (Miller, 2014, p. 149)

In fact, Miller argues, some uses of multimedia in teaching have been shown to *detract* from learning, instead of supporting or enhancing it. For example, if you are showing a slide presentation to students, and narrating over your slides – as you might do for a simple video in an online course – the impact on student learning might well depend on how you decide to handle the content of the slides. Simply reading the words on the slides can produce what the research calls the *redundancy effect*, which will actually hurt student learning; but you can err at the other extreme as well, and interfere with learning by not paying enough attention to the slides. What works best – Miller describes it as the "Goldilocks" principle – is a close but not perfect relation between slides and narration, and when the narration occurs in conversational language (Miller, 2014, p. 154).

The point being made by all of these experts in the field of educational technology just represents an extension of what we argued in Chapter 1: Every decision you make in designing your online course should extend from the learning objectives you have designed for your course. Develop those objectives first, and then figure out which technological tools will help you and your students meet them. You'll likely not be using chairs with wheels with your online students, but you might well find that the latest fancy teaching tool or program that you have heard about from a colleague just does not fit well with your course, and that some simple alternative will get the job done more efficiently.

MODELS

A faculty member in construction management wanted his students to draw on actual blueprints, but he only had one set. His solution? Students worked in groups and took a picture of the blueprint with an iPad. Using an app, they drew on the blueprint according to the instructions. They were then able to share their image with the rest of the class on the large projection screen so the class could review and discuss.

A group of faculty had worked for three days in a teaching seminar. At the end of the seminar, teams were to present their work. The other participants wanted to contribute in real time and also record the interaction and material for later reference. Their solution? Each faculty team created a shared Google Doc. As they presented, other participants contributed additional resources and ideas directly into the doc. By the end of each team's presentation, a rich, robust set of materials existed, more fully developed than the team members themselves had started with.

I teach advanced jazz dance, but my body does not perform the advanced turns and leaps like it did 20 years ago. My solution?

I pause class, gather my dancers around me, and play a YouTube video on my smartphone of a young and agile dancer executing the leap with perfect technique. I describe what she is doing so my students get both good instruction and a helpful visual example.

All three of these real-life scenarios feature a purposeful technology tool to accomplish an objective or solve a problem. The construction management professor only had one set of blueprints to work with. The faculty teams wanted to contribute to each other's work in a meaningful way. I am just plain getting old; new aches and pains remind me that my body no longer soars and spins the way it once did.

Both in the classroom and online, our technology should solve teaching problems or open new possibilities for teaching excellence. We have plenty of opportunities to accomplish that goal using the small teaching approach.

Create Short Lecture Videos

One of the pervasive problems of online classes is that they can be text-heavy, dry, and boring. Students are often confronted by an off-putting wall of text. An increasingly feasible solution? Creating short videos to deliver content.

Some faculty are charged by the prospect of upping their online teaching game with informative videos. Many more are intimidated by the idea. Creating lecture videos, for many, seems like it will be "big teaching" – that is, so much work that it never happens. But once again, it does not have to be that way. For small teaching, we advocate use of content videos: Invest a small amount of time and effort to achieve a big reward in student engagement and learning.

When thinking about how to incorporate lecture videos, many online faculty imagine posting videos of their classroom lectures in the course. This is certainly one way to do it, and some institutions are investing in elaborate lecture-capture systems to facilitate this process. But lecture capture requires expensive tech and a team of skilled professionals. The small teaching way is to record short narrated slideshow videos or webcam-style videos speaking directly to the camera on your computer monitor.

The key word here is *short*. "Traditional in-person lectures usually last an hour, but students have much shorter attention spans when watching educational videos online," writes Philip Guo in a blog post about a study he and his colleagues conducted (Guo, 2013). The researchers compiled data from 6.9 million video-watching sessions to track engagement patterns of online students. Their findings led to a strong recommendation that online class videos should be no longer than six minutes. In a conference paper that presents more in-depth results of the study, Guo and his colleagues note that informal videos led to greater engagement and that high production value might not be effective. The researchers warn that a great deal of pre- and post-production effort will be needed "if instructors insist on recording live classroom lectures" (2014). That sounds like big teaching to me.

Instead, you can create a mini-lecture video yourself without expensive technology or a team of experts, and without a big investment of time. Guo's research actually showed that students engage less with formal professionally edited videos. So set aside half an hour at your desk and record your own content without worrying too much about high production value or perfectly polished delivery.

You can do this using a wide range of video-recording tools and software. For example, Canvas includes a native recording option. Other LMSs may not have that feature, but institutions are increasingly licensing third-party video tools to embed within the LMS, such as Kaltura or Panopto, so that it's seamless to use. Alternatively, find one of the many free or low-cost options available online. At the time of this writing, Screencast-o-matic (for screencasts only) or Loom (for screencasts or webcam recordings) are both good options. They are relatively simple to use to record short informal mini-lectures. Explain Everything offers recordable interactive whiteboard functionality. You could even record yourself using Zoom or other videoconferencing software if you have more experience with those formats.

The two most common forms of mini-lecture videos involve talking through a short set of slides or speaking directly to the webcam. Both can be very effective. Some instructors are not comfortable seeing themselves on camera: if you are one of them, start by recording a five-minute screen capture of your slides. With practice, you may find that you become more comfortable recording yourself talking to the camera. (Incidentally, this approach is a great way to reinforce instructor presence, as discussed in Chapter 4.) Remember the research cited by Michelle Miller, which showed that, when we narrate over slides, conversational language works most effectively. Keep your narration casual, and make sure you frequently refer to the material on the slides without just reading it word for word.

Most tools offer at least minimal editing ability, and that's really all you need. Do not edit out the occasional trip over your tongue. That makes you and your video authentic. When I record webcam mini-lectures, I capture a few extra seconds of me smiling at the camera after I finish talking. It's quick and easy to cut there or fade out so students do not see me fumbling around trying to find the right button to click to end the recording.

Remember to provide one or more alternative forms of your video content so that you are facilitating successful interactions for all your diverse learners. Captions, transcripts, and even text-based outlines of your video content can provide choices for how your students consume the material (Tobin & Behling, 2018). Some video-recording tools provide an auto-captioning tool that can speed up the captioning process (though you may have to quickly edit your captions for accuracy); if you like to type out your mini-lecture script before you record, then you'll already have a transcript ready-made. You may also want to provide guiding questions that students can answer while viewing the mini-lectures to help your learners actively engage with your videos instead of passively consuming them.

If you create your mini-lectures in your LMS, they are already embedded where you want them. If you record them using another tool, find out how best to stream them in your online class. Consult your local instructional designer or LMS support team for guidance on this and other support services to make your videos easily viewable and accessible for students on whatever device they are using to engage in class.

Most importantly, remember the small teaching philosophy. Start with one mini-lecture video. Is there a concept that has always been hard to convey in your online class? There's the subject of your first mini-lecture video. Next time you teach that class, add a couple more.

The good news is that you can reuse these videos for future classes if you are intentional about what you include. Do not include a semester-specific due date because that would be irrelevant next time you teach the course. In a recent article for *Inside Higher Ed*, David Joyner, Computer Science faculty at Georgia Institute of Technology, recommends additional strategies to make sure you can reuse your videos (Dimeo, 2017). For example, be careful about referring to other videos within your course. If your videos are too closely connected,

> modifying one area of the course might demand that you modify several others as well to stay up-to-date ... avoid this by keeping the videos as individually independent as possible. Rather than using phrases like, "Recall

the example we used last semester," say "Imagine this example." If the previous area of the course is unmodified, students will draw the connection on their own, but if that example has been dropped, the video does not come across as unconnected. (Dimeo, 2017)

This level of planning may not come naturally, but keep at it. Invest a little time figuring out what to include in your mini-lecture and how best to record it. It'll take less time with practice, you'll benefit from the return on your time investment for multiple semesters, and your students will be glad to have a break from the wall of text.

Spur Engagement with Online Content

Unfortunately, busy online students have developed a predictable pattern. At the risk of overgeneralizing, many students will not watch even the most engaging, informative, or important video if there is no accountability for doing so. Online students are becoming ruthlessly efficient in how they spend their time on classwork. We can hardly blame them for this, as so many of them have busy and challenging lives outside of their studies, which can include special challenges like caring for sick relatives or even fighting food insecurity (Goldrick-Rab, 2016).

A colleague of mine, completing an online master's degree, carefully examines the end-of-module assignment first, then skims the assigned textbook chapters for the necessary information to complete the task. I am guessing his instructors believe their students are thoroughly reading all assigned material, but that may not be the case at all. Just as my colleague does, online learners usually have both work and family obligations. Many of your students will have been drawn to the online format precisely because they need schedule flexibility in order to pursue college-level learning while maintaining other commitments. So if there is not an explicit reason to watch a video, even if it's less than two minutes long, some students will not watch it. At the same time, we know that the content we have created will benefit their learning, so we have to think deliberately about how to spur their engagement with the course materials.

An effective and simple way to create that engagement and add accountability is to include a short, graded assessment after each required video. This strategy can also help students actively work with the content, which helps them to "process information and monitor their own understanding" (Brame, 2015). Some video tools allow embedded quizzing, although not all do as of this writing, and embedding quizzing adds a layer of complexity to your work. Still, this approach can hold students accountable for engaging with your videos.

If you prefer to keep it basic, add an auto-graded quiz immediately following the video. Use your LMS quiz tool to create a five-question multiple choice or true/false test to check for understanding. You can include feedback in the quiz answers to enrich student understanding. For example, if a student gets a question wrong, you can direct the student to review a section of the video at a particular timestamp. You can set the quiz to show this text to students upon submission of the test. For correct responses, you can also provide additional guidance, perhaps suggesting where students can find additional resources on the topic.

Instead of an auto-graded quiz, in my technology and leadership class I assign a short-paragraph written response—or this could be a recorded audio or video response—worth five points after each mini-lecture video. In the instructions, I tell students they have to demonstrate to me that they watched the video, thought about the content, and are applying it to their context.

I am willing to read and grade these manually because I like that these short responses require higher-order thinking. It typically takes me less than one minute to grade each submission. That small investment of time pays big dividends in terms of increased engagement with the course content.

The most helpful and interesting videos are worthless if students do not actually watch them, or watch them without full attention. Make watching the videos worth a few points. You are likely to get far higher levels of engagement with the video content as a result.

Leverage Video for Spontaneous Updates

In addition to mini-lecture videos, short recorded announcements in which you respond to developments in your class can have a powerful impact. We all take advantage of "teachable moments" in the classroom. Ever alert, we seize unexpected opportunities to reinforce a concept based on an unplanned comment or occurrence during class. The same thing is possible, even desirable, when teaching online. When you spot student confusion, for example, take a few minutes to record yourself clarifying instructions or answering questions that pertain to the whole class. These short updates require even less planning than your mini-lectures; just identify a few salient talking points and record yourself using a native or embedded video capture and streaming tool in your LMS. Or you can use the tools already mentioned (Loom, Screencast-o-matic, or Zoom) or the YouTube app on your phone and then stream the announcement video in your class. The idea is to watch for those teachable moments, then record a quick video to address the situation.

Again, students prefer informal videos in which you are authentic to stiff, formal, or professionally edited videos. They want to see and hear you being you. You needn't record and re-record until you achieve the perfectly polished presentation. Do you always articulate every word perfectly when teaching in the classroom? If not, don't worry about doing so in your teaching videos.

For many faculty, this might be a new and uncomfortable experience. Some of us don't like the way we look or sound on camera. I'd encourage you to try recording yourself speaking to the camera, even if you begin with a very short one-minute greeting in the "Start Here" section of your online class.

We all practice public-speaking skills when we teach in the classroom. This is simply a variation of that skill. Were you perfectly comfortable standing in front of a room full of people when you first started teaching? For many of us, it took practice to gain confidence in that setting. Give yourself time to practice and build confidence in creating online class videos, too.

The more practice you get, the more comfortable you'll be with sharing your thinking in real time with your students via video. A couple of years ago, I was grading assignments while using my treadmill desk. I wanted to give a couple of points of general feedback to my students, so I used the native recording function in my LMS to make a few comments as I walked. This stretched my comfort zone; I'd never shared something as casual as that, but it was authentic and it got students' attention. Indeed, just a few weeks ago one of my students from that class, who is also a faculty member at NAU, told me he still remembered that announcement because it was so unusual to see an instructor talking to students from their treadmill desk. As another example of authenticity, last year I answered a student's question via video so I could talk through a few considerations. I recorded a 90-second response using the YouTube app on my smartphone. In the middle of my recording, two of my daughters popped up behind me and started clowning around. In the past I would have stopped the recording, banished them from the room, and started again. This time I briefly introduced them, asked them to settle down, and continued with my recording. My students told me they appreciated seeing that side of me, a working mom in my home office, and they got useful course-related information, too.

Over the years that I have been recording these in-the-moment updates, I have become increasingly fond of the informal, casual approach. When I record using the webcam on my laptop, I literally jot down three to four bullet points on a Post-it Note, affix that note immediately to the right of the camera lens, and review my talking points in a conversational tone, making sure that my eye movement to the right to read the note while talking is not apparent in the recorded video—this became easier with practice, as most skills do. Recall Philip Guo's research that shows a less formal approach can help to engage online learners, whose attention span is shorter than it would be when attending class in person.

However, if you are new to recording video announcements, or if you prefer to plan more meticulously than I do for my off-the-cuff approach, you may want to emulate Joana Girante's method (2015). Girante, an economics professor at Arizona State University, explains how she creates and uses weekly videos on ASU's TeachOnline website (which, incidentally, is a great resource for finding innovative strategies and support materials for online teaching). Girante uses her weekly announcements to set the stage for the week's content and, like me, to address things that occur to her that very week, perhaps referring to a current event or further explaining a concept that her students are struggling with. But these videos are more highly produced than mine are. Girante narrates PowerPoint slides and incorporates images, animated graphics, and short video clips to attract and hold the attention of her students. She writes a script, complete with cues for advancing slides and animations, and she uses video editing software on her computer to edit her recordings. If this approach resonates with your teaching style, invest some time in learning to create this kind of announcement video. With practice, you'll likely soon become adept at the process so that you become more efficient, able to quickly create your videos as needed throughout the semester.

While mini-lecture videos are probably best created prior to start of the term, try these short videos for updates on the fly. After all, that's what you would do in the classroom, right? You'd say a few words to clear up confusion, not hand around a sheet of paper with some written comments and explanations. If you choose to speak directly to the camera, your facial expressions, combined with your vocal intonations, can do a lot to help students understand your meaning. Provide them with these nonverbal cues using quick casual recordings.

Source Existing Media

I firmly believe that it's essential to include some videos of yourself in your online class. Your students want to see and hear you, their instructor. But you don't have to reinvent the wheel for every topic you want to present. As I am sure you know, you can find rich sources of high-quality media on every subject on the planet and beyond. Take a little time to find relevant videos, audio recordings, and images. If you are not sure where to start, ask your campus librarian for help. There's a huge amount of material available online. Find and share impactful pieces of content that add depth and breadth to your existing instructional materials. This will help students gain a richer understanding of the nuances of your subject.

For example, a faculty member teaching organizational psychology found that his students could not quite grasp the concepts in the textbook. He discerned that these ideas, presented in dry textbook-ese, did not resonate with his students.

His solution? He posted scenes from *Office Space* (as appropriate under copyright permissions) to make the concepts come to life. Students instantly understood the principles at work when presented in engaging, humorous film clips.

Notice once again that technology solved a problem. This instructor did not share *Office Space* solely because he thought it was funny. Doing so would have fallen under the questionable category of "edu-tainment." Rather, the instructor identified a problem and applied an effective technology solution. When considering adding media of any kind, think carefully about how it supports the achievement of course learning outcomes and what problem it solves. If you don't have a good answer for both of those questions, leave it out.

As you look for relevant videos, audio, and images, keep two additional considerations in mind. First, think broadly about categories and sources of media. News outlet archives. TED Talks. Images from credible sources of natural disasters, war zones, refugee camps, shrinking polar caps. Khan Academy videos. Song lyrics on YouTube. Even humorous summaries of the classics. Students in my recent First-Year Seminar on Heroes, Villains and Monsters amused themselves (and, I'll argue, learned a lot) by finding and sharing videos such as the Overly Sarcastic Productions version of *Beowulf*. (Look it up. It's funny—and informative).

Second, always be wary of the shiny. In *Minds Online: Teaching Effectively with Technology* (2014), Michelle Miller provides an excellent overview of multimedia theory, which, she notes, "is most commonly associated with Richard Mayer" (p. 153). Miller explains, "Central to the framework is the multimedia principle, which holds that adding pictures - or diagrams, or other similar representations - to text produces enhanced learning compared to text alone." Miller further explains that, although this concept seems to make sense, "a host of variables interact to create enhanced learning through multimedia" (as cited in *Multimedia Learning*, Mayer, 2009) and proceeds to give a useful overview of these variables and the various ways in which they interact. "The moral of the story? Don't bring in graphics except those with a substantive connection to what you are trying to teach. Pictures for pictures' sake make your lesson prettier, but less effective" (Miller, 2014, p. 155). Intentionally selected, images and media can powerfully impact student understanding. This seems logical, but it's important to consider the opposite of this statement. Adding images, visuals, and audio that are not directly related to content can overwhelm and confuse learners. Ensure your media resources are relevant, not distracting.

As a quick reminder, you'll want to pay attention to copyright considerations when you source existing media for your online (and other) classes. You will likely find someone at your institution, perhaps a librarian or instructional designer, who can help you navigate legal concerns. Another useful resource is the Stanford University Libraries' copyright and fair use website (https://fairuse.stanford.edu/overview).

Find the Right Tech Tool for the Job

In the 2016 second edition of their book *The Online Teaching Survival Guide: Simple and Practical Pedagogical Tips*, Judith V. Boettcher and Rita-Marie Conrad acknowledge that "digital tools are changing faster than we can describe them" (62). The challenge of "describing specific tools that will be obsolete before the book is published" led them to focus instead on technology tool categories that accomplish specific pedagogical purposes. This is an effective approach, done thoroughly in that book so I have chosen not to replicate it here. I can highly recommend *The Online Teaching Survival Guide* for a practical treatment of concepts and approaches we touch on in this text.

For small teaching with online technology tools, we can focus on implementing technology solutions in feasible yet impactful ways. Remember that our focus is on solving problems. Don't select a tech tool just because you heard of someone else using it and you thought it sounded cool. Instead, to help you teach most effectively, choose a usable technology tool that solves your problem.

Most of us have the greatest success when we make minor changes, little by little. If your roof is leaking from heavy rain, start by getting a bucket. Don't tear the roof off. Small tech tool fixes can be remarkably effective. By contrast, large-scale implementation of a complex tech tool may very well backfire and cause more problems than it solves.

So how do you identify appropriate and purposeful technologies to implement in your class? Perhaps the most efficient way to conduct your research is to search online for apps and ed tech tools aligned to your course objectives, which should reflect the range of levels of cognition in Bloom's Taxonomy. Here are just a few examples of how to intentionally align tech tools with the cognitive domain of Bloom's:

- *Use Zoom to help your students understand complex concepts.* Schedule an optional synchronous study session in which you answer students' questions in real time.
- *Quizlet can help students remember facts and vocabulary terms.* Students create flashcards that can be accessed via an app on their smartphone or tablet for studying on the go.

- *Hypothesis helps students analyze.* Have students, individually or in groups, annotate online texts to draw out deeper meaning or important concepts.
- *Google Docs and Slides help students synthesize and create.* Assign group research projects or presentations, using Google tools to foster seamless collaborative work, as learners compile findings and create papers and slide decks to report on their research.

There's a seemingly endless array of available technologies, with more coming out every day. By the time you are reading this, the above tools may have been superseded by even more effective solutions. The point is to find a tech tool that accomplishes your objective and aligns with the desired level of thinking for the learning activity you use it for.

Finally, again, I cannot emphasize enough the importance of the small teaching approach when implementing tech tools in your online class. To be most successful, start small. Make sure you yourself are comfortable with the tech. If you cannot easily and confidently use the tool, it's not the right choice for you. Remember, too, that you can teach very effectively using only the basic set of tools in your LMS. Boettcher and Conrad offer excellent advice about beginning your online teaching career with readily available LMS tools such as Announcements, Discussion Forums, Assignments, and Quizzes. "The first time you teach in any new environment or with a new set of learners," they note, "it is wise to keep it simple and use the basic set of tools well supported by your institution" (Boettcher and Conrad, 2016, p. 63). The authors further explain, "Fortunately, most communication tools for teaching and learning are now included in institution-provided learning management systems (LMS)" (p. 65). After providing a brief introduction to the basic tools available in the LMS, such as those noted above, Boettcher and Conrad share this invaluable advice:

> Give yourself a break and don't expect perfection of yourself the first time you teach in this new-to-you environment.... You are learning new digital tools, what they can do, and how to recover when things don't always go as expected. (p. 68)

This last reminder, that things don't always go as planned, is another important reason to stick with the tools that are available in the LMS and are supported by your institution if you are new to teaching online.

However, if and when you are ready to expand beyond the LMS, try one new minimal implementation of a purposeful tool next semester. The next time you teach the class, expand and refine your use of that tool, making incremental advances as you go. Before you know it, you'll be teaching effective and engaging online classes, taking full advantage of the enhancements offered by a range of powerful technology tools, improving student learning and engagement all the while.

One note of caution: Consider the impact on your students of using technologies outside of your LMS. These may require a separate account or a subscription fee; your selected tool may not be accessible for students using a screen reader or keyboard-only commands; social media tools could mean that students have to put themselves out there in a public space in a way they may not prefer to do. Think through the implications and consult with your local instructional designer to help you think about issues you might not even be aware of. Whatever tools you decide to use to engage your students and foster their learning, make sure they are the right tools for the job at hand.

PRINCIPLES

Purposefully incorporating technology tools in online classes can have a significant positive impact on student learning. Follow these guiding principles to help ensure a successful addition to your teaching toolbox:

Identify the Objective

You began creating your class by writing your objectives, and those objectives should help determine your technology use. What tools will help you achieve your goals – and what tools will help you solve the problems that would prevent you from achieving those goals? You can and should certainly explore and learn all about the many technological tools that are available to online instructors, but explore with a critical eye. Which ones of them will help your students learn? Which ones align with your objectives? As you proceed throughout the semester, you will see new challenges arise, learning moments missed, and unexpected obstacles. These pain points are opportunities to explore and implement new tech tools. Having a good understanding of the problem you want to solve will help you find the best technology solution and help to ensure that you are using the technology purposefully.

First, do No Harm

The ancient Greek physician Hippocrates is popularly credited with this basic premise. In providing medical care, doctors are to abide by the overriding principle of not hurting their patients with prescribed treatment. Likewise, our teaching methods should not make things more difficult for our learners. Select technology tools that don't hinder learning. Some common barriers to ease of use include a difficult log-in process, out-of-pocket expense, nonfunctionality with keyboard use only, or levels of complexity that require learners to use all their cognitive resources to navigate the tech. These kinds of barriers will not promote student learning and success, so carefully analyze and test the usability of your tech tools to ensure that you are not making things harder for your students.

Provide Alternative Means of Access

Including media and using technology tools can do a lot to liven up online classes. But ensure that all materials and tools are accessible in multiple formats (your institution's disability or accessibility resources department can usually help with this). The principles of Universal Design for Learning tell us that an adjustment that helps make technology accessible for one student may also help many others be successful (Tobin & Behling, 2018). For example, captioning videos enables hearing-impaired students to consume the content – but it also benefits non-native English speakers by providing another way to take in what is being said. I have manually captioned my short lectures and announcements directly in YouTube. It takes me roughly four minutes per one minute of video to type the audio. Or, try the auto-captioning tool in YouTube, cleaning up the captions with quick edits after they are produced. You can also provide full-text transcripts for videos or audio recordings. Make sure all images are tagged so that a screen reader being used by a visually impaired learner has meaningful content to convey. If you choose to include a tool that is external to your LMS, check the accessibility first. In short, don't keep your students from being able to access and participate in your online class; provide alternative options that benefit all your diverse learners with all of their unique preferences and needs.

SMALL TEACHING ONLINE QUICK TIPS: USING MEDIA AND TECHNOLOGY TOOLS

Online classes can be text-heavy and static. Create more dynamic and engaging courses with the intentional use of media and purposeful technology tools.

- *Create short, three- to five-minute mini-lecture videos.* Narrate over a slideshow or record yourself talking to the camera on your computer monitor or smartphone. Use a native video recording tool in your LMS or an external tool or app.
- *Include assessments to ensure students are attentively watching your video content.* A short multiple-choice quiz or written or recorded reflection can hold students accountable for consuming – and actively engaging with – the content you provide.
- *Build depth and nuance with existing video content and your own informal video announcements and updates.* Source clips from any number of media forms and outlets ranging from TED Talks to popular films. Add timely clarification with authentic casual video clips you record. Remember the significance of nonverbal cues to communicate effectively. Find and create video content to bring these cues into the otherwise isolating online classroom.
- *Select technology tools that solve a problem you have identified and that align to the intended outcomes of a given activity or of the course as a whole.* When thinking about using a new tool, whether it's within or external to your LMS, stop and ask yourself why you want to use the tool. If you don't have a good pedagogically sound purpose, leave it out.

CONCLUSION

A few years ago, I decided to keep a food journal to help me achieve some health-related goals. Looking for a pocket-sized notebook that I could keep on me, I spent a couple of hours searching through hall closets, junk drawers, and cupboards full of kids' activities and art supplies. I was pretty sure my young daughters had some stashed from when they used to play Restaurant and take each others' orders while pretending to be servers.

It was only after my fruitless search that it dawned on me that I carry around a device in my pocket all day long. I am never without my smartphone. And chances were good that I'd find an app to function as a food journal. Feeling slightly foolish about the time I'd spent looking for that nonexistent notebook, I searched the App store and indeed found several robust options to track nutrition, activity, and more.

In this case I had a problem, and, although by a circuitous route, I found a technology solution. Soon I had formed a daily habit of tracking calories consumed, such that I hardly noticed I was doing it. In this way, the technology became transparent, seamlessly incorporated in my everyday routine.

Media and tech tools have great potential to improve the student educational experience, identified as national priority number one in a 2017 report from the American Academy of Arts and Sciences, *The Future of Undergraduate Education: The Future of America*. Let us employ these tools to help our students learn more effectively in our online classes. Implement transparent media and technology solutions, being careful not to make things harder or use tech for tech's sake.

These are powerful tools – powerfully beneficial or powerfully distracting. Be purposeful.

Teaching Humans

P art I of this book focused on the importance of deliberate design in online classes. Regardless of your experience level, teaching online arguably requires more planning than teaching in person, especially if you've taught in the classroom for a while. Many of us are adept at improvising during class. We likely have materials that we've used for years: slides, handouts, active learning prompts. An online class requires different kinds of materials and activities. Teaching online also requires a different form of interaction, a different demand on our time than does teaching in person. In short, we need to bring intentionality to online teaching in ways that differ from our approach in the classroom.

In this section, we focus on the humans we are teaching—the real people behind the names on the screen. The social and emotional components of learning are powerful (Eyler, 2018; Cavanagh, 2016). Online courses require deliberate attention to all three potential relationships in the course: the one you have with your students, the one your students have with you, and the one the students have with each other. In the online classroom, where students are likely completing coursework in isolation, alone with their computer, they can easily forget that there are other people in the class who can help. This is vastly different than what we experience in an in-person class, where the other people in the room are clearly visible. The existence of others gets obscured online.

To address this challenge, in Part II we look at small teaching ways of building connections between ourselves, our learners, and the course material. This takes far more intentional effort than it does in person. Yet it can be done, and multiple studies show that doing so impacts learning. Personal interactions are instrumental to online student success, just as they are in face-to-face environments.

In Chapter 4, we'll examine the importance of building community. When we facilitate the development of a robust and dynamic community of learners in an online class, we significantly increase the potential for individual student learning and success. When we don't attend to this essential ingredient, we see high attrition rates, low engagement, and minimal participation. I've entered online classes and observed tumbleweeds blowing forlornly across the deserted, dusty road. To prevent this sense of neglect, we'll explore evidence-based methods of being actively present in our classes and helping our students do the same.

Another essential component of learning is receiving input on our performance. Feedback provides crucial guidance to help us see where we are in our effort to achieve mastery. This measuring stick powerfully impacts our students' ability to learn, but like many other teaching activities, giving regular feedback requires deliberate effort in an online class. Take a moment to consider the importance of feedback in learning. People *can* learn new information and skills through one-way transmissions such as reading books (like you're doing now) or watching YouTube videos (an easier and faster method of acquiring new information), but that kind of learning requires more effort, dedication, and commitment on the part of the learner. Chapter 5 presents small teaching ways of providing the ongoing feedback that helps sustain a more typical student. These strategies can enable us to give students frequent and meaningful guidance without creating an unsustainable demand on our time.

We explore a third aspect of teaching real people in Chapter 6: helping our students successfully complete our online classes. Without set class meetings and the physical presence of an instructor and other students, the flexibility afforded by online learning can work against busy online students, who may not fully understand the time commitment and level of self-direction required to be successful in an online class. Therefore, we'll consider ways of helping our students persist.

When we keep tension on the line, we're often more success-ful in reeling in the fish. Neglecting to do so allows the fish to get away, sometimes with our favorite lure. An online course requires that same kind of regular tension on the line to keep everyone engaged. With it, we'll see more of our students successfully com-plete our classes. And when we consider that we're helping stu-dents achieve one more milestone in their journey toward degree completion, we are motivated to employ small strategies to help.

Several years ago, I set out to learn to play the bodhrán. I acquired this handheld Irish drum and found a good series of tutorial videos. Can I play the bodhrán today? No. I lost interest in the video instruction and did not persevere. The outcome would likely have been different had I bought lessons from an instructor, learned more about the instrument and its rich history, and attended the local weekly Celtic music jam session to learn from other musicians. Interacting with people, building community, and receiving input on our efforts help us to persist. We'll look at feasible ways of fostering these interactions with the people in our classes in order to help our students succeed.

Chapter 4

Building Community

INTRODUCTION

"The Storm Troopers are actually the good guys," I said. "They're just trying to keep law and order. It's the Rebels who are causing all the problems."

The room erupted in noise. Students couldn't contain themselves. Some argued with each other in spontaneous little groups. Some wildly waved their hands in the air, talking over each other as they fought for my attention. The ones who knew me pretty well by this point in the semester contented themselves with folding their arms and smirking at me from a posture of defiance. Prove it, their facial expressions said. We don't believe you.

I called on the student who was the most agitated, whom I feared might explode if I didn't allow her to express her passionate opinion on the matter. She made her point; another student argued vociferously against it. A third student opened his comment by saying, "Going back to what she said … " and proceeded to agree with the first girl, building upon her argument.

Our heated debate continued for well over 20 minutes. Periodically, I would lob in a new argumentative ingredient to stir the pot, to challenge students on their viewpoints, to demand evidence from the movie to support their position.

I certainly didn't persuade my students that I was right. I wasn't even convinced myself of the argument I was defending. But we did enjoy a lively exchange of opinions, substantiated by carefully recalled scenes from the films. By the end of the class, we likely had more questions than answers, but we were committed to continuing the conversation in our quest for new understanding.

Students later told me, in their end-of-term course evaluations, that the debates we had in that class helped them to see others' viewpoints, to consider perspectives that differed from their own – to expand their thinking. This was music to my ears: One of my primary goals for my first-year seminar class was to cultivate new ways of thinking, and our interactions in class had done just that.

The importance of exchanges such as this cannot be overstated. As social beings, we learn from each other. We may learn what not to do, we may seek to emulate others because we admire them, or we may understand complicated concepts differently as a result of someone else explaining it to us in a way that makes more sense than the teacher's explanation had.

Interacting with others is a key component of our ability to learn new things. This can happen naturally in the classroom, but it doesn't always happen so easily in an online class. As we have seen, online students are typically isolated, sitting alone behind a computer screen, engaging with class content by themselves. They experience little, if any, real-time exchanges or collaboration with other people, whether students or the instructor.

Although social experiences may not naturally happen in online classes, we can look to research old and new to help us understand how to make small changes to our teaching that could foster the robust dialogue and engagement we enjoy in the physical classroom.

IN THEORY

Creating a sense of community in an online course involves both effort and intention, but it should form an essential part of your thinking. The sense of community among learners in a course – something not always achieved very effectively in face-to-face courses, it should be noted – plays an essential role in the effectiveness of the course in producing learning. Two sources can help explain why this is so: one close to a hundred years old, which helped establish the importance of peers and community in learning; and one that appeared just after the turn of the millennium, and has provided a conceptual framework for understanding how to foster that sense of community in online learning experiences of any kind.

Lev Vygotsky was a Russian psychologist and polyglot whose research and writing took place mostly during the first decades of the twentieth century. Although he wrote about a wide number of topics, not all of them related to education, he remains most well-known today for a theory he developed about the importance of students working in collaboration with peers and instructors in order to achieve their full cognitive potential. Vygotsky posited that individual learners can be identified at specific levels of development at any point in time: we might say, for example, that a student learning math is capable of solving problem types A and B, but nothing yet beyond that. The type of problem that remains just outside of that student's reach, problem type C, is one that they will be able to achieve when they work in a social context with a more experienced learner (such as a teacher) or with their peers.

Vygotsky labeled the space between the student's current state of knowledge and the potential state of knowledge they might achieve with the help of peers as the *zone of proximal development.* In an essay first published posthumously in 1935, and later included in the 1978 collection of his work *Mind in Society: The Development of Higher Psychological Processes,* Vygotsky describes it this way:

> We propose that an essential feature of learning is that it creates the zone of proximal development, that is, learning awakens a variety of internal developmental processes that are able to operate only when the [student] is interacting with people in his environment and in cooperation with his peers. Once these processes are internalized, they become part of the [student's] independent developmental achievement. (p. 90)

In other words, an essential part of the student's movement from problem B to problem C is her observation of those around her, her collaboration with them on tasks (and even play), and her imitation of those who have already mastered problem type C – at which point problem type D becomes her new zone of proximal development. We can take Vygotsky's research as a foundation for our claim that connections and community are important to create in online courses. Students need more than access to videos, text, and disembodied voices commenting on their work. They need the presence of their peers and instructor to help them learn.

Lev Vygotsky was not alive long enough to help us understand how we can facilitate learners helping one another in online environments; for that, we can turn to a conceptual framework developed by a group of Canadian researchers in the years immediately preceding and following the turn of the millennium. From 1997 to 2001, these researchers sought to identify the characteristics of online learning experiences that could both provide guidance to online instructors and establish a framework for future research on the effectiveness of online teaching and learning. The initial presentation of their research, in a seminal 1999 paper, established the idea of a "community of inquiry" as a framework for both creation and evaluation of online teaching and learning (Garrison, Anderson, and Archer, 1999). Their initial paper has led to a fully developed field of research on the importance of community in higher education teaching and learning, one that includes an online community of inquiry devoted to research on communities of inquiry, curated by some of the key scholars in the field.

The three primary aspects of a community of inquiry established in the initial paper continue to guide that research today. The effectiveness of an educational experience, they argue, depends on *presence* in three core areas:

1. *Cognitive presence.* They define this as "the extent to which the participants in any particular configuration of a community of inquiry are able to construct meaning through sustained communication." Such construction of meaning depends on whether learners engage in activities like reflecting deeply on the course content, drawing new and creative connections with course material, or opening themselves to new ideas and ways of understanding.
2. *Social presence.* This essential feature consists of "the ability of participants in the Community of Inquiry to project their personal characteristics into the community, thereby presenting themselves to the other participants as 'real people.'" Social presence can be established or indicated in a community of inquiry through such factors as "emotional expression, open communication, and group cohesion."
3. *Teaching presence.* This last form of presence works in concert with the first two in order "to support and enhance social and cognitive presence for the purpose of realizing educational

outcomes." Practically speaking, this can occur through both the "design of the educational experience" and "facilitation" of learning within the course (Garrison et al., 1999).

These three distinct elements quite obviously work most effectively when they work in concert. The teacher begins by establishing her presence in the design of a learning experience through taking into account the actual learners who will be in the course, and builds into the structure of the course plenty of opportunities to engage with those learners through direct instruction and feedback. But a well-designed course will also provide opportunities (and incentives) for learners to interact with one another, both to help each other learn and to build that sense of community. When these two forms of presence have been established, the learners in the course are more likely to engage in the kinds of active, collaborative processes that help them construct new knowledge through their cognitive presence.

The most important and also most challenging of these three forms of presence, for the creation of online courses in higher education, will likely be social presence. "Social presence," the authors argue, "marks a qualitative difference between a collaborative community of inquiry and a simple process of downloading information" (p. 96). But you can better understand how to create social presence in your online courses if you contextualize it within the other two forms of presence, which both provide the rationale for doing so and clarify your role in the process. You want to establish that social presence because it will help students become more cognitively present in the course – in other words, more actively engaged and thinking. And you can help create that social presence through *your* presence as a teacher, which you establish initially through thoughtful design and then continuously through your interactions with learners.

In both of these areas, small teaching can help.

MODELS

Once we accept the importance of building community in what can be an otherwise very isolating learning experience, it is not difficult to implement strategies to help us do this. First, consider the impersonal nature of online class interactions. Even for experienced online learners and instructors, it's easy to forget that a name on the screen represents a human being who can benefit from your presence and benefit your learning with their presence. Reading static text in a discussion forum, course message, or written assessment does little to remind us that a unique individual wrote those words, someone with prior experiences or expertise that can help shape our understanding of course concepts. To create community in online courses, then, we should help learners see both ourselves and one another as human beings behind those names.

Structure Student Interactions

In the Community of Inquiry framework, as well as in Vygotsky's work, student-to-student interaction helps create new learning. It's not enough for students to work with your content. It's not even enough for students to work with you. They must work with each other, too, to learn and succeed in our online classes.

Joshua Eyler's 2018 book, *How Humans Learn: The Science and Stories Behind Effective College Teaching*, provides additional compelling arguments in favor of the value and importance of social interactions for learning. In order "to know more about the interplay between teaching and learning," he explains, "we have to delve into our nature as social beings. In fact, it is not a stretch to say that much of what makes us human stems directly from our sociality" (p. 66). Eyler goes on to highlight the centrality of social interactions for effective learning:

> At a very fundamental level, we need others in order to live functioning lives. As an extension of this, our sociality drives our learning in many essential ways. Sure, we can learn things on our own, but we rarely learn them as deeply, because so much of our learning derives from our social nature and our visceral need to communicate with other people. (pp. 66–67)

To help our students learn from each other as well as from us, their instructors, Eyler encourages us to design and teach our classes in such a way as to "place our social natures as human beings front and center in the learning process" (p. 83).

One of the most common ways to harness the power of social interactions in online classes, especially student-to-student interactions, is to include online discussions as a central element of the course design. A tried-and-true method to create community from the beginning is to have students post an introduction in the first week of class. These introductions can be in the form of text or video. Be sure to incentivize students' replies to each other as well. Perhaps students can ask a follow-up question of at least one peer, to help them get to know each other. Guide them to engage with class content right away by sharing two or three goals or expectations for the class, or by identifying metacognitive strategies they plan to employ to be successful (McGuire and McGuire, 2015) or by describing what they may already know about the subject. In other words, introduction posts can be more than just an ice-breaker; they can be a purposeful in-road to class material as well.

If appropriate for your learning outcomes, consider requiring video introductions of your students. Several of mine have told me that they've worked with the same people in their online program for multiple semesters, without ever being able to put a face to a name. We can learn a lot about and from each other through the relatively simple means of seeing and hearing each other. YouTube and other tools make this quite feasible, and the payoff in creating strong community from the start can be significant.

Continue class conversations through meaningful online discussion prompts. Contrary to popular belief, online discussions can be just as rich and engaging as a lively classroom discussion. Indeed, in *Creating Engaging Discussions: Strategies for Avoiding Crickets in Any Size Classroom and Online* (2018), Jennifer Herman and Linda Nilson point out that online discussions can "avoid the problems related to the traditional classroom, such as time limitations, dominating students, and large class sizes" (p. 49). To maximize the potential of online discussions, be sure to create discussion topics that are "discussable" – that is, avoid closed-ended questions and prompts. Instead, offer students the chance to debate, persuade, share their experience as related to a class concept, discuss a case study, or otherwise engage more deeply with class material and with each other. Key to this strategy is to require students to submit an original post and then to reply to a minimum number of their peers' posts. To foster originality, in many Learning Management Systems (LMSs) you can require students to post their own submission before they can read others' posts.

Also, setting two deadlines for each discussion forum, an earlier one for initial posts and one a few days later for replies, can help students hold a meaningful and timely conversation. Many instructors have increased success when the grade for an online discussion includes several components, including meeting staggered deadlines, replying to other students, and achieving standards for both the length and the quality of the post. Getting students to apply class concepts in a discussion with their peers can help them process and retain material more fully as they think critically, defend their argument on a particular topic, and reflect on their own and others' experiences related to class content (Herman and Nilson, 2018).

Writer and educator John Orlando presents an intriguing alternative approach to fostering meaningful online discussions in a 2017 *Faculty Focus* article. Orlando calls into question the common online class discussion requirement of one original post and at least two reply posts per student. If the purpose of this requirement is to "generate creativity," he argues, "then a response to someone else's point might contain more insight and creativity than an original [post]" (2017). Orlando proposes requiring "one or two original thoughts" instead of both original and reply posts, which, as many online instructors have found, can feel a bit unnatural. After all, when conducting a discussion in the classroom, do we require at least three contributions from every student? And that one must be a new point, while the other two respond to a peer's comment? No, we don't. That would feel inauthentic and too scripted. Orlando encourages us to similarly relax some of our standard expectations for online discussion participation in order to foster stimulating, authentic, and creative social interactions in which students can learn from each other.

Some faculty find that whole-class online discussions can feel overwhelming, with too many posts and replies, so that meaningful conversation – and learning – gets lost in the shuffle. To address this concern, consider using the group functionality available in most LMSs to create small discussion groups. Cognitive psychologist and veteran online educator Morton Ann Gernsbacher recommends this approach particularly when you're teaching large-enrollment classes. "If the pedagogical goal is to enable interaction and engagement between and among students about what they read," she explains, "then you need to divide and conquer" (Gernsbacher, 2016). Creating these smaller groups can make "a class of 80 can feel like a class of six to eight." To set this up in your LMS, you can create group discussions in which only the members of each group can access that group's discussion board. This keeps the interactions more focused and organized than they would be in the whole class discussion. The group tool itself usually offers several options, such as randomized enrollment, manual placement of students into groups, or allowing students to self-enroll. You might use this last option if each group is studying a unique topic, for instance. Students choose the topic they are most interested in exploring, which would give them some control over their experience in your class – more on this in Chapter 7. The many available options in group creation and functionality mean it's likely that you could find a way to encourage meaningful peer-to-peer interactions using this tool.

I hope by now that you agree that structuring student interactions to enable them to learn most effectively is a worthwhile thing to do, especially in online classes. In order to foster the best learning in our classrooms, Joshua Eyler notes that we "should include strategies for cultivating a climate that is conducive to learning and to productive social interactions" (2018, p. 86). However, Eyler calls into question something that many of us who teach online have often wondered, whether the technology-enabled social connections that take place in online classes can truly facilitate learning, "whether the technology allows us to tap into our sociality *enough* to maximize learning" (p. 107). A fair question. A valid question. One to which, when online environments and interactions are intentionally designed and facilitated, I would answer yes. Purposefully used, technology can allow us to sufficiently learn from and with each other. The key is to use tech for social interactions the small teaching way: by making deliberate design and teaching decisions based on the science of learning.

Show Up for Class

The importance of the social and teaching presences in the community of inquiry framework suggests that you have the potential to impact the sense of community in your online class in a way that no one else in the class has. You set the tone and the example, both at the very beginning of the class and throughout the semester. Although you may feel yourself present in class just through your role as instructor, you have to make your presence *known* to students. This can be a simple practice to implement, but it can produce significant results in keeping the attention and engagement of your students.

An often-cited case study reveals the impact of online instructor behaviors on student satisfaction with feedback and teaching quality (Ladyshewsky, 2013). The researcher compared student evaluation results on several sections of the same online class taught by two different instructors. Bear with me: Before you dismiss student satisfaction as a questionable measure of instructor effectiveness, recall that a primary goal of effective online teaching *must* be to retain the attention and engagement of our students. It's so easy for online learners to disengage that we must employ all reasonable tactics to keep them attending and participating in class. When students are satisfied with instructor behaviors, we can likely surmise that we're successfully doing our job.

In particular, Ladyshewsky focused on how the two instructors interacted with students and gave feedback in online discussion forums. Instructor 1, who earned significantly lower satisfaction ratings, posted much less frequently than Instructor 2. In addition, Instructor 2's responses to student discussion posts were more personal, using students' names, expressing gratitude for their contributions, and adding personal anecdotes to further illustrate a student's point, for example. Ladyshewsky concluded that Instructor 2, through more frequent and personal discussion posts, exhibited greater levels of social presence in addition to the cognitive and teaching presence established by the less frequent, shorter, and less personal posts of instructor 1 (p. 13).

This research reinforces the importance of frequent and supportive instructor engagement in online classes. Remember our opening analogy, about a student showing up to class on the first day of class, but no one is there? The same principle applies throughout the semester. If your students begin to feel that you are never in class, they'll stop showing up, too, and the energy of the online learning community will take a nose-dive. It's vitally important to be active in your class in order to help sustain the interactions in the class.

Online classes are not meant to be like your favorite slow-cooker recipe. They are not "set and forget." It's impossible to foster meaningful relationships with that approach. In order to be effective, you as the instructor should log in often. Actively participate and engage your students. Think of it as checking on a simmering pot, stirring often, tasting to see whether to add more salt. Your interactions in class can be minor. The important thing is to be present, and to make sure your students know it, on a very regular basis.

One of the simplest ways to make your presence known is by posting frequent text or video announcements. This serves two purposes. Frequent communication helps to keep your students focused and progressing. Plus, you can use announcements to accomplish important teaching goals: clarifying misunderstandings, summarizing the week's highlights, helping students to prepare for an upcoming exam. In some LMSs, you can even schedule announcements to post at whatever date and time you choose. In this way, you can appear to be present even when you will not actually be present – for example, if you have a travel commitment that interrupts your regular class activity. Schedule or post announcements to create an ongoing reminder that students should be paying attention to classwork.

It is also helpful to engage with your students in the online discussion forum, as Ladyshewsky found. Establish a regular routine. Maybe you will post comments, questions, and additional guidance in the online discussion board on Tuesdays, Thursdays, and Fridays. It only takes a few minutes to read student contributions and add your own thoughts. It's highly motivating for students when you are in the discussion with them – and the opposite is true, too. Many students are seriously demotivated when their instructor never joins the conversation online.

Once again, think about our analogy with the in-person classroom experience. If you were to ask your students to discuss the assigned reading as a large group, and then you walked out of the room, would you expect that 20 minutes later there would be a lively debate taking place? The more likely outcome would be that students would be on their devices, attention focused on their individual screens, if they remained in the room at all. You have to stay in the room, to lead and guide and shape the conversation in order to uncover new understanding. This is also true in an online discussion. Be present and active in the conversation in a meaningful combination of all three presences: social, teaching, and cognitive. Ladyshewsky calls for online instructors to "facilitate student engagement in discussions" (2013) so that we support students by our social, teaching, and cognitive presences.

In addition to interacting with students in discussions, it's important to make yourself known to your students by giving timely feedback. From the student perspective, submitting a paper or a project online can feel like sending something out into outer space. If there is a lengthy silence, if it takes you too long to acknowledge that you received it, let alone to grade and return the submission, students get frustrated. Post your typical turnaround time in your syllabus, and do your best to stick with your policy. Try something like, "I will typically grade and return assignments within seven (7) days of the due date. If this changes due to unusual circumstances, I'll communicate that as needed." Be sure to post an announcement or send a course message if you do get behind in grading. That certainly happens for a variety of valid reasons. Just be sure to tell your students what's happening and when you expect to catch up, so that they are not worrying whether you're still there and still actively reviewing their work.

Our students need to know we are there, we're actively participating in class, we're teaching and guiding and giving feedback and interacting and doing all the things good teachers do. Further, Michelle Pacansky-Brock, a faculty mentor for digital innovation in the California Community College system, identifies the particular importance of being there for our increasingly diverse student populations in a recent *Inside Higher Ed* article. "Relationships are at the core of meaningful college experiences," she notes, "and they're particularly important to underserved students who are more likely to doubt their academic abilities. Underserved online students need the presence of an engaged instructor" (Lieberman, 2018). We can support our learners who may otherwise become marginalized in online classes simply by being actively present and engaged with them.

For the sake of all our online students, each one of whom deserves our teaching best, show up to class. Often. Too much prolonged silence on our part is a sure way to kill the energy in an online class. But taking a little time to be fully present contributes to the energy that sustains the social aspect of learning so important in an online class.

Reveal Your Personality

Another way to establish your teaching presence, in addition to your regular communication with the students, is to help your students see you as a real person. Establishing presence in an online class "doesn't just naturally happen," note Rosemary Lehman and Simone Conceição in *Creating a Sense of Presence in Online Teaching: How to "Be There" for Distance Learners* (2010, p. 4). Because online instructors and students are not in the same physical space at the same time, they argue, it's essential to be deliberate in our efforts to be present with our students.

A great way to "be there" for our students is to share more of who we are as people. We'll present some practical suggestions for how to do this, but remember, it is not necessary to try all of these ideas at once. In fact, it would not be advisable to do so. Instead, pick one or two of the following to try. Demonstrate that you are a real person who cares about your students, and they will respond with warmth and increased engagement, like a flower turning toward the sun.

When preparing for a new semester, think carefully about the experience students will have the very first time they enter your online course. Just like in person, first impressions count. What will they learn about you when they click into your class for the first time? Starting off on the right foot is truly important, so think about small teaching approaches you can implement before the class even begins.

For example, create media-rich course content to share some information about yourself. Show your students a bit about who you are as a person and a professional. Linda Nilson and Ludwika Goodson, in their excellent book, *Online Teaching at Its Best: Merging Instructional Design with Teaching and Learning Research* (2018), suggest you should also share information about "your interest in the course content, and your positive feelings about teaching it" (p. 85) since that helps to create a welcoming environment in which students can learn. There are lots of ways you can do this, ranging from more simple to more technical or complex. The key is to help your students put a face to a name and to get to know you just a bit.

A relatively simple strategy is to create a "Meet Your Instructor" section of your online class. Post a photo of yourself, whether it be a professional headshot or an image of you camping with your family. Or both. Write a brief biography that summarizes your academic background, your research interests, and also your personal hobbies and pursuits.

Some instructors like to create an automated slideshow video to reveal something about themselves to their students. There are several online video creation options, such as Animoto, that pair your still photos, videos, or music clips with their templates and soundtracks. The result is a professional slideshow video that takes mere minutes to create. This can be a highly visual, impactful way to convey something about yourself and your interests. Your students will know that you are more than just a name on the screen. Keep in mind, the time you invest in creating a video such as this really pays off, because you can reuse the same video for different classes or for several semesters in a row.

A third option is to record a short webcam-style video in which you introduce yourself to your students. As I've suggested elsewhere in this book, this does not have to be fancy or professionally produced. Just use the camera on your computer monitor or on your mobile device to record a two- to three-minute greeting. Talk a little bit about why you got into teaching your content in the first place, why you think it's relevant for today's learners, what you hope to accomplish in the class. Briefly share some information about your family, pets, or favorite pastimes. Once again, several websites and mobile apps can facilitate the recording and sharing of quick videos. And don't worry too much about how polished your speech is. If you trip over your tongue just a bit, if a stray hair is out of place, if your dog barks off camera, it's fine. As we have discussed already, these imperfections help our students see us as real people. They go a long way toward establishing the relationships and trust that foster effective online teaching and learning.

One additional consideration: including images and videos in online classes helps to create a more dynamic and engaging learning experience. But we want to be sure that our materials are accessible for all learners. Pay attention to details like the quality of the audio, even for an informal video. Using a headset or earbuds with a built-in microphone can help.

It's equally important to provide alternative means of access. Videos should ideally be captioned, or should be accompanied by a text transcript. Many institutions can help you caption your videos or otherwise check the accessibility of your content. Providing alternative ways to access your content helps all learners, no matter their circumstances (Tobin and Behling, 2018).

Sharing your personality with your online students helps establish both teaching and social presence. Begin the semester by introducing yourself in a way that helps students get to know you. Continue this effort throughout the course by writing or recording announcements in your authentic voice. If you're traveling to a conference, or attending an out-of-state wedding, let your students know you'll be offline for a few days, but that it doesn't mean you've abandoned them. And otherwise share select details about yourself, your personality, and your life. Doing so is well worth the effort required to create and establish relationships person-to-person.

Design and Teach for Cultural Inclusion

An often-overlooked yet increasingly important issue in online education is the lack of provision for the needs of culturally diverse learners. Differences in ethnicity, sexual orientation, political affiliation, gender identity, faith backgrounds, and many other nuanced and multifaceted forms of culture exist in the online classroom, but these differences are rarely planned for or accommodated in the design and teaching of online classes. In order to build community, support all of our learners, and help each individual feel a sense of belonging, we must begin to increase our awareness of the ways that cultural contexts influence online student behaviors and levels of engagement.

How People Learn II: Learners, Contexts and Cultures calls for recognition of "the cultural nature of learning," (National Academy of Sciences, 2018, p. 136). The report authors emphasize the importance of this recognition because "the influences of environment and culture ... affect what takes place in every classroom and every student. The characteristics of the learning environment, of educators, and of the students themselves are all shaped by their cultural context" (p. 136). I think many of us would agree that this must be the case, yet we do very little to acknowledge the impact of cultural differences in our online classes.

Courtney Plotts is the national director of the Council for At Risk Student Education and Professional Standards (CASEPS). In her work, Plotts advocates for the needs of culturally diverse learners and helps faculty to see the importance of increasing their awareness of this issue. When we are better informed, we can better support our students and include them in the online class community we work so hard to create. Plotts argues that although support services exist for multicultural and LGBTQ students on our campuses, for example, equivalent support structures are not as frequently available in online spaces. "Culture on the outside permeates online learning," she contends, "but we don't do anything about it" (C. Plotts, personal communication, January 10, 2019). What we tend to do instead is to ignore cultural differences in our online classes. That's a mistake, however, because it leads to marginalizing whole populations of our students, even if unintentionally:

> Standards for teaching marginalized students don't look the same as they do for teaching other students. There are ways and mechanisms of having rigor in your curriculum, but also it's important to include a pathway for students who don't have the self-efficacy that others may have . . . . There are cultural contexts for why some students do or don't reply to your email or post in discussions. [If you ignore these] you'll lose the same students over and over again. (C. Plotts, personal communication, January 10, 2019)

To begin to address this situation, Plotts recommends seeking professional development in culturally responsive online teaching and also evaluating the diversity of online faculty at our institutions. On an individual level, we can all ask ourselves what the role and impact of diversity in online classes is currently, and perhaps what it should be.

In a 2017 article titled "A Fundamental Look at Cultural Diversity and the Online Classroom," Karen Milheim suggests we should consider "how a student's cultural background might manifest itself in a virtual learning environment." She contends that simply "acknowledging that culture does, in fact, influence learning is an important step in designing for and instructing a culturally diverse student body" (Milheim, 2017). One practical suggestion from both Plotts and Milheim is to carefully monitor online discussions for culturally sensitive language and behaviors, such as a student making a derogatory comment, or students simply neglecting to reply to some students, perhaps because of cultural differences, more than others. If we discover such "archived marginalization" (C. Plotts, personal communication,

January 10, 2019), we can take action to address or remedy the situation, perhaps by deleting an offensive post or modeling appropriate discussion replies to students who are coming from cultural contexts that are different than our own.

Here's another idea from Obiageli Sneed, an instructional designer at ASUOnline (2016): Include an awareness activity from the *Critical Multicultural Pavilion EdChange project* by Paul C. Gorski. In particular, Sneed recommends the "Name Stories" activity (n.d.) as part of the discussion introductions. You and your students can share stories about how you got your names, meaning, nicknames, what you prefer to be called, even pronunciation tips. As others reply, perhaps with compliments and questions, a natural opportunity emerges to discuss cultural values and elements that are important in our unique backgrounds and heritages.

You can find a wealth of additional resources at the *Critical Multicultural Pavilion EdChange project* website. Look for additional ideas for awareness activities, equity awareness quizzes, case studies, and support materials to help you incorporate these kinds of activities and resources. These materials are not necessarily geared to online teaching, which is fine; think creatively about how to apply some of these approaches in your online as well as your face-to-face classes. But as we work to make small changes in the specific ways we foster the social element of online learning, let's commit to cultural inclusivity as a defining characteristic of our practice.

Convey Caring and Support

A final way to create community in online classes is to demonstrate that you care about your students. Getting to know each other as people is a two-way street. The more our students know about who we are, the more likely it is that they will engage with us and with our online content. Similarly, we want to know our students as people as well. Like us, they are not just names on a screen, although it can sometimes feel that way. Our students are living, breathing people. They come to us with hopes and dreams, pressures and concerns, competing demands on their time. It's important to remember that students have lives outside the LMS. Their whole world does not revolve around our class. From time to time, they may need additional support or flexibility.

A recent phenomenological study of 12 instructional designers highlights the importance of keeping the online student's experience firmly in view when planning and teaching online courses (Vann, 2017). "Findings showed that all participants considered empathy for learners to be an essential concept in the instructional design process," (p. 235) and that "empathy should guide the decisions that inform the instructional strategy for any given instructional design" (p. 236). This study uses the term *empathy* to indicate that we should carefully consider what our students will experience in our online courses, which I wholeheartedly agree with. However, in a 2018 blog post, writer and educator Kevin Gannon argues that a pedagogy of empathy might not appropriately capture the idea of supporting our students in these kinds of ways: "A pedagogy of care, on the other hand, welcomes students on their own terms, includes them for who they are, and – most importantly – commits us to doing the type of work to maintain that climate and approach" (Gannon, 2018a). This is a useful distinction; the point I'm making here, whether we think of it as empathizing with or caring for our students, is that online learning presents unique challenges, and we should do "the type of work" Gannon calls for to build trust and relationships with our students. Acknowledging and planning for those unique challenges allows us to do just that.

Andrea Deacon similarly argues for the importance of caring about our students' needs as online learners (2012). In her insightful article, "Creating a Context of Care in the Online Classroom," Deacon rightly asserts that too often, online faculty overlook – or have not yet been prepared to address – the social and affective elements in an online learning environment. Without deliberate attention to this aspect of teaching and learning, Deacon notes, online students might easily perceive the "classroom as a cold and impersonal space, a space where their ideas and experiences are not valued or important and their instructor does little to showcase a caring attitude or foster a learning community." She encourages us to take time to "think carefully about how the affective and social domain of their teaching becomes transformed in an online classroom" (Deacon, 2012, p. 6). If we don't, Deacon claims, students are likely to perceive that "their instructor does not value, respect, or care about their needs as learners" (p. 7). When we stop and think about it, I suspect most of us would say that we *do* care about the needs of our online students, but it takes intentional effort to create an online learning environment that conveys this attitude – that we value and respect our students and want to help them succeed. Fortunately, we can find many small approaches to do just that.

The importance of considering online students' needs was brought home to me in a recent conversation with a former student who took my online graduate course on technological fluency and leadership. Students in this program seek a master's degree for career advancement. Almost all of my students are working professionals with family obligations. This fully online program allows these individuals to earn an advanced degree without disrupting current obligations.

Partly because I know that my students are juggling a lot of different commitments, I had created a mechanism to allow students to have up to three deadline extensions, no questions asked, during the course. My former student told me, months after the fact, that she was able to complete the class on time, despite the fact that her home was significantly damaged by severe storm activity while the course was in session. The stress and time pressure that resulted from this damage to her home might otherwise have caused her to withdraw from the only optional pursuit in her life – her online class. But I had empathized with my busy online students in the design of the course by allowing deadline extensions. Consequently, she did not even have to expend the emotional energy required to fill me in on the details of her situation. Instead, she finished her coursework when it was possible to do so and successfully completed another class toward her master's degree.

Demonstrating this kind of understanding of students' lives and pressures shows that you know they are real people too, that you care about them, and that you're invested in relating with them in a way that allows them to persist. Over the years, I've had innumerable students come to me with personal issues that impacted their ability to succeed in class, as have you, if you've been teaching for any length of time. I think sometimes we develop a healthy skepticism about reasons students provide for not completing work on time. But I've learned not to immediately jump to the conclusion that a student who needs additional time is taking advantage of me. I try to assume positive intent. As a real person with real pressures, it's very possible, even likely, that something negative really did occur in the student's life. Rather than being overly strict and demanding, a little flexibility can go a long way toward helping our online students succeed.

My favorite small teaching strategy in this respect is the Oops Token, which allows students some wiggle room on class assignments. I first read about this idea in Linda Nilson's 2015 book, *Specifications Grading: Restoring Rigor, Motivating Students, and Saving Faculty Time*. Think of this as a "Get Out of Jail Free" card. You can offer one or more of these opportunities as appropriate for your class. Students turn in a token for a no-questions-asked deadline extension, the opportunity to revise and resubmit an assignment, or otherwise make up for an unexpected challenge or honest mistake. We'll take a closer look at Oops Tokens and Specifications (Specs) Grading in Chapter 7, "Creating Autonomy," as this strategy can also be quite effective in helping students learn to take responsibility for their own learning. Personally, I've found Specs Grading to be quite effective in accomplishing both goals – that is, building in flexibility to demonstrate that I care about students' lives outside the LMS, and helping students recognize that there are consequences for not doing their work up to standard. It's kind of a silver bullet, really – but more on that later.

Meanwhile, if you're wondering how to manage something like this, one solution is to create a hidden and ungraded grade center column for each token. If a student uses a token, enter a "1" in that column. In this way you can streamline your tracking of each student's use of tokens. You can also offer extra credit to students who don't use any of their tokens. Just check the grade center column or columns and add five points if no tokens were needed during the course.

Oops Tokens are a good way to convey empathy. You can find other approaches too. One that is quite simple yet very effective is to schedule five-minute phone or videoconference calls with your online students. It's truly amazing how impactful a short conversation can be. Hearing your tone of voice, or if using video, seeing the expression on your face (and vice versa) really helps us connect with our students. You can require this of all students, maybe at the beginning of the term. Or you can reserve this strategy for struggling students. Last semester, for example, I talked on the phone with a student who had completed all her work in the first week of class, then disappeared for three weeks. I was considering having her administratively dropped, but decided to reach out before I did so. When we spoke, she explained that her fiancé had suffered a relapse of his debilitating illness and they'd gotten into financial trouble because he couldn't work. Like my student with the severe home damage, this student had let slide her only optional commitment and fallen behind in class. As we spoke, it was clear that she was amazed that I understood and was willing to give her a chance to catch up if she could. The relief in her voice when she explained that doing so would allow her to remain in good standing for financial aid was palpable. You might think I was too soft on her; I don't always make such arrangements. And your class may not accommodate this degree of schedule flexibility; some of mine don't, either. But when we can, let's talk with our students in real time to see what might be possible. Speaking with students can clear up misunderstandings, clarify confusing concepts, and generally demonstrate your support in a tangible way.

Finally, you can show that you care about your students by asking them how the class or how their semester is going. This simple action indicates that you care about them as individuals, and students appreciate and respond well to that. You might pose the question generally in an announcement, followed by an expression of gratitude and support for their ongoing effort. Sometimes, when I sense a particularly low-energy atmosphere in my online class, where the whole class seems less engaged than I usually experience, I'll send an individual course message to each student. I paste the body of the email into each message, which makes this a relatively efficient process. I ask students how they're doing and how I can help them. Most students reply with a quick, "Thanks for asking, I'm fine" type of a response. I can work with the few who reach out with a more particular concern without an overly burdensome demand on my time. But as you can imagine, getting a personal question about their well-being has a big impact on students, and I've seen renewed energy and engagement as a result of taking the time to send these messages.

You may have too many students in your online class to implement this particular approach; again, I reserve this step for semesters when the online energy is unusually low. But the basic idea, that is, enacting scalable and authentic demonstrations of caring and support, can truly help to establish trust. As we know, this is a crucial element of creating community in online classes. Therefore, it's worth considering how it might be done in your online classes, or indeed your face-to-face and blended classes, which could of course also benefit from this kind of outreach.

PRINCIPLES

As should be clear by now, building community in an online class can be quite feasible. Demonstrate that you are a real person. You care about your students. You are there to support their success in an otherwise isolating environment. Your students will respond with greater engagement with you and with their peers. A few principles can help shape your own small teaching methods of building community:

Create Zones of Proximal Development

Intentionally structure student-to-student interactions. Design engaging and meaningful discussion forums. Build support mechanisms such as staged deadlines and grading rubrics to help busy online students stay on track. Consider implementing small groups to lead the discussion in an assigned module. With this approach, each group of students could develop expertise on one chapter or topic. They then lead their peers in a way that helps others advance further in their zone of proximal development. We can leverage the social interactions in our online classes to help our students learn from others who are further along in their development.

Establish Teaching Presence

One of the defining characteristics of an effective online class is the frequent presence and ongoing support of the instructor. Do your students ever see or hear you? In written text, do they get a sense of who you are personally and professionally? What are you doing to guide their learning throughout the semester? Many online instructors don't know how to "teach" in an online class, since the material can be canned or predetermined and set in place, like a textbook. You *can* actively teach your students online. They're hungry for your expertise, your guidance, your reacting in the moment, just as you do in the classroom when you detect confusion or a lack of understanding. Do this online through discussion posts, announcements, summary posts that highlight the week's main concepts, short videos to clarify a concept, and even through an old-fashioned phone call when warranted. You'll find that these guiding interactions are intrinsically rewarding as they increase your own satisfaction with teaching online.

Support Social Presence

Would you rather attend a professional conference or complete a self-paced online professional development module? Most of us value the opportunity to congregate with like-minded people, to network, to share ideas and interact with each other. Many students will feel the same way: They would prefer the in-person learning experience that results from attending classes on campus. But the flexibility offered by online classes is the only way that many students can earn a college degree. Appreciating that this mode of learning may not be their first choice, indeed that they may feel anxious and alone, will help you shape your approach to creating and establishing a thriving online community. Be sure to sustain your efforts: speaking from personal experience, it's easy to start out strong, and then fade away from class interactions as the semester gets busier and busier. There is no better way to squelch student engagement and learning. Develop efficient ways of interacting with your students, and *sustain those efforts* until the final week of class. The continuity of your personal engagement will help your students stay actively engaged with the course and each other as well.

SMALL TEACHING ONLINE QUICK TIPS: BUILDING COMMUNITY

If you've taught online, you know it is very hard to retain your students' attention. It's like flying a kite. It's vital to keep the tension on the line. If you're not paying attention, you'll lose the kite. The same is true for our online students. Their drifting manifests itself in minimal participation, low achievement on assessments, and doing the least possible amount of work to pass the class. It's important to keep tension on the line, to actively engage and constantly capture students' attention, in order to foster their success. Building community is an effective way of doing this.

- *Require peer-to-peer interactions in your class.* This can take the form of online discussion boards, small-group discussions or projects, and having students record brief introduction videos and respond to each other to get to know each other a bit.
- *Show up to class as often as you are able.* In my experience, the more we participate in class, the more our students will, too. Post frequent announcements, engage with students in online discussions, and provide feedback on assessments in a timely way. When our students see us in class, they will be more motivated to engage there as well.
- *Prior to the first day of class, post some information about who you are as a person.* Create a text-based page with one or more still photos or develop a video to show students something about your life

and interests. Reveal your personality throughout the semester by interacting with students in your authentic voice.

· *Develop your cultural awareness.* Consider how ethnic and other cultural contexts influence your students' experience and interactions in your online class. Strive for inclusivity in your class design and teaching. Incorporate activities such as "Name Stories" as one way to get started.

· *Cultivate and demonstrate genuine caring for your students.* Create margin in your class, room for a bit of flexibility in case life happens, for you *or* your students. Use Oops Tokens or other approaches to soften class policies when needed.

CONCLUSION

Online classes and degree programs still struggle with a reputation of being subpar to the in-class experience. A big part of this phenomenon, in my view, is the fact that early online classes felt like an electronic correspondence course (and unfortunately, many still do today). Historically, an individual online student worked through content alone and submitted assignments from afar. Some highly motivated students can succeed in such an environment, but many cannot.

Lots of us thrive in an engaging, dynamic, interactive environment in which we can learn from and with our peers. Indeed, this is exactly why the Community of Inquiry framework came into being. The team of Canadian researchers set out to understand and address the importance of building community in an online class, in order to prevent the electronic correspondence course phenomenon. Small teaching applications of this framework, plus intentional design to create zones of proximal development, result in a robust learning experience for our students.

The good news is, it's not that hard to create an engaging environment online. If you are skeptical about this, just consider the lively interactions we see on social media. Someone posts something impactful, be it attention-grabbing, joyful, tragic, incendiary, or ironic. Instantly numerous people respond and join the conversation, and these conversations can be sustained over days, weeks, or even months. Social media shows us that it is possible to engage people remotely.

With careful thinking about your course and your learning outcomes, you can implement strategies that will build relationships, establish trust, and help your students realize their full cognitive potential.

Chapter 5

Giving Feedback

INTRODUCTION

"How long does it take you to grade a paper?" asked my niece. I started to explain that it depends on the length and type of the writing assignment, and made up a number: "Oh, an average of about 20 minutes, I guess, depending on how thorough I'm being in my comments."

I stopped myself there, realizing that she was not actually interested in the details. "Why do you ask?" I said. My niece said she was wondering how long it usually takes an English teacher to grade and return a set of papers. Again, I asked why she wanted to know. She proceeded to tell me that over the course of the previous school year, she never once received a paper back with comments in her accelerated English class. No one did. They submitted their papers and never saw them again.

"But how did you know what you needed to do better next time?" I asked, horrified. "Exactly," she replied. "I didn't." She explained that she and her fellow students could look up the grade for each assignment online, but they never received targeted feedback about what they had done well and how they might improve as writers.

This lack of feedback occurs more commonly than we might like to admit in online classes. Maybe it has something to do with not having an appointed time to see our students. When I teach

English in person, I determine in advance what class meeting I intend to return students' papers. In my first semester teaching, I actually returned all papers the very next day. I knew my first-year students were anxious about their performance. Out of compassion – and perhaps some perverse form of pride – I made it a point to grade and return papers the next time I saw them.

That practice didn't last long. But when we know we will see our students every Tuesday and Thursday at 9:30 a.m., we have a built-in mechanism reminding us to return exams and papers in a timely way. If we hold them too long, students start to ask when they'll get their work back. They can do this because they know where we will be and when they will see us. Class meets on Tuesday morning; they know we'll be in the classroom. They can pin us down and get a real-time response to whatever current questions they have.

The same does not necessarily hold true for online courses. It may not be clear exactly when we will be in the classroom, available to answer questions. And since we typically don't have a preset meeting time in an asynchronous online class, we don't see our students and remember that they are waiting to find out how they did on that major project, or even on their minor projects along the way. They can fall out of sight and out of mind.

These separate but related issues – teachers not providing feedback in a timely way, and students not having clear avenues to request or receive that feedback – contribute to a regrettably common experience of online students: feeling unsupported, on their own, with no real sense of how they are doing or how to get their questions answered when they have them. I've seen some egregious examples of this neglect. A colleague told me about the time he took a 10-week online class. He posted a question about the final project in the Q&A discussion forum in Week 2. In Week 8, he still had no answer.

A couple of years ago, I participated in a six-month online professional development certification course. Acknowledgment of submissions and indication of whether I'd met expectations was intermittent. Perhaps the developers didn't think professionals needed feedback; it didn't seem to be part of the design of the learning experience. Or maybe, as has happened to many of us, assessing learning took longer than expected, and the facilitator struggled to keep up with participant submissions. Whatever the reason, my experience served to remind me of the importance of helping all learners in all contexts know just how they are doing at any given time.

Of course, we online instructors, many of whom might be teaching different courses at multiple institutions, must protect our time. When I first started teaching online I found myself in class first thing in the morning and last thing at night, checking posts, answering questions, and generally interacting with students. I had to learn that instructor presence does not mean being available 24/7. But it does mean supporting our students by responding to questions and providing feedback on their work in a reasonable amount of time. It means assigning grades and giving comments before too many other assessments are due. It means notifying our students if we expect to be offline due to conference travel, for example, and not to worry if a response is delayed.

You'll notice that we have primarily been discussing two very practical aspects of feedback: making sure students receive it, and making sure they receive it in a timely way. My experience as an online instructor, student, and coach of other online instructors has convinced me that these elements are often missing from online courses, so we'll focus on them in this chapter. But of course we want to make sure our feedback is meaningful and effective, so we'll consider first what the research tells us about how to ensure our feedback helps our students learn, and then present models for providing that feedback in a consistent, timely way in your online courses.

IN THEORY

It's worth stepping back to remind ourselves of the general context in which feedback typically occurs: grading student work. Within that context, feedback serves one of two purposes: Justifying the grade we have given to students, or providing them with specific instructions on how to improve for their next assessment. The first kind of feedback relates more to *summative assessments*, which are the judgments we make about student performance; the second kind relates more to *formative assessments*, which are the opportunities we provide for students to try their hand at a task and get feedback on it *before* they are measured for their high-stakes grades.

Of course we have an obligation to measure the performance of our students through summative assessments, even though many of us would prefer to teach without that responsibility. Almost any online course you might teach will require you to provide summative judgments about the work of your students, and translate them into grades. We have seen very few instructors who completely shirk their obligation to grade student work, and to offer at least some explanation for the grades they have given.

But what students crave, and what too often they don't receive, is feedback specifically designed to help them get better – especially through frequent, low-stakes assessments. When we actively engage students throughout the semester with formative feedback on their work, we can significantly improve their learning. In their book *Effective Grading: A Tool for Learning and Assessment in College* (2010), Barbara E. Walvoord and Virginia Johnson Anderson argue that student "involvement in learning is in part determined by their perception of faculty members' interest and friendliness toward them, including the fairness and helpfulness of the testing and grading system and the teacher's communication about their work and their grades" (p. 14). If we want online students to actively engage with the course, we have to engage them as frequently as possible through fair and helpful feedback.

Two core principles should help guide your thinking as you consider how to provide such feedback to your students in online courses. First, make it timely. "Assessment without timely feedback contributes little to learning," write Arthur Chickering and Zelda Gamson in their seminal article on "Seven Principles for Good Practice in Undergraduate Education" (1987, p. 4). The research on *how* timely that feedback should be is not entirely clear. One meta-analysis of more than 50 studies on this question found that feedback on lower-stakes assessments such as quizzes or classroom activities was more beneficial when it was immediate; feedback on more major assessments, such as tests, was more beneficial following delay, perhaps allowing students some time to rest their brains and process their performance before reviewing the assessment and hearing the feedback (Kulik and Kulik, 1988). So don't hesitate to take a little longer with those higher-stakes assessments, but stay focused on turning around the shorter, low-stakes material more quickly.

Second, ensure that all of your assessments of student work include clear directions for how to improve for the next time – and do not simply justify a grade or number you have stamped onto their work. Walvoord and Anderson call focusing on grade justification a "common trap" that leads us to focus on the negative aspects of student work. But "our chief responsibility," they argue, "is to help this learner move forward." They recommend we ask ourselves this core question with every comment we provide on student work: "What does this learner need from me at this time?"

(Walvoord and Anderson, 2010, p. 110). Our response to that question becomes the driving force behind our feedback.

With all of that said, of course students will want to know why they have received the grades you have given them, and we should provide them with that information. But you might consider how you can distinguish for your students the summative and formative aspects of their performance on assessments. Jim has taken to dividing the comments on his students' major assessments into two categories, which are clearly labeled "This Time" and "Next Time." The comments under "This Time" focus on assessing their performance on the completed assessment; "Next Time" comments give students instructions for how to improve. Similarly, Flower's categories are labeled "Strengths" and "For Improvement." The comments under "Strengths" highlight what the student is doing well; "For Improvement" comments provide specific ideas for, well, improving. As you formulate feedback strategies for your online course, consider how you might help your students keep most clearly in view the feedback that will help them learn.

We stay firmly focused in this chapter on providing feedback to students, which means we won't delve much into the many thorny questions surrounding grades and grading systems. Walvoord and Anderson's book is an outstanding resource for considering such issues more deeply, and is worth a read if you are looking for help in those areas.

MODELS

Being available for our students, and providing timely feedback to support their learning progress, doesn't have to be an overwhelming time drain. If you're teaching a traditional in-person class, you will likely spend anywhere from a few to several hours in the classroom and engaging with class-related activities each week. The models presented here help you spend a comparable amount of time effectively, strategically distributed throughout each week, in order to powerfully impact student learning and success.

The online feedback coin has two sides, both equally important: giving *timely* feedback and giving *effective* feedback. The first two models in this chapter provide practical advice on timeliness, the last two focus on the quality of feedback, and the one in between bridges both timeliness and efficacy. Some of these suggestions are simple, small, and relatively easy strategies to implement; some are more complex, something that may be more successful if you have more time to plan or more online teaching experience under your belt. Taken together, these five models should give you plenty of ideas about how to make small changes in your approach to provide useful guidance to your online learners.

Set Deadlines Strategically

I taught online for years before figuring out that if I didn't want to deal with panicky student emails on Sunday evening, I shouldn't make the weekly module assignments due on Sunday at midnight. Having learned that lesson, now I'm more strategic about setting assignment deadlines. For example, if I know I won't have a chunk of time to grade until Saturday, I don't make the project due the previous Sunday night. If I know I'm traveling abroad for a week, I don't assign a complex task during that time, one that will likely generate lots of student questions and an additional need for time-sensitive support.

In short, consider your own availability for providing feedback just as much as you consider appropriate pacing of learning activities when creating the course schedule.

This leads back to my earlier point about students not necessarily knowing when you will be online for real-time responses. Their lives online in other contexts have conditioned them to expect immediate responses. Traditional college-age students are used to sending their peers a text message or Snapchat and receiving an instant response. As one post on the website *Netsanity* pointed out, "When a teen sees that a friend or partner has received the message but hasn't responded, it can cause anxiety and frustration" (Netsanity, Are Messaging Apps, 2017). These students may carry their expectations about immediate feedback into your online course.

But this problem doesn't apply only to students in their late teens and early twenties; all of us have been conditioned to technologies that provide instant responses. Many online shopping sites, for example, offer real-time assistance through a synchronous chat function. When we're conducting transactions online, we almost expect there to be a way to get a fast and customized answer to our specific question. Yet some Learning Management Systems (LMSs) don't offer this kind of a chat tool. Even if yours does, there's no way you can be online at all hours of the day and night, as your students are. It's often the case that students can't get help in the moment that they need it.

I closely observed my husband's behavior in the online summer class he just completed. As a diligent and mindful student, full-time university employee and father of three, he carefully scheduled class time each evening after dinner. Often, he'd have questions about some of the finer points of the learning activity he was engaged in. But his instructor was not in class in the evenings, which is understandable, but still challenging. There would be no way for him to get an answer within his allotted class time for the day. Instead he would methodically analyze every angle of the assignment instructions, make a decision about the best way forward, and hope for the best.

We don't have to be available for student questions at any time of day or night. Instead, we can be intentional in how we set due dates and communicate expected turnaround times so that our students know not to panic if they don't receive an instant response.

My online modules now close on Mondays at midnight. This way I have time at my desk on Monday during the day to field last-minute questions prior to the deadline. I figure that many of my students, most of whom work full-time, will do their course-work over the weekend. If they email me questions on Sunday, I can reply on Monday; they can revise their work as needed Monday night and still submit on time.

Have Real-Time, Just-in-Time, Conversations

This small teaching strategy is also related to timeliness in responding to students' needs. It's relatively simple, but requires more planning than setting deadlines strategically. This approach makes sense for many online instructors, yet it is often overlooked.

Many of us are conditioned to think that online classes are asynchronous. Some online classes take place entirely (or almost entirely) synchronously, with live virtual class meetings, but most of today's credit-bearing online courses in higher education don't require a great deal of synchronous class activity. In other words, no one *has* to be engaged in any activity at the same time as anyone else. Indeed, this is a primary reason that online learners choose to attend class online, as I've noted elsewhere in this book. They need the scheduling flexibility in order to pursue a college degree around their current work and family obligations. But just because most of the course takes place asynchronously, it doesn't mean that synchronous, or real-time, interactions are completely off-limits.

If you've ever picked up the phone to call a colleague after exchanging 12 emails without making progress on the topic, you'll know how effective it can be to have a quick conversation. When we talk to each other, we can answer questions, clarify misunderstandings, address issues, and reach consensus. Achieving resolution can take much less time when speaking by phone as opposed to a seemingly endless back-and-forth by email.

The same holds true in our online classes. Sometimes a short, real-time conversation is a far more effective mode of communication than the most thoughtfully created text instructions, recorded videos, or email replies can ever be.

Before looking at some small teaching ways of structuring synchronous interactions, it's important to clarify what I am *not* suggesting. You shouldn't *require* attendance at any event you've scheduled to take place on a particular day and time. Some instructors, with all the best intentions, mandate participation in office hours, a class orientation, or a study session, for example. But if your online learner works second shift at the local manufacturing plant, your thoughtfully scheduled 7 p.m. session will never be possible. You might think that's an ideal time for students who also have full-time jobs to meet with you, and even pat yourself on the back for giving up some of your evening to accommodate your learners' needs. But the truth is there will never be one single meeting time that fits all of your students' schedules.

Workarounds include offering multiple sessions for the same event, making attendance completely optional, or recording the synchronous session for later viewing by students who could not attend. Just don't mandate that online learners be able to commit to a real-time session – for many, it won't be possible.

For this reason, I don't tend to hold virtual office hours – but I'll offer some suggestions for how to do so, if you want to take this approach, in the next model. Personally, I've found that my content is not complex enough to warrant live sessions for mini-lectures and Q&A sessions. My online courses are very practical, based on technology we use every day at work and at home.

Therefore, I prefer scheduling either mandatory or as-needed conversations with individual students. Recall our discussion in Chapter 4 on the importance of being present for your online learners. What better way to be there for students than to make time to talk to your student, when they're struggling with a particular concept or need a bit of individualized support? Whether you require a real-time conversation with each student or simply make the opportunity available for those who want to take advantage of it will depend on many factors. If you teach a large-enrollment class, you may not want to require a 10-minute conversation with each student. But let's say you have a reasonable class size and you anticipate student anxiety stemming from difficult content. It may be well worth your time to briefly connect with each learner in the first week of class.

You can ask students to sign up for a timeslot using a Google Doc or Sheet. Create a schedule on which you list several meeting days and times. Students select their meeting time on a first-come, first-served basis. Or, use one of many online scheduling services available, such as youcanbookme.com. The advantage of using a system like this is that it offers more functionality than a homegrown sign-up sheet. For example, it can interface directly with your calendar and sent automated reminders to your students before their appointment time. However you choose to schedule it, you and your students both may appreciate the oft-forgotten simplicity of a phone call. I've often found this to be the most efficient and convenient option since students have their phones with them all the time, or so it seems. It's an easy way to connect, sometimes even on short notice. Or, of course, you can use a videoconferencing solution available through your LMS, or a platform such as Zoom, which is quite easy to use.

Whatever communication tool you choose, spending just a few minutes talking with a student can have a significant impact on their engagement and learning.

I know some instructors who do this. They tell me the payoff for investing those 10 minutes per student is significant. They communicate warmth, interest, and confidence in the student's ability to succeed, all in just a few minutes. If you add this element to your course, you may want to provide students with a prompt or topic for discussion, or perhaps a series of questions you plan to discuss. The conversation can be primarily social, or related to class content, or a mixture of both – you can decide what makes the most sense for your teaching preference and subject matter. After that call, your students will likely be more willing to reach out for help, knowing you, their instructor, is a caring human being who is committed to their success.

Although I see the value of scheduling a mandatory call with each learner, I have not used this method in my own classes. Instead, I reserve this option for students who need one-on-one attention. Perhaps a student clearly doesn't understand assignment instructions, as evidenced by an initial effort that falls far short of the mark. Perhaps someone is experiencing a set of unexpected challenges in their personal and professional life. In each case, a 15- or 20-minute call, which we hold during a mutually convenient time (you can make time slots available using the online scheduling service I mentioned above), can do wonders to help your student get back on their feet and resume progress in the class.

I'm convinced that my understanding and supportive tone of voice does more to reassure the student of the feasibility of success than anything I actually say during the conversation. In Chapter 4, I described a recent phone conversation with a student who had fallen behind because of a health crisis. As I said there, in all of these kinds of conversations, the relief I hear in my student's voice is palpable. In a short, real-time conversation I can literally hear pressure being relieved. With such phone and videoconferencing calls, I've done more to impact my student's learning and success than I can accomplish in a hundred written or recorded messages.

Get Creative with Virtual Office Hours

Holding online office hours can be a great way to support your students in their learning. These sessions can replicate what happens in the physical classroom better than any other method. However, many faculty members have found them to be less than satisfying, for several different reasons. As alluded to in the previous model, we face numerous challenges when attempting to hold online office hours. Students won't all be available at the same time, so attendance is frequently quite low – even when students could attend, often they choose not to. If they do show up, we may experience technology challenges such as audio and video problems that interfere with the learning opportunity and lead to frustration on the part of both you and your students.

Wondering why his attempts at holding online office hours were often unsuccessful, Patrick Lowenthal, together with his colleagues, investigated how to make video-based synchronous office hours most effective for online learners (2017). The researchers made several changes to previous, unsatisfactory attempts to hold online office hours, surveyed the students regarding what was working and what wasn't, and adjusted the new approach accordingly. The resulting virtual office hours were better attended, more interactive, and generally more successful in terms of students valuing the experience. Lowenthal and his colleagues make several useful design recommendations, a few of which I'll highlight here:

· *Rebrand your office hours.* Knowing that students rarely attend instructors' office hours, Lowenthal called his synchronous sessions "Happy Hours." Other possible names he suggests include "Coffee Breaks," "Afternoon Tea," or "Consultations" (p. 188). Using a more inviting name can imply that these sessions are less formal, more supportive, and less intimidating.

- *Reduce the frequency of these events.* Although it's common to offer virtual office hours every week, Lowenthal found better success when he held 60-minute Happy Hours only four times per semester (p. 189). He scheduled these strategically, according to when the time together would be most useful. For example, you might offer a synchronous review session just before an exam. Or consider holding a live feedback session after a major project or paper is due, to address common errors and help students see how they can do better next time.
- *Announce the scheduled sessions ahead of time.* List them in the syllabus and talk about the schedule during the first week of class (p. 188). Encourage students to put these on their calendar and plan to attend.
- *Alternatively, use a scheduling tool like Doodle to determine times when most students can attend (p. 189).* This strategy might be particularly useful if you have students in multiple time zones.
- *Encourage students to submit questions prior to the synchronous event.* This way, you can tailor your presentation or prepare some talking points to address common areas of confusion (p. 189).
- *Offer incentives such as the opportunity to earn points for attending.* Be sure to offer a "comparable learning experience for those unable to attend a live session. For example, give those students specific questions/prompts to respond to while watching the recording" (p. 189).

As I think you'll agree, the research conducted by Lowenthal and his colleagues offers a rich source of evidence-based and creative solutions to the common challenges associated with online office hours. If you're interested in many more design recommendations based on this study, please read the full article, "Live Synchronous Web Meetings in Asynchronous Online Courses: Reconceptualizing Virtual Office Hours" (Lowenthal, Dunlap, and Snelson, 2017). You will likely find several ideas for how you can reimagine your online synchronous sessions so they're both timely and an effective means of providing feedback and guidance for your learners.

Use Tech to Streamline Grading

This model moves squarely into the category of providing quality feedback – the other side of the feedback coin. You can actually do some things better and more easily in online classes than you can face-to-face. Streamlining grading using readily-available technology tools falls into that category.

An effective yet surprisingly underutilized tool for assessing student work in online (and blended, and face-to-face) classes is the rubric tool within your LMS. When I was full-time faculty, I graded hundreds of online students' research papers manually before I became aware that I could create a rubric in the LMS. In my current role as an instructional designer, I see numerous faculty grading with a rubric created in Microsoft Word instead of using the LMS rubric tool. They are doing better than I was when teaching full-time: at least their students are provided with a rubric. But downloading, marking, saving, and uploading a rubric in Word for each student submission takes far more time than it does to assess work using the LMS rubric.

As is often the case with grading, investing a little bit of time and effort up front can save you an exponential amount of time when evaluating student assignments or discussion posts. Spend some time creating an effective rubric in your LMS. This may not be as simple as it sounds. Rubrics are complex assessment tools: Used appropriately, they can save you a significant amount of grading time while still providing rich, robust feedback to your students. Invest the time to research and design your rubric—you'll be able to use it for several semesters to come.

An excellent resource to help you with this task is *Introduction to Rubrics: An Assessment Tool to Save Grading Time, Convey Effective Feedback, and Promote Student Learning* (2012) by Dannelle Stevens and Antonia Levi. This practical guide includes how to create effective rubrics, the advantages of using rubrics, using rubrics with faculty colleagues and teaching assistants, and discipline-specific rubrics. If you are new to creating and grading with rubrics, this book is likely to prove invaluable.

To facilitate the design process, you may find it helpful to create the original rubric in Microsoft Word or similar. Once you're happy with the criteria, levels of achievement, the wording and the scoring distribution, it doesn't take long to create an LMS rubric. Copy and paste the text from your document into the tool. Often, you can choose whether each column, or achievement level, shows points possible, a percentage of the total points possible, or a range of points or percentages. You have the option to customize your rubric and scoring method to align with your subject matter and your outcomes.

Depending on your LMS, you may need to associate the rubric with the assignment. In other words, it may not happen automatically. Once this is done, you can set the rubric to be visible to students, which helps them explicitly see your expectations for their work.

As you begin grading with the LMS rubric, you'll find that your time spent engaged in the task is reduced significantly. LMS rubrics are typically easy to use. They calculate a student's grade automatically as you click the radio buttons for the appropriate level of achievement for each column, and they import the score or percentage directly into the LMS grade center. The rubric tool makes it easy to give robust and specific feedback on strengths and areas for improvement in a remarkably short amount of time. Keep in mind, this time-saving tool is equally effective in your face-to-face or blended classes, too, if you have students submit their assignments online instead of on paper.

Of course you want to make sure that your rubric aligns closely with your instructions, and that the descriptions you provide in each cell are useful for students. If you can be sure of that, you can save yourself a lot of grading time without shortchanging the quality of feedback your students receive.

Give Meaningful Comments via Media Tools

Another approach to providing quality yet efficient feedback is to record your comments using audio or video tools. Although I'm clearly a fan of the written word (hence the book you are reading), nuances can get lost in translation when feedback comes only in written form. No matter how clearly you write, no matter how careful your word choice and sentence style may be, writing lacks additional cues that help to orient both partners in a conversation. Vocal intonations add emphasis, or empathy, or enthusiasm. Facial expressions convey encouragement, concern, optimism. Body language communicates interest, attention, support. All this is forfeit when the only thing we have is written text.

To compensate for this loss of nuance in your feedback, consider giving comments using audio or video. A pair of researchers evaluated the impact of audio versus written feedback in one undergraduate biology class and one postgraduate biology class, both of which took place in person (Voelkel and Mello, 2014). In the undergraduate class, a treatment group of students received audio feedback on a formative essay; in the postgraduate course, all students received audio feedback on their formative essay. The researchers found no significant difference in the learning gains of the undergraduate students who received audio feedback;

undergraduate students performed almost exactly the same on the final exam regardless of whether they'd received audio or written feedback on the formative assessment (p. 25). However, all student respondents indicated increased satisfaction with the audio feedback; it felt more personal, they reported, and they found it to be more useful because the audio feedback included more explanation and suggestions for improvement than the written feedback did.

Interestingly, the researchers found that the audio feedback, which they captured using digital voice recorders, took on average five minutes longer to create than did the written feedback. However, the audio feedback was more robust: "On average 34 words per minute were produced by spoken feedback whereas only four words per minute were written in the form of comments" (Voelkel and Mello, 2014, p. 28). An analysis of the audio and written feedback confirmed the students' sense that the audio feedback was more detailed and personal. The researchers concluded that "it might be well worth spending the additional time necessary to provide high quality feedback. Staff training and increasing experience may over time shorten the time needed to produce audio feedback" (p. 29).

Another study of audio versus written feedback found similar results, that audio feedback did not significantly impact student performance (Morris and Chikwa, 2016). However, an important finding for online teaching in particular emerged in a study of instructor and student perceptions of audio feedback in online composition classes (Cavanaugh and Song, 2014). As in the study of biology students, these researchers found that students had more positive perceptions of audio feedback than they did of written comments and noted that audio feedback may be particularly effective in online classes. In the physical classroom, they point out, if a comment is unappealing to a student, "there is at least the opportunity for the instructor to present a friendlier face in class and cushion the student's impressions" (Cavanaugh and Song, 2014, p. 126). Providing audio feedback allows online instructors to add encouraging vocal intonations and oral markers of support.

A great example of this strategy in action is my colleague's use of recorded comments in her online First-Year Seminar class. I was unfamiliar with this idea when she first told me about her approach, but as I've considered it I've come to see that it is quite simple yet highly effective.

My fellow instructor explained that recording her comments about students' papers allowed her to convey support for her students in an impactful way. She knew that her freshmen online students were likely feeling some level of anxiety and doubt, so she went the extra mile to encourage them. She demonstrated to me how she said things like, "I can see that you tried to include supporting evidence here, and I know this can be hard, but we really need to surround the evidence with explanation to make a strong argument." Even here this sentence communicates only so much. When my friend spoke this to me out loud, she infused empathy, understanding that the task was challenging, appreciation for the effort put forth, but also clear emphasis on what the student needs to do to improve. She used vocal intonation and an authentic intention to help her students succeed to great effect.

In Canvas, you can record audio or video comments directly from the grading screen. Look for the "play" button under the text box for comments. Clicking that button allows you to record audio or video, or to upload media you may have already created.

If you're not teaching in Canvas, you may not have such a seamless way to create the comments, but it may be worth looking into the options. If your institution has licensed a media service such as Kaltura or Panopto, you can create audio comments using that tool and then provide the link in the comment text box. Or consider using a digital voice recorder and emailing the .mp3 files to students, as some of the researchers did in the studies just cited.

Alternatively, you could capture a quick video of yourself talking to your student using YouTube or similar apps on your phone, or using a media recording solution available in your LMS. In a 2015 study on the use of video feedback in undergraduate and postgraduate education courses, researchers found that both students and faculty found video feedback to be more useful and motivating than written comments (Henderson and Phillips, 2015). An efficient way to share your video comments with your students is to paste the link from your recording into the text comment box. Adding the visual of your face, ideally wearing a positive expression and conveying optimism in your students' ability to succeed, enables you to provide a richly nuanced and effectual way to communicate with your online learners.

As you're reading this, you may be uncertain about whether to try video or audio feedback, if recording comments is a new skill. Some of you may prefer to use video instead of audio. Another variation is to record a screen capture in which you talk through a student's paper as displayed on the screen. Great idea – but it requires a little technical know-how. If you like the idea of providing media comments, start small. Audio recordings take less prep and therefore less time than video, yet still deliver a powerful bang for the buck.

Want to help your online students know what you really mean in your feedback? Talk to them. It's as simple as that.

PRINCIPLES

Given the unique dynamic of an online class, intentional effort must be made to support students through regular and ongoing feedback. These principles can shape your way forward.

Be Timely and Responsive

At the risk of repeating this point too often, let me reinforce the importance of being available to answer questions and to help students know how well they are doing in the class. When you teach in person, students know where and when to find you, and, importantly, they have also committed to that meeting time in their schedules. The same is not true in an online class. Reduce student anxiety by being responsive to questions and returning assessments as soon as is reasonable. Explicitly state in your syllabus when students should expect you to reply to emails and return graded work. If you become unexpectedly unavailable, let them know. Explain why and when you'll be back. A little transparency goes a long way. Make yourself accessible for students. The payoff – increased student commitment and effort – will be well worthwhile.

Take Advantage of the Tech

We can do many things more effectively when teaching online than we can when teaching in person. Using technology to provide highly efficient yet powerfully meaningful feedback is one of them. Put the affordances of technology tools to work for you. Take advantage of embedded or readily available technologies such as LMS rubrics, audio- or video-recording capabilities, and even the oft-forgotten phone to communicate with both efficiency and impact. You can give individuals targeted specific input on their work. Doing so doesn't have to dominate your schedule when you apply the right tech tools to the task.

Put Yourself in Your Students' Shoes

Think of situations in which you've been anxious about your performance – such as from your own student experience, or from waiting for the peer review comments on the article you've submitted to a respected journal in your field. Perhaps in your employment, your supervisor is opaque; you don't have a sense of how you are doing or where you may need to improve. Not receiving guidance or timely answers, not having a clear sense of your standing in a situation, can increase anxiety. Equip your students for their best success by calling to mind how it feels when you lack the input you need to move forward productively. Demonstrate empathy and caring by being available to help.

SMALL TEACHING ONLINE QUICK TIPS: GIVING FEEDBACK

Your students need your targeted and timely guidance in order to develop a sense of self-efficacy. They need to know how they are doing in your class and what they can do to improve. Don't let them languish under a cloud of doubt. Instead, empower your students to achieve greater success through efficient and effective feedback. Help them see how their performance matches your expectations. Your students will detect your support and respond with renewed effort.

- Schedule deadlines to coincide with your availability to answer questions in advance and return graded work after.
- Talk to your students in real time, by phone or using any number of videoconferencing tools. Schedule a call for each student, or offer this on an as-needed basis for students who need additional support. Create the human connection and achieve greater understanding through the simple means of talking to each other.
- Take a creative approach to offering virtual office hours, working to ensure they are meaningful and a productive use of your time as well as your students' time.

- Create LMS rubrics to swiftly evaluate student work while simultaneously providing detailed individual feedback.
- Record audio or video comments on assessments to provide richly nuanced input, adding emphasis and empathy through your voice.

CONCLUSION

"The uncertainty is the hardest part," my 14-year-old daughter said to me over dinner one night. "Put that in your book. Uncertainty is the worst." She was referring to the unknown of beginning her first year of high school, but her point seems especially relevant to this chapter.

Indeed, this was the greatest challenge my husband faced in his online summer class described earlier in this chapter. Although he was diligent to do his work, he received very little feedback from his instructor, whether in the moment he had a question or otherwise. Sad to say, he completed 75% of his course without hearing from his faculty member on his performance or progress. Given this striking lack of guidance, this uncertainty about how he was doing, my husband was tempted to conclude that he must be failing the course. But he persevered and eventually earned the reward for his hard work and self-directed learning in the form of an A for the class.

Although my husband, who is both mature and highly motivated, was able to persist in the face of such uncertainty, many of our students won't. When they don't know how they are doing, it's hardly surprising if they become anxious and unmotivated. Eliminate the uncertainty. Administer small feedback to help your students thrive.

Chapter 6

Fostering Student Persistence and Success

INTRODUCTION

"Cheerleading *has* to happen!"

My colleague in the biology department was describing for me what she does to help her students complete her rigorous accelerated online course. Acknowledging that some faculty may balk at the thought of themselves as cheerleaders, she revised her statement to include words like *coaching* and *mentoring*. It was abundantly clear to me, however, that this biology professor was passionate about her students' success. Her enthusiasm was evident in every syllable she spoke. She would get her online students over the finish line or die trying.

Later that same day, I had another conversation with a faculty member in advertising and public relations. "I used to think that my job was only to teach the content," she said. "I used to be uncomfortable addressing students' unprofessional behavior. Now I believe that a big part of my job is to help students become functioning adults." In other words, she sees part of her job as helping her students learn what it takes to be successful in today's society, a task that extends far beyond the confines of her class content.

I really enjoyed these interactions because both instructors reflected back to me my own passion for excellent teaching to foster student success. Clearly, they both care deeply for their students. They're willing to go above and beyond the call of content-based duty to help their students succeed. That doesn't mean that they dumb down their content or inflate their grades. Instead, they've embedded support structures within their teaching that enable students to rise to the occasion, work hard, and persist.

An overarching theme of my own teaching has always been to help students in just this way. Sometimes this happens in the college classroom. Sometimes it happens in the dance studio. Sometimes in my Pilates class. In all of these environments, learners need encouragement. They need empathy and support, especially if the context is new, unfamiliar, or anxiety-inducing. They need reassurance that with effort, persistence, and resilience, they will achieve their learning goals.

One Saturday a month I teach a beginning Pilates class at my local gym. Last month, a member nervously came up to me before class as I was setting up the music. "I've never taken Pilates before," she said. "I'm not sure what to expect."

"Great!" I beamed. "You're in the right place. This class is for you. This is a beginning level class, so I'll give lots of instruction and tips along the way. You'll always know what to do and how to do it – I'm sure of it."

I proceeded to give her a few pointers, such as that she would not need shoes and that we would remain on the floor throughout class, targeting core muscles and weaving in relaxing stretches as well. I helped her to know what to expect, but my main goal was just to reassure her, to encourage her that all would be well. After class she thanked me, said how much she enjoyed it, and promised to be back next time. As the result of hearing a few encouraging words and seeing a confident smile, my new Pilates student had overcome her nerves and taken the first step on a new fitness journey.

I do the same thing in the adult jazz class I teach on Fridays at lunchtime. I get students who used to dance as children, years ago. Others always wanted to take dance but never had the opportunity. Some are trying dance for the first time as a way of varying their wellness routine, of getting more movement in their life. All of my adult dance students display some degree of nervousness, some level of not knowing what to expect.

I tell them, repeatedly, that I admire them for trying something new, something slightly out of their comfort zone. I spend almost as much time instructing them to be patient and keep practicing a new step, to stick with it, as I spend on giving instruction on the new step itself. I draw their attention to dancers who have made good progress simply by persisting through the challenge of learning an entirely new skill. Indeed, one of my current students was brand new to jazz dance when she started three semesters ago. Although the movement was unfamiliar to her, she worked hard, came back for more, and was patient with herself. She's come a long way in the time we've danced together, and I hold her up as an example of persevering despite occasional mild frustration.

Similarly, I like to highlight how far dancers have progressed just within the course of one semester. Around Week 6 I start saying things like, "You couldn't have done this step back in September. See how far you've come?" And I repeat that refrain every time we learn a new step of increasing complexity, one that requires increasing skill. "You can do this," I tell my dancers. "You've got this."

If we want our students to succeed in our courses, and in their lives beyond school, they definitely need some of this kind of cheerleading. But they need more than just our words; they also need concrete strategies to help them succeed, ones that are both built into the structure of the course and capable of helping out in a pinch. When we combine these structured supports with our positive, encouraging attitude, we are giving our students the best possibility to succeed in our online courses and beyond.

IN THEORY

The original *Small Teaching* includes a chapter on helping students develop what researcher Carol Dweck has termed a *growth mindset*. Decades worth of experiments by Dweck and others have suggested that when learners believe their intelligence is flexible and capable of improvement, they are more likely to be successful at learning tasks. By contrast, some learners have what Dweck calls a *fixed mindset*, which means that they assume that intelligence is a static thing – that you had your IQ stamped on your forehead at birth, and that you're stuck with whatever you were given (Dweck, 2007).

Mindset researchers have been arguing for some time now that we can help learners succeed by convincing them to abandon such fixed mindsets about learning and intelligence. When learners bring a fixed mindset into an academic context, it can limit them in numerous ways. If they believe their intelligence is fixed at the low end of the scale, it causes them to give up in the face of challenges. I'm just not smart enough for this, they might think. If they believe their intelligence is fixed at the high end of the scale, they might not want to complete required work. I don't need to do the homework assigned by the teacher, they might think; I'll just pick it up on my own. Whether they believe they are naturally smart or naturally stupid, in other words, a fixed mindset can interfere with their learning.

Dweck and many other researchers in this field have demonstrated, fortunately, that mindsets can be changed. People can be educated out of fixed mindsets and into the understanding that intelligence is a flexible commodity, one that can be grown with effort. But the past few years have seen increasing debate about the value of such efforts in education, as some critics have argued that the benefits have been oversold. Progressive educators, for example, have argued that focusing too much on the mindsets of students might cause us to ignore structural problems in the education system, or inequalities in the classroom or in our society. We can't cure all of our educational ills by changing the mindsets of students.

But the research that supports the power of mindsets – which is strong, but not unlimited – remains solid, and only continues to grow. The problem really lies in the fact that it has been oversimplified and packaged into a cure-all. Changing the mindset of a student won't erase the challenges that are faced by students who come to our courses beset by poverty, or victimized because of their race, gender, or sexual orientation. Too many teachers (and their administrators) have attempted to slap mindset into their curriculum with simplistic applications: praising students for their effort, for example, instead of their performance.

In 2015, Dweck addressed the backlash against mindset, and these oversimplified applications of the theory, by explaining:

> [E]ffort is key for students' achievement, but it's not the only thing. Students need to try new strategies and seek input from others when they're stuck. They need this repertoire of approaches—not just sheer effort—to learn and improve . . . effort is a means to an end to the goal of learning and improving. (*Education Week*, 2015)

In this language you can see the logic behind the models we outline below, and in the original *Small Teaching*. Students need more than effort to succeed. They need a teacher who has created opportunities for them to "try new strategies and seek input."

They need a teacher who keeps their eyes pinned on "the goal of learning and improving." These are elements we can seed into our communication with students (as you'll see in the first model below) and into the structure of the course (as you'll see in the next three models).

Mindset theory falls more generally under the umbrella of thinking about how to help students succeed in our courses. We are less concerned here with the specific tactic of identifying mindsets and changing them, although that theory helps explain why we believe efforts to support student success matter, and can make a difference. Instead, consider what we offer in this chapter as concrete steps you can take not only to remind your students that learning benefits from effort, persistence, and reflection, but to build those reminders into the very fabric of your course.

MODELS

Online classes suffer from a relatively high attrition rate compared to traditional in-person classes, at least 10–20% higher (Bawa, 2016). Some studies have found that online student attrition rates may be significantly higher, up to seven times higher, than in face-to-face courses (Patterson and McFadden, 2009). This is a known issue in online higher education. Many of us who regularly teach online can attest to discouraging online attrition rates, though we have little recent national research to support our anecdotal observations. Still, the issue of online students failing to complete their classes is widely acknowledged as a pressing concern.

We have many strategies we can use to combat the easy tendency of students to drift away. Indeed, we can do a lot simply by being actively present in our class, by interacting frequently, and by providing timely feedback. Chapters 2, 4, and 5 present numerous small teaching strategies to help us be there to support our students' learning in our online classes. But there's more we can do, and we should. I believe we have many good reasons to help our students persist and earn a college degree. Here are some ways we can do more of this in our online classes.

Nudge Targeted Students

A personal email from you, especially if sent early in the semester, has significant potential to help a student who needs a little extra attention. Colleges and universities are increasingly developing and putting in place support systems to help us identify and reach out to students who may be struggling. But a personalized message from your email address can be much more impactful than these other approaches.

My passionate-for-student-success biology colleague, when teaching her eight-week online classes, checks on every student on Day 3 of a new session. If a student has not yet accessed the course or the publisher content, she sends a personal email to that student. The message asks whether she can do anything to help, and reminds students of the importance of getting a strong start in her fast-paced course. She tells me that her students, perhaps surprised that an online instructor is paying attention, typically respond by logging in and getting started with the course. Or they may drop the course before the deadline, ensuring that they don't throw away precious tuition dollars on a course they can't commit to completing at this time. Either way, my colleague's timely email helps her students take appropriate action.

A similar approach has yielded powerful results for Zoë Cohen, faculty in the College of Medicine at the University of Arizona. In "Small Changes, Large Rewards: How Individualized Emails Increase Classroom Performance" (2018), Cohen shares her strategy of emailing individual students who failed the first of three exams in her in-person Physiology of the Immune System course – typically, about 20 students in a class of 200. Cohen's approach is a perfect example of a small teaching way to help students persist. She sends a personal email in which the body of the message is the same, but she addresses it to each individual student. "Hi _____," it reads,

> I was looking at the exam #1 scores for PSIO 431 and saw that you didn't do as well as expected. Since it's still early in the semester, now is the time to try and figure out what went wrong and how we can fix it.

She proceeds to ask some guiding questions about how the student prepared for the exam. "Did you come to class and participate in the discussions? Do you have a study group? Did you come to office hours to discuss the material?" Cohen ends on an encouraging note, expressing her interest in working with the student "so that the rest of the course goes more smoothly."

The first time she sent these emails, Cohen was surprised at her students' responses. She expected students to blame her for not adequately preparing them. Instead, she received several replies thanking her for showing an interest, and resolving to change practices in order to do better. Three years after sending that first email, Cohen now makes it a regular practice. She has seen the impact and considers this small investment of time to be well worthwhile.

Cohen teaches in person, but her strategy, known as a *nudge*, can be easily applied online. The idea of gently steering students toward making wiser decisions stems from an impactful book titled *Nudge: Improving Decisions about Health, Wealth, and Happiness* (Thaler and Sunstein, 2008). The basic, yet revolutionary, premise is that we can influence people to make better decisions simply by the way we present the choice or encourage them to do so.

Helping our students form better study habits, for example, can be the result of a communication strategy such as Cohen's personalized emails.

Nudges are becoming more widely used, and studied, in teaching in higher education. Researchers are finding that these small interventions that encourage positive behavior are making a difference in students' performance. One recent study measured the impact of two personalized emails from the professor to individual students reminding them of various avenues of support (Carrell, Kurlaender, and Bhatt, 2016). Not surprisingly, the treatment group earned higher grades than the control group.

Nudges such as these may be even more important in an online class. Show your struggling students that you're paying attention. Demonstrate that you care. Send a personal email, written in a kind and supportive tone of voice, early enough in the semester for them to change their behavior to be more successful. Like Cohen, you may be surprised at the impact this small outreach can have.

Assign a Goals Contract

Although online learning is rapidly expanding, it is still new enough that many students have little experience with online classes. For example, college students have generally spent at least 12 or 13 years in the K12 classroom. They know what to expect in that setting. Rarely have today's college students spent anything like that amount of time taking online classes.

Because of this, students need help understanding what will be required of them in the online environment, where self-directed learning is essential for success. We can teach students how to make and honor their commitment to a course by asking them to submit a Goals Contract in the first few days of class.

Although learning contracts are not new, they can effectively help students develop their own strategy for success. The University of Waterloo Centre for Teaching Excellence website encourages faculty to use this approach in their classes. "Learning contracts give ownership to students over their learning at the outset of a project or class, they prompt students to reflect on how they learn, and they establish clear goals and project timelines" (Self-Directed Learning: Learning Contracts, n.d.). Helping our students take ownership of their learning is a strategic way to help them persist and complete online classes, and therefore is well worth considering.

The first half of the Goals Contract can help clarify your expectations for students in the course. Decide what behaviors are often lacking in online students who fail to complete your course. Create a list of statements for students to agree to. For example, you may want to present some statements such as these for students to initial their agreement:

- I have read and understood the syllabus.
- I carefully reviewed the course schedule and noted deadlines in my calendar.
- I understand that to succeed in this eight-week class, I will work 16–18 hours per week on coursework.
- I have scheduled time in my weekly routine to log into class at least four different days of the week, some of which are not consecutive.
- I can and should post questions about the course in the Q&A forum on the discussion board.
- I will attend online tutoring if I start falling behind.

Have students print the document, initial next to each statement, and sign and date the contract. Then ask them to take a picture with their phone or tablet and upload it for a low-stakes quiz grade. You may want to make this activity required in order to release the remaining course content.

The advantage of this strategy is that you have students' agreement in writing in case a complaint arises later on. The downside, of course, is the same flaw of every end-user agreement you've ever signed. We are all prone to checking the box next to a statement that says, "I agree to the terms of use," without reading the terms of use, simply in order to move on and begin using the application. Students may initial, sign, snap, and upload without really thinking about what they've agreed to do.

For this reason, I like to add a second essential component to the Goals Contract. Recently, I attended a professional development workshop in which we were asked to set some goals for the upcoming academic year. The activity was elegant in its simplicity. The prompt asked us to write two goals, state one thing we committed to doing to help us achieve those goals, one challenge we anticipated would interfere with our ability to achieve those goals, and one strategy for overcoming that challenge. The opportunity to write down these statements, to articulate our plans in this way, made concrete the otherwise vague intentions we formed in the workshop.

A Goals Contract combines the teacher's statements of expectations with goals established by the students. Provide a document with a few statements and space to initial. Below that, have students identify their two goals, one thing they commit to doing, one challenge, and one strategy. Students print the document, initial, hand-write the goals section, then take the photo and upload the pic. Adding a component in which students have to think through what they plan to do to succeed can make this activity quite powerful. This simple activity helps them to set goals, and importantly, to see for themselves that they can achieve those goals (Nilson and Goodson, 2018, p. 116).

As an alternative to having students write out the goal section of this contract, you could offer them the option of recording a video of themselves stating their goals and plans. Some students might find it more compelling to verbalize their positive intentions in that format. Whether in writing or in video form, ask students to articulate that they understand what it takes to succeed, and to identify how they plan to do so.

Use Mastery Quizzes

My cheerleading biology friend uses another technique, mastery quizzes, that can really help at-risk students in her online course. The concept is simple. My colleague requires a vocabulary quiz worth zero points at the beginning of each module. Students must earn 100% on the quiz, even though it does not count toward the final grade. What it does, however, is make the rest of the module content available. Until students earn 100% on the vocabulary quiz, they may not proceed with the module.

To enable them to earn 100%, students have unlimited attempts. They may take the quiz as many times as they need to in order to get that 100%. But until they do, students may not move forward.

In a series of articles on authentic learning, Theresa Gilliard-Cook and Brandon West explain that mastery quizzing can be used to get students to "demonstrate a baseline knowledge or vocabulary" and to "reinforce their comprehension" of these baseline concepts (2015). The authors further note that mastery quizzes are effective for two main reasons. First, they are low-stakes since students can take the test multiple times to achieve success (most learning management systems (LMSs) allow you to determine a set number, such as three attempts, or you can set the quiz so that students have unlimited attempts). Additionally, mastery quizzing "requires the students to reflect on what they don't know and gives them an opportunity to go back to address the gaps in their knowledge" (Gilliard-Cook and West, 2015). Whenever we can help our students reflect on and address any gaps in their knowledge, we should probably consider doing so.

We can help our students to earn the necessary 100% (or whatever level you determine is mastery – perhaps for your content, 80% is sufficient) on such quizzes and also develop self-reliance by embedding guidance and directions in the test feedback. "Such feedback is simple to prepare yet often neglected," point out Nilson and Goodson (2018, p. 84). If we take a bit of extra time to set up this automated feedback for each LMS quiz, we can direct students to address their own gaps in their knowledge. Keep in mind, too, as with many small teaching suggestions, your time investment pays off when you reuse these quizzes semester after semester. For example, you can set the feedback that displays if the wrong answer is selected to say, "Incorrect. Please review pages 342–344 of your textbook." Or it might direct students to review the relevant section of your mini-lecture video according to its timestamp. So the feedback could say, "That's not the best answer. Review the video from 2:15 to 3:00 to help you rethink your response."

In my colleague's class, the purpose of the mastery quiz is to make sure students can speak the language of biology. She argues that students can't learn concepts if they don't understand the terminology. To empower students to learn new information, she requires them to demonstrate mastery of the vocabulary. In the process of doing so, she gains new opportunities to provide support to her students and structure for their learning.

Many of the students in her online, 8-week general education biology class have failed the in-person, 16-week class. The lack of structure in the face-to-face class seems to contribute to their failure. Just showing up to a lecture, without specific guidance about things like making sure they know the vocabulary for the day's lesson, has not resulted in successful completion of the class. Some of her online students take these Mastery Quizzes up to 13 times before they earn 100%, my colleague tells me. She will sometimes provide very detailed guidance, like suggesting they write down the words on the quiz, and look up and write down the definitions, before they reattempt the quiz. "Students thrive on the structure provided by these gateway quizzes," my friend said. "They don't have the basic study skills they need to be successful. The mastery quiz forces them to practice good study habits in order to complete the class."

Again, no points are attached to these quizzes. The implied message is that this is a basic study skill. Working to learn these terms is necessary to make progress through the course. This teaches the value of laying a strong foundation before trying to acquire new understanding.

Providing guidance on where to find the correct answer helps students pass the quiz and proceed with module content. Consider adding meaningful guidance to your feedback for correct answers, too. Encourage students to find out more, and suggest an additional resource or two. Recommend complementary topics for parallel self-study. Show students how and where to further explore on their own. Use embedded feedback to remediate or challenge, right in the moment when it's most relevant.

You can set up mastery quizzes in your LMS using the settings on the Quiz tool and the conditional release function. Set the quiz to allow unlimited attempts, or whatever number you decide is best. Exclude the score from the final grade. Set the conditional release to only display the rest of the module content after the quiz shows 100%. Your local instructional designer or LMS support team should be able to help you do this if you're not sure how.

Scaffold Assignments

Many students are anxious about what they will experience in their online class. That may change over time, as students become more experienced with online learning. But for now, it's helpful to build structures that reassure students that they are on track.

Noted psychologist Albert Bandura's self-efficacy theory (1977) tells us that when we achieve success on a task, our belief in our ability to succeed increases. "Successes raise mastery expectations," Bandura explains, "Repeated failures lower them, particularly if the mishaps occur early in the course of events. After strong efficacy expectations are developed through repeated success, the negative impact of occasional failures is likely to be reduced" (Bandura, 1977, p. 195). In light of this, it's vitally important to structure learning tasks that allow learners to succeed early and often.

For example, in recent years the push bike has become very popular for teaching preschoolers how to ride a bicycle. Gone are the training wheels. There aren't even any pedals. Instead, the young child uses their feet to make the bike go and to make the bike stop. Since there are no pedals to worry about, beginners can experience success sooner than they might otherwise – and with fewer crashes that result in skinned knees and elbows. This increased belief in their ability to succeed allows the child to master other necessary skills such as balancing and steering. Once the child feels confident in their ability to coast around on the push bike, it's a small step to teach them to use pedals and brakes in order to truly ride a bike.

You can create a similar sequence in your online class by offering frequent opportunities for students to succeed in low-stakes tasks as they work toward more complex and high-stakes ones. Remember, according to Bandura, repeated failures have the equal and opposite effect, so we must be careful not to create tasks that set our students up to fail. Instead, think carefully about what small and achievable tasks you can create, activities that are likely to lead to students successfully completing them, and thereby becoming more expectant of their ability to succeed on the next, slightly more complex, task.

One of the assignments in my educational technology class, for example, is to create a teaching video mini-lecture on a topic of interest. Many of my nontraditional students have not had much experience recording themselves. These students are often nervous about this task. They have low self-efficacy when it comes to creating a polished teaching video. However, I have specific pedagogical goals for this assessment, so I want them to build the skills to demonstrate their knowledge in this format as opposed to other modalities.

Before I knew about scaffolding learning activities, I may have concluded they would just need to figure it out. I might have told them in Week 1 that the video would be due in Week 8, and suggested they start practicing. I might not have told them even that much—out of ignorance about helping students succeed, not out of malice. But over the years, I've come to see the value of building support structures that empower students to take small steps, to achieve small successes, to grow in confidence as the task becomes more complex. So now I deliberately build multiple opportunities for feedback and growth in a project such as this.

First, students post a short (60- to 90-second) video introduction of themselves, due on Day 4 of the eight-week course. Because students are talking about something they know a lot about, it should not be too cognitively demanding. What they do need to figure out, however, are some of the basics of creating and posting a video. This task is like putting them on a push bike. There's no need to worry about everything yet, but students need to decide which device or app to use to record. They need to find a headset or earbuds with a microphone, so that viewers can hear them adequately. They need to learn how to upload their video to YouTube or NAU's video streaming solution, Kaltura, and request machine captioning. They need to embed their video or paste a link into an online discussion forum, and submit it before midnight on the day it is due.

For some students, these tasks aren't challenging. But for many of my older students, recording even a 90-second video involves several new steps that each require skill development and practice.

I know my students are nervous about this (because they say so in the opening seconds of the video), so I make it a point to reply to these posts and grade them as soon as I possibly can, generally within one day of the deadline. I put on my cheerleader hat, award all-or-nothing points – a good-faith effort earns full credit – and include confidence-boosting comments.

Video tasks build in complexity over the course of the class. After creating their video introductions, students continue developing skills through frequent assignments that enable them to practice and gain confidence in recording and editing videos. These tasks increase in length and difficulty. For example, in Week 2, students post a 2- to 3-minute video discussing their key takeaways from an assigned journal article. The following week, they propose their teaching video topic, including their rationale and a brief summary of supporting materials, in a slightly longer video, not more than 3 to 5 minutes. And the task continues to build from there both in difficulty and duration. By the time the 8- to 10-minute teaching video is due, students have practiced recording meaningful videos multiple times.

Importantly, I assess each submission and return feedback well before the next video task is due. It's difficult to develop a new skill in a feedback void. We need constant instructions, encouragement, and coaching in order to progress. As soon as possible after each video deadline, I grade and return the assignment so that students have time to improve their method before creating the next video.

This intentionally structured process allows my students to become more confident in their ability to succeed on the teaching video assignment. Those who were nervous in the first week of class now have a much higher sense of self-efficacy for this task. I like to think that they can apply this same practice elsewhere in their lives, in various settings and contexts. For me, helping students see what it takes to succeed is important for their lifelong well-being.

PRINCIPLES

I suppose I am so interested in helping students persist and succeed because more than the grades are at stake. Like my friend in the advertising and PR department, I have bigger goals for my students. Whatever the class I'm teaching, I want students to mature and grow in confidence. We can apply small teaching strategies to help our students pass our classes. More importantly, these approaches will help our students become more effective in their personal, professional, and civic lives.

Help Students Commit to, and Achieve, Success

As their instructor, *you* know what it takes for your students to complete your class. Help *them* to understand what it takes. Help them commit to doing the necessary work. Assign tasks that cause students to evaluate their readiness for your class. Ask students to think about what they are willing to do to get through. Have students articulate their plan of action. At strategic points of the class, check in with students. Ask them if they are meeting the goals they laid out in Week 1. Suggest ways they can continue moving forward, even if they've had a setback such as a failed exam. Help your students see how to succeed and, importantly, take action that allows them to do so.

Provide Lots of Structure

Online learners are often unaware of the level of self-direction it takes to persist and succeed in a class. Without the supports of a set class time and physical presence of the instructor in the classroom, students must create their own classwork schedules and plans for success. Guide the development of this kind of self-direction by creating strong structure. Oblige students to demonstrate mastery of foundational concepts before proceeding to more complex processes. Teach students good study habits by not allowing them to progress in your class without them. Foster a growth mindset by allowing multiple attempts on tests and papers. Help your students become better at directing their own learning by providing the framework that they may lack. Over time, we'll develop the leaders of tomorrow by holding students to account today.

Create the Personal Touch

Personal outreach from you can have a major impact on your individual students. Create minor impact on your time through small and targeted methods of contact. Develop a strategy that enables you to personally interact with students without too much demand on your time. This could be a reply to each individual's introduction post. Or comment briefly but meaningfully on a task in the first week within as short a time frame as you can. Send a personal email after the first test to anyone who did not do well. Whatever your approach, help students see you as an individual who cares about their individual success. Create person-to-person contact to motivate and guide students to succeed.

SMALL TEACHING ONLINE QUICK TIPS: FOSTERING STUDENT PERSISTENCE AND SUCCESS

Attrition rates in online classes are distressingly high. Increased access to college resulting from the flexibility of online learning is meaningless if students don't persist and attain a degree. We can apply small teaching strategies to help.

- *Nudge students in need of a little extra support.* Send targeted, personalized emails at strategic points of the course with reminders about steps they can take to recover lost ground.
- *Ask students to commit to a plan for success.* Have them complete a Goals Contract in the first few days of class. Submission of this contract could release the rest of the class content to underscore its foundational importance in the course.
- *Require students to demonstrate mastery of foundational concepts.* Create gateway quizzes, which must be passed with a score of 100%, in order for students to proceed with module content.
- *Deliberately build self-efficacy through scaffolded assignment design.* Students achieve success in small tasks to help them develop confidence for more complex ones.

CONCLUSION

The other night, I attended my daughter's open house at her new high school. I was impressed in general with the school ethos of supporting student success while encouraging practical behaviors to achieve it. In particular, I was struck by the pre-AP English teacher's comments. She related how she always hears deep dark confessions from her new students, such as, "I've never been good at writing," or, "I'm a terrible speller."

"I can work with those things," she said. "That's my job." She went on to say that what she can't work with, what truly hinders progress, is a poor work ethic. "I can't help students who won't do the work."

Students might not be doing the work in your course for a variety of reasons. Some of them might have overextended themselves; some of them might not be ready for a college course. But many of them will not do the work because they doubt their own abilities, or because they don't understand the amount of work and self-discipline required to succeed in an online course. For all of these students, the kinds of small teaching nudges we have considered in this chapter should provide support to help them on their academic journeys – both in your course and beyond.

Part III

Motivating Online Students (and Instructors)

T he challenges presented by online learning differ from those presented by traditional instruction. Attrition rates are among the most significant of these challenges for online courses. Many students find at least some of their online classes to be dry, boring, and unengaging. We as online teachers may similarly experience a lack of teaching and learning energy in the online classroom. Just the other day a faculty member in our Applied Indigenous Studies program expressed this sentiment to me. "I really get jazzed in the classroom," he told me. "My online classes don't hold my attention."

Bearing in mind that online learning is still a recent phenomenon in the world, I'm confident that researchers and practitioners will develop a broader range of evidence-based solutions to the unique issues we face in online classes, more extensive than we have available today. In the meantime, both parties in the online learning partnership can be, at times, guilty of investing less time and energy than are required to create a synergistic learning experience. Given the apparent need for support in this area, in Part III we'll focus on the challenge of maintaining the needed momentum for a successful online course. Here we'll consider strategies for keeping our students – and ourselves – motivated, inspired, and engaged.

Our approach in this section is shaped by the control-value theory of achievement emotions developed by Reinhard Pekrun, a researcher at the University of Munich in Germany. Pekrun and his colleagues studied how the emotions that students experience while learning impacts their motivation to engage in the learning itself. Sarah Cavanagh provides a succinct overview of Pekrun's theory in her 2016 book, *The Spark of Learning: Energizing the College Classroom with the Science of Emotion*. The first element in this theoretical framework is the level of *control* students have over their learning experience. Cavanagh describes this as the extent to which "students feel in control of the activities and outcomes that are important to them" (2016, p. 148). *Value* is the second factor in this theory; value represents the degree to which "the activity or material represents meaning or worth to students" (p. 148). Cavanagh summarizes Pekrun's body of research in this area by explaining that when students evaluate a learning environment, feeling a sense of "high control and high value will both independently and synergistically contribute to which emotions students experience and how those emotions contribute to motivation and learning" (p. 148). These two notions of control and value provide a manageable entry point for thinking about how to motivate students in our online courses.

To help students develop a sense of control, Chapter 7 presents small teaching strategies for fostering learner autonomy. Online learning requires a high level of independence. Students must take ownership for their learning in order to succeed in an online class. It's vital that they learn to direct their own learning in ways that may not be as necessary when taking an in-person class. We'll consider doable adjustments to our online teaching that help students become less reliant on you, their instructor. Such adjustments allow students a degree of choice so that they feel more in control of their learning. They can teach students how to take responsibility for their learning, arguably an important life skill in many contexts outside of your class. Giving students more control – or at least the perception of more control – can lead to increased motivation to engage with you, your material, and the other students in the class.

Similarly, we should help students see the meaning or value of class activities. Chapter 8 explores the importance of making connections between new knowledge and pre-existing knowledge or experience. These connections help students to form the dense webs of interrelated ideas that we as experts have in our neural networks. When students see how new concepts relate to each other and to what they already know about the material, content becomes more meaningful. Chapter 8 will examine ways to help students form these connections for themselves. In so doing, we help students to find worth and perceive the value of what they are learning and how it applies to their lived experience.

Finally, in Chapter 9 we turn our attention to *us* as online instructors. It's certainly important to find ways to foster motivation in our students. But how do we keep ourselves motivated? Here I'll seek to inspire you to keep finding purpose in your online teaching, to continue to develop your own sense of control, your own sense of the value of what you are doing. Online classes aren't going away. Excellent online teachers are positioned to make a tremendous impact, not only on individual students, but on our society as a whole, as we teach tomorrow's thought leaders today.

When our online classes are as engaging as our dynamic in-person classes, we'll know that we've arrived. When we are just as jazzed in the online classroom as we are in the physical, we'll know we've succeeded. When both parties in the online learning partnership are highly motivated, an energizing atmosphere results in which deep, meaningful learning takes place.

Chapter 7

Creating Autonomy

INTRODUCTION

About five years ago, I was hired by our educational leadership department to design and teach a new, updated version of their course on Educational Technology in the College Classroom. This online graduate-level course is a requirement for students in two master's programs: one in educational technology and the other in community college and higher education. I completed a significant redesign of the course to incorporate content in the areas of instructional design, the learning sciences, and principles of effective teaching with technology. Modeling best practices in online course design and delivery was a primary goal of the redesign. I invested a lot of work in the new development, and I was quite pleased with the resulting course.

My students, however, were not.

After teaching the course a few times, a major problem became increasingly apparent. The course served two master of education programs, but not all students in these programs are educators. Both programs had been designed for flexibility, to meet the needs of a range of learners with varying career goals. This meant that about 50% of my students were neither college instructors nor K12 teachers, and they never would be. Many of my students were pursuing a master's degree in higher education to advance their administrative careers at the community college or university. That they were required to take an entire course on teaching with technology made no sense for them. They complained, and I agreed. The institution had inadvertently created a clear misalignment of content and learner goals. It was impossible to create relevance in a course about teaching methods for students who had never taught and would never teach.

To address this concern, I proposed that we expand the scope of the course to meet individual learner needs and goals. Those students who were educators could focus exclusively on how to *teach* well with technology. Students who were not educators could take a separate path, one that allowed them to focus on how to *work* well with technology, no matter what their job was.

A curriculum committee approval process ensued, leading to a new course title, Technological Fluency and Leadership. I embarked on another major course development project. My overarching goal for the new course was to allow students to customize their learning so that whatever their workplace or career goals, they could learn how to improve their work with effective use of technology. I expanded this approach to include the use of technology in our personal lives and in our volunteer roles in the community as well.

In this new course, students have complete freedom to choose where to focus their learning. They take responsibility for learning what will benefit them in their unique context. They decide what will help them achieve personal and professional goals. They are almost completely autonomous when it comes to how they spend their time and energy in my course. And just as Reinhard Pekrun's theory would suggest, now that my students have significantly more control over their learning experience, they're much more highly engaged as a result.

Students will not succeed in an online class if they do not take responsibility for their own learning. My new course has been more successful because I have been able to rebuild the curriculum to meet multiple needs. Fostering student autonomy is woven into the fabric of the new design. You may not have the freedom to completely redesign your course and content, however, so the models in this chapter will focus on the elements that most instructors *can* control, especially the ones that fall at the level of small teaching.

IN THEORY

In Chapter 2, we introduced you to *The Meaningful Writing Project*, a book that described the conclusions of a massive survey that asked students about what made writing assignments meaningful to them. The implications of those conclusions, in our view, extend well beyond the scope of written assignments, and can help us think more deeply about what makes any kind of learning experience meaningful to our students. *The Meaningful Writing Project* articulates three core elements that were reported most frequently by students as contributing to that sense of meaning. We discussed one of those three items, regular *engagement* with peers and instructors and course content, in Chapter 2. A second feature is *connections*, which means that the students could see connections between the course work and their own experiences: past, present, and future. We will discuss that idea in more depth in the next chapter.

The third element is *agency*, a concept that underpins the models recommended in this chapter. When students feel like they have some ability to control or have a say in the process of completing their work, they are more likely to find that work meaningful. As the authors of the book point out, we can't give people agency; we can, however, provide the conditions and support for it to flourish: "We can intentionally build optimal conditions for agency to emerge. Agency is strengthened by offering experiences that get students to notice they have the capacity to direct energies for themselves, in and beyond classrooms" (Eodice, Geller, and Lerner, 2016, p. 53). This quote reflects the premise underpinning many of the recommendations in this book and the original *Small Teaching*, that our goal as teachers is to create environments that spur and support learning – not simply to present content to students and hope they master it.

If we want to motivate students to learn in our courses – in person or online – we have to provide them with opportunities to be active agents, just as Flower did in the course described in the opening of this chapter. But we want even more than that, which is why we are using the broader term *autonomy* in this chapter, one that you see more typically cited in the educational literature. The contrast we would make here is that students with a sense of agency feel like they have the power to act in a given situation; students with *autonomy* have a broader awareness of themselves as independent learners who have both the responsibility and control of their own learning.

The findings of *The Meaningful Writing Project* fit well with what research on learning and motivation has been telling us for quite some time now. James Zull's *The Art of Changing the Brain: Enriching the Practice of Teaching by Exploring the Biology of Learning* (2002), which explores the biology of the brain in relation to teaching and learning in higher education, argues that "one important rule for helping people learn is to help the learner feel she is in control" (Zull, 2002, p. 52). You can probably relate well to this idea, since most college faculty were willing to spend months and years settling into the pursuit of a question that fascinated them while earning their doctoral degrees. We don't undertake such pursuits because someone has commanded us to do so; we undertake them because they fascinate us, and we get to follow the pathways that interest us. Your students are no different in this respect; they are more likely to pursue their work (and find meaning in it) when they are tracking down the questions that interest them, rather than the ones you have set for them.

At the same time, you of course are the expert in your field, and you will have a better understanding of the important questions or content in your field, as well as of the teaching strategies and assessments that will help them learn. The key is to strike a balance by providing plenty of support and guidance, while still allowing your students enough freedom to help them develop that sense of autonomy – which was exactly what students reported as most helpful to them in *The Meaningful Writing Project*. While students valued assignments that gave them agency, they also valued guidance and support from their instructors. The authors describe it a sweet spot that falls somewhere "between *allow* and *require*" (Eodice, Geller, and Lerner, 2016, p. 48); one of the students in the survey calls it "guidance without boundaries" (p. 38).

In the models that follow, we have tried to strike that balance as well. Throughout the first six chapters of this book we have provided plenty of guidance for you in terms of how you can create great online courses for your students, and in this section we encourage you to identify the places within those course structures in which your students can exercise some control over their own learning, or the ways in which they demonstrate their learning to you. Providing those opportunities, and supporting learners as they take advantage of them, will help them develop the autonomy that we hope online education can foster in our students.

MODELS

Helping students develop autonomy has lifelong implications for their future success. The small teaching strategies outlined here encourage students to take responsibility for their learning in our online classes and beyond.

Offer Choice in Online Discussions

Online discussions have potential to significantly impact learning. The peer-to-peer instruction that can take place there, when prompts are structured carefully, can go a long way to deepening student understanding of core concepts. However, discussions can also become a tedious exchange of required original and reply posts that bears little resemblance to the lively conversations you facilitate in the classroom. A simple solution to the challenge of creating engaging online discussions is to let students choose what they want to talk about.

We know that students take more ownership of their learning when they find the task relevant to their personal experiences or intriguing to them in some other way. Designing for increased agency can be as simple as helping students feel they have more control over their work, and therefore, help them see more value in the task. As Cavanagh (2016) explains, "The most straightforward route to maximizing students' sense of control and value is quite simply to give them control by giving them choices in activities and assignments wherever possible" (pp. 150–151). Cavanagh goes on to explain that providing students with choices leads to "greater completion, interest, enjoyment, and perceived competence" (p. 151). These sound like great benefits, don't they? You can reap those benefits and build an element of learner agency into an online course by providing options for online discussion topics.

I like to do this in a whole class discussion. Students in my technology fluency class have four or five questions to choose from for each module's discussion. For example, they can write about which of the readings they selected. As another way to add choice, I provide 12–15 articles related to the module topic;

students read five that most interest them – and then write about what they found significant about the readings they chose. This way, students inform each other about the readings so that all articles are covered without each student having to read all of them.

I always post three or four other discussion questions in addition to the one related to module readings. Students might choose to write (or talk, for video discussions) about the online resources that they contributed to our shared Google Doc, to summarize what they found and explain why it interested them. Or they might talk about a piece of content I provided in the module, perhaps my mini-lecture video or the guest lecturer for the week. They can also discuss the unique project for that module, reflecting on their process, what they learned, and how they plan to do things differently as a result.

Each week also includes a question about how what we did that week impacts them personally. I'll ask how the readings affect my students' experience at work, or what change they've made in family life as a result of our activity in class. Students love the opportunity to talk about themselves (don't we all?). They engage much more enthusiastically and naturally, as they would in a spirited conversation you might facilitate in the classroom, simply by way of having a choice about their contribution. As an added bonus, they often describe tech solutions to common challenges that I face as a busy working mom. I'm still using an app that one of my students identified, Picniic, that helps to organize hectic family life, with options for weekly menus, recipes, grocery lists, calendars, individual chores and task lists, and more. This is just one example. Giving students the option of pursuing topics that interest them means I'm always learning from their experiences. What better way to keep yourself fresh and enthusiastic in a course you regularly teach than to keep learning from your students?

Creating choice in online discussions is quite simple, though it requires a bit of creativity to devise multiple possible discussion questions for each module. My forum instructions state that they can write about any or all of the questions. There's no requirement that they have to address at least two or three; if they choose to write about just one, but their contribution is well crafted and substantial, that's fine. The goal is to allow students to engage with topics they find interesting, and then interact with other students who likely wrote about something else of interest. This way there are multiple mini-conversations happening in the forum. The end result is a rich stream of conversation that brings out nuanced themes and various angles and facets of the module's topic. Best of all, I now have 25 co-creators of content. Student contributions create a far more robust exploration of the topic than I could ever engineer on my own.

In some weeks I require students to record a video instead of writing their post. In other weeks, in line with Universal Design for Learning (UDL) principles, I tell them that they can choose whether to record or write. Sometimes their replies come via video. The course offers continual, yet relatively simple, options for students to choose how they want to engage each week. This helps keep module discussions fresh and relevant, instead of the stale and forced interactions that often characterize this component of an online class. Let students choose what to talk about. Structure multiple ways for them to engage. They'll contribute more than the minimum, and you'll likely find it more rewarding to interact there as well.

Create Self-Enroll Scaffolded Groups

Another way to help online students develop independence is to design a group process that simultaneously allows choice and fosters self-sufficiency. This strategy weaves together two essential ingredients of creating autonomy: personal interest or relevance, and supporting students early in the process to equip them for success without your active involvement.

Create groups that students can enroll themselves in based on topics of interest. Each group has a limited number of spots, so enrollment happens on a first-come, first-served basis. If I were teaching an educational technology class today, for example, I might create a group for each of the following topics:

- AR/VR (Augmented Reality and Virtual Reality)
- Mobile Learning
- Universal Design for Learning
- Open Educational Resources
- Gamification

Based on their interest in the topics, students sign up for the appropriate group. Because they've chosen an area of interest to them, students should naturally be more invested in, and take more ownership of, their learning and contributions to the group.

Once students are in their groups, scaffold their process of becoming a well-functioning team in which learners honor their commitments both to themselves and to the others in the group. Robert John Robertson and Shannon Riggs offer valuable insight into the research on and implementation of asynchronous online group projects in their chapter on collaborative assignments in *High-Impact Practices in Online Education: Research and Best Practices* (2018). Robertson and Riggs highlight both the benefits and challenges of online group work and present a convincing argument for creating effective collaborative projects, identified by George Kuh (2008) and the Association of American Colleges and Universities (AAC&U) as a high-impact practice, despite the challenges involved:

> Interestingly ... historically underserved students comprise many of the same student populations that online providers of higher education are trying to serve by bringing higher education to where they are.... Given this overlap between the student populations that online providers are trying to serve and the student populations identified as benefiting from high-impact practices (HIPs), promoting collaborative activities online is becoming more essential. (Robertson and Riggs, 2018, p. 72)

Although there are good reasons for including group work in online classes, one of which is their claim that such tasks prepare students to work in an increasingly global, asynchronous professional environment, Robertson and Riggs are quite open about the obstacles involved with collaborative learning tasks, especially those that are unique to an online course. Of particular interest is their point about the potential inauthenticity of learning to collaborate, which may not be as necessary "for mature students, especially those who have been in the workforce or military" (p. 78). Younger students who are moving straight from high school to college benefit from more practice working in teams, they argue, but for students who have already been on the job, this may feel "forced and unnecessary" (p. 78).

Their advice, therefore, is to carefully design collaborative projects to promote healthy group functioning and authentic, meaningful learning that will be valuable in students' future workplaces. Here's a quick summary of some of the other important characteristics of collaborative assignments in online classes you'll find in this chapter, though I encourage you to read it for yourself because it's so rich and helpful. In order to be effective, a collaborative project in an online class should:

· Reflect your pedagogical purpose.
· Begin with a structured team-building activity.
· Include a plan to prevent conflict, or work through it constructively if it occurs.
· Require transparent group communication.
· Have explicit grading criteria and processes (Robertson and Riggs, 2018).

With these features of a well-designed group project, you can have every hope that the task will achieve the learning goals you set for it and will benefit your students in ways that reach beyond the content of your course.

So how do you do these things in practice? Here are some small suggestions to consider. Once students have signed up for their topic of interest, make sure the task instructions are clear. You may want to record a short explainer video since students may struggle to read through lengthy written directions. Next, have students participate in a team-building activity that functions as an ice-breaker and also helps students to identify and select team roles. Both the task and the team roles should ensure a collaborative, interdependent approach in which the positive contributions of each team member impact the success of the whole. The 2017 movie *Jumanji: Welcome to the Jungle* illustrates this concept brilliantly. Without giving too much away, I'll explain that the main characters find themselves in a video game. In order to escape the game, they must overcome a series of obstacles and achieve the objective so they can go back home. As in real video games, each character has strengths and weaknesses. Through a series of adventures and mishaps, these characters learn that they must simultaneously play to their strengths while covering each other's weaknesses. If they don't work together, they will fail the objective and physically die in the game. It's an excellent analogy of how we expect students to work together in groups, maximizing individual strengths and helping each other succeed.

Sounds good, in theory. To help students achieve this harmony in reality, you may want to require a team contract in which students negotiate expectations, agree on standards of respectful and considerate behavior, and establish a procedure to address conflict or any failure to honor the contractual agreements. Ask students to discuss and create their contract in a videoconference call and then report periodically on their process and progress at the beginning of the group task and at incremental periods or after staged deadlines throughout the project.

When you structure the group project with these kinds of supportive elements, you help students in a group hold themselves and each other accountable for doing what they said they would do. They learn to take responsibility for their learning, to develop autonomy, as they uphold individual commitments and rely on each other for success. Given that the ability to learn and work both independently and in teams is highly sought after by today's employers (Agarwal, 2019), we contribute to our students' future success by helping them develop a sense of responsibility for their own work and for their contributions to the team.

Apply Specifications Grading

In Chapter 4, I briefly mentioned Specifications Grading, an assessment strategy described by Linda Nilson in her book by the same name (2015). There, I presented one piece of the Specifications, or Specs, Grading approach: Oops Tokens, a way of adding flexibility to your class and demonstrating caring and support for your learners. But I didn't really do justice to Specs Grading in my earlier treatment of it. The real beauty of this approach is that it helps students take *responsibility* for their learning by holding them accountable for doing the *work* of learning. As author Terry Doyle explains, "The one who does the work does the learning" (2011, p. 13). Yet, many of our assessments that truly get to higher-order thinking require us to do more work while grading these artifacts than our students did while creating them – at least, it often feels that way. Nilson points out that there is a flaw in that system, and I think she's quite right.

Nilson presents a compelling argument for holding students to a higher standard of work; her practical approach shows how to do this while simultaneously minimizing our grading burden. True to small teaching form, a couple of years ago I decided to try a few little elements of Specs Grading in my online technology fluency class.

First, here's a brief summary of Specs Grading in the way that I've applied it. Nilson provides a useful analogy from the software engineering industry. When a customer orders a new product, the engineers receive a list of criteria, or *specifications*, for what the product should be able to do. If the finished software program does not meet those specifications, the customer does not take it and say, "Ok, I guess that's about 78% there, that's good enough." No. "Either a program meets all these specs, or it doesn't," Nilson explains. "And if it doesn't, it fails and must be revised or abandoned" (Nilson, 2015, p. 56).

Yet, this is exactly what we do – that is, accept work that is below par – when we assess student work on a typical grading scale that allows for partial credit. We train students to think that they can submit less-than-standard work, that they can earn a C or a B or even a low A. What Specs Grading does, by contrast, is to require students to meet *all* the basic criteria, or their work is not acceptable. Nilson advocates for a rigorous all-or-nothing grading strategy – applied strategically, maybe not for every assessment – that holds students accountable for doing the work at the level we expect. This might be at 90%; you can determine that, depending on how you write the task specifications. Specs Grading requires students to work hard to that meet our high expectations; simultaneously, our grading load is significantly lighter since we can use a checklist or rubric to efficiently grade their submission. If it meets the criteria, the student earns 100% of the points. If the work doesn't meet all specs, the student earns a zero.

Again, this is a very brief summary of Specs Grading, one that does not even touch on another element that is a form of contract grading. In this application, students can determine what grade they want to earn in the class, then do that amount of work. Although this sounds intriguing, I've not implemented this component, so I'll limit my remarks to how I used one small part of Specs Grading in my online class.

One of the changes I made was to grade all discussion forums on the all-or-nothing basis that Specs Grading makes so feasible. If you've taught online classes with a discussion component, you know that it can be challenging to determine the difference between a low A and a high B, for example. Or if not difficult, at least time-consuming. We want students to make meaningful and substantive contributions that move the conversation forward, not simply parrot the reading or what their classmates have already said. But drawing distinctions such as that an "A" post will contain at least 250 words and a "B" post will have between 175 and 249 words seems arbitrary and meaningless to me. Students are expert word-count-fillers, having had years of practice.

Instead, applying Specs Grading to my online discussions allows me to quickly – I'm talking mere seconds – assess whether students' contributions are significant enough to get full points. If not, they get a zero. My discussion rubric has exactly one row and two columns. The row summarizes the instructions for the forum. The columns are labeled "Meets Expectations" (full points) and "Does Not Meet Expectations" (zero points). No longer do I debate whether a submission is more like an 88% or closer to a 91%. Students earn 100% or zero. I can tell at a glance which one.

In this system I have found that, as Nilson claims, students figure out pretty quickly that they can't get away with half-hearted effort. The first time a student earns a zero for what may have otherwise been an 86%, they sit up and take notice. Students can't skate by with minimal effort. This is not "Cs get degrees." Specs Grading requires students to read all the specifications (assignment criteria) and then submit work that is at least up to that level.

If you've taught for any length of time, you may have developed a certain skepticism that students actually read assignment instructions. You may feel that some students require too much hand-holding or spoon-feeding. Specs Grading is a way to help students mature in their approach, to grow in their ability and willingness to take ownership of the quality of their work – a desirable trait for tomorrow's workforce to possess.

One caveat: Nilson recommends, and I wholeheartedly agree, that you include a "Get Out of Jail Free" card in the form of one or more Oops Tokens. Students earn that zero one time, submit an Oops Token to be allowed to resubmit the task, and from then on invest a whole lot more effort to produce work that is up to snuff. In Chapter 4 I described using these tokens for deadline extensions as a way of showing compassion for students' life circumstances. I find that they add just enough wiggle room to allow me to hold students to a high standard while acknowledging that life happens.

Consult Nilson's *Specifications Grading* (2015) for a more in-depth description of the approach. I've only implemented one small part of it. I share my method here to show one way in which Specs Grading and a Learning Management System (LMS) rubric can facilitate meaningful assignments that require higher-order thinking without placing an undue grading burden on the instructor.

Annotate, Tweak, and Co-Design Your Syllabus

One final suggestion for helping your students become autonomous learners is to get them actively working with your syllabus, even potentially helping to shape the final document. This is a great way to give your students some control over their learning and help them see the value of the work they are doing in your course. Of course, this strategy can be just as effective in your in-person or blended classes as in your online ones. All our students can benefit from becoming more adept at directing their own learning – allowing students to meaningfully interact with your syllabus can help to accomplish this goal.

Many of us treasure our syllabus as the heart and soul of our course, the repository of the essential course design, content plan, and contractual agreement between ourselves and our students. Indeed, in his 2018 syllabus creation guide for *The Chronicle of Higher Education*, Kevin Gannon writes, "An effective syllabus is a promise that, as a result of our course, students will be able to do a number of things either for the first time or at least better than they could before" (Gannon, 2018b). Sounds great, doesn't it? Quite promising, actually.

However, many of our students don't see the syllabus as full of "promise." It's not exaggerating to say they often see the syllabus as a boring document that fails to provide meaningful guidance. Some of them (most of them?) don't even read it.

One way to engage students in their own learning and with your syllabus is to solicit their active feedback and input on its content by having them annotate the document. Hypothesis, for example, is a free online program that students can use to annotate any document on the web.

Researcher and educator Remi Kalir writes about this approach on his blog in a post titled, "Annotate Your Syllabus" (Kalir, n.d.-a,b). He outlines multiple benefits to inviting students to annotate your syllabus. They can ask questions about assignments or course policies. They can comment on major assignments, indicate where they have concerns, and ask for potential tweaks. They can share practical advice with each other about how to be successful in the course. They can voice opinions on familiar texts and suggest supplemental ones or optional additions to the course schedule. They can discuss instructor and institutional policies to get at the nuances of how these play out in practice.

Getting students to read, think, and talk about the syllabus in a meaningful way is a challenge in both traditional and online courses. This assignment addresses that issue. And, Kalir notes, it provides ongoing benefit throughout the semester. In his blog post on this topic, Kalir refers to an August 2018 tweet in which he points out, "Because the annotated syllabus is available to students throughout the semester, this record of Q&A is a persistent resource. This shifts the classic 'It's in the syllabus, did you read?' approach to a more constructive 'We discussed this when annotating our syllabus, pls revisit our convo'" (Kalir, n.d.-a,b). This step toward building learner independence seems rewarding and purposeful in and of itself.

To truly encourage learner autonomy, however, Kalir recommends using the annotated syllabus to facilitate course co-design between you and your students.

In my courses, I seek to create the conditions whereby students craft their own learning pathways, pursue their interests, and make the course of use to their immediate and longer-term goals. Practically speaking, this means that assignments change during the semester. And that readings are thrown out and replaced. That units of study are adapted. That instructional activities are created and facilitated by students. And that I welcome students' critical feedback and respond respectfully to their needs from one week to the next. (A Strategy for Course Co-Design section, para. 1)

Consider the value of helping students determine their own learning pathways to investigate what is most interesting and relevant to them. What better way to cultivate the self-determination that offers so many benefits in online classes and beyond? Allowing students to co-create the course is a powerful means of getting them to take ownership of their learning.

Kalir acknowledges that this is a "challenging, intensive and emotionally-present approach to pedagogy and course design." If this sounds like giving up more control than you are comfortable with, consider a small teaching approach to dipping your toe in the course co-design water. A special education professor I know leaves one blank course learning objective on his syllabus. Students write their own objective, then design and execute an assessment to measure their achievement of it. In this way, he allows students to choose one facet of what they want to learn in the course and decide how they will demonstrate that they've learned it.

Practically speaking, you can use Hypothesis to annotate the syllabus in whatever manner you decide to begin with. Students create a free account using a personal or school email address, then begin to post and interact on the syllabus posted in your LMS or on a site like docdrop.org. Rather than a tired old document that no one ever reads, the syllabus becomes a living document in which you and your students can "collaboratively discuss learning" (Kalir, n.d.-a,b).

Not sure about using Hypothesis? In a follow-up post, "Annotate Your Syllabus 2.0," Kalir encourages us not to let the technology get in the way of the approach (Kalir, n.d.-a,b). He suggests that Google Docs may be an effective tool, if that's what you and your students are already using, or even flipchart paper and markers, if you're teaching a blended or face-to-face class. Kalir reminds us not to let technology get in the way of your pedagogical purpose: "Use familiar technology," he suggests. "Annotating your syllabus doesn't necessitate that you or your students learn a new tool or set of technical skills. The goal is to annotate, ask questions, share thoughts, and start a discussion about learning together" (Kalir, n.d.-a,b). Excellent advice – a great reminder to find the right technology tool for the job and resist the temptation to try a new tool just because it's the latest greatest thing. Keep your teaching and learning purpose firmly in view. Then find the best tech – be it an online tool or pen and paper – to help you accomplish your goal.

PRINCIPLES

Helping online learners develop autonomy should result in increased engagement and success in your class, and will benefit them in countless learning and workplace contexts moving forward. We can draw out a few principles to guide your process.

Offer Choice to Increase Learner Agency

When we are interested in what we're doing, we naturally invest more time and energy in the task. Take advantage of this by creating multiple ways for students to choose what they want to work on, talk about, and create to demonstrate knowledge. When they find relevance and inherent value in the task, students will be much more inclined to take ownership of their learning. Offer options wherever possible to cultivate the autonomy needed for online student success.

Foster Independence

Many college faculty today wrestle with knowing how much support to provide. At which point does this turn into spoon-feeding? We do our students no favor by coddling them. Higher education should prepare students to be self-motivated employees who don't require micro-managing. However, this way of thinking can lead to the opposite extreme, where we throw students in at the deep end with no support whatsoever. It's important to find the balance, and for online learners, it may be necessary to lean toward providing more support early in the semester. But we can gently remove the training wheels if we systematically create mechanisms that help students become more independent and take more responsibility for their learning over time.

Hold Students Accountable for Their Work

Expect – and require – only the highest-quality work. Raise the bar. Provide the support needed to help students clear it. Give students clear expectations for success, assignment criteria, rubrics, and exemplars. Don't lower your standards in the name of grading efficiency. Instead, refuse to accept junk effort. Reject work that does not demonstrate excellence. Teach students the importance of ensuring their work is on time and meets expectations. They'll benefit from this lesson for years to come.

SMALL TEACHING ONLINE QUICK TIPS: CREATING AUTONOMY

Today's students may come to us with a background that has not taught them to take responsibility for their actions. As is often bemoaned by those of us teaching in higher education, our current K12 system does not seem to do enough to prepare students for the rigor of college classes. Yet we don't want to overgeneralize or blame systems that may be outside of our control or even our influence. Instead, we can take responsibility to foster autonomy in order to help our students succeed in their online classes and beyond.

- *Provide multiple topics and questions in online discussion prompts.* Include some that allow students to relate the topic to their personal experience.
- *Let students sign up for groups based on a topic they want to delve into.* Provide support structures that help groups develop into productive teams as they increase in independence.
- *Use Specifications Grading to set a high standard for student work.* Establish an all-or-nothing grading approach for some elements of your class to help students learn to take responsibility for their efforts.
- *Use Hypothesis or other online annotation tools.* These will allow students to become co-creators of the course syllabus with you.

CONCLUSION

Consider the process of raising a child to be a healthy, productive adult. You pass through countless stages of increasing independence along the way. Newborn babies are completely helpless, unable to do anything for themselves. But developing children don't stay that way. Wise parents guide their learning to enable them to do more for themselves, from rolling over to scooching around on the floor to pulling up to taking those first tottering steps. And that's just one analogy – children go through innumerable other phases of self-sufficiency as part of growing up.

Let's apply the same intentional approach required of parenting to the development of our online students. I've come to believe that helping others increase in autonomy is about more than success in our individual courses. We have a unique opportunity to help those we teach, both in class and in life, learn to take more responsibility for their learning and their actions, to take ownership, to grow in independence.

Our increasingly interconnected global economy requires critical thinkers. Creative problem-solvers. Engaged citizens. We can help to develop tomorrow's leaders now in our online classes. Put the affordances of the flexibility inherent in online learning to work toward this end. Acknowledge the challenges presented by the need for students to direct their own learning. Embed small teaching strategies that create autonomous learners. You'll do them – and our global society – a great service.

Chapter 8

Making Connections

INTRODUCTION

Blood, sex, and gore. Love, betrayal, murder. Injustice, bigotry, revenge. Our responses to society's enduring themes shape who we become. Join us as we explore legendary heroes and monsters in iconic classics ranging from Odysseus to Othello to Luke Skywalker to Harry Potter. In doing so we seek to understand the potential we each have for both heroism and monstrosity.

So reads the course description for the First-Year Seminar I developed and taught last fall, *Legends, Heroes and Monsters*. Was I trying to get the attention of 18-year-olds? You bet. Did I exaggerate the shock value of events and themes found in these texts and films? Nope. These themes and issues not only resonate in the works referenced above, but in the daily news. I made it my mission in the course to help my students see how both ancient and contemporary stories reflect and inform our lived experience today.

In this class, I conducted a running activity throughout the semester. Every few weeks we would zoom out from the details of the current text or film and make a list on the whiteboard of heroic qualities common to one or more protagonists we'd studied. For example, in the second class meeting of the semester, we listed admirable characteristics on the whiteboard that we'd observed in the assigned reading from Homer's *The Odyssey*. I like to have fun with this activity, provoking both laughter and debate by adding things such as Odysseus' fabulous wavy hair or his massive rippling thighs. The students would eventually persuade me to erase those items and replace them with more standard traits such as courage and physical strength. In this way, they practice building a persuasive argument from a literary text.

As we finished one text and prepared to start the next, I'd carve out a few minutes of class time to add to or revise our running list. Each time we engaged in this task I instructed students to copy the lists in their notebooks, so while I didn't have a permanently saved version, we could recall earlier discussions and refer back to their notes if needed.

Little by little, our list of heroic qualities evolved into something nuanced and debatable. We looked for attributes shared by more than one protagonist. We looked for opposites, too. Odysseus repeatedly saves his own skin at the expense of his men. Harry Potter frequently sacrifices his well-being, eventually his very life, in order to save his friends. Beowulf never shirks from danger, finally dying in his final glorious battle with the dragon. Sir Gawain gives in to the temptation to cheat out of cowardice, a desire to preserve his life.

As we engaged in these pursuits, we were linking course content that can often seem remote to today's college students – ancient stories from foreign cultures – with their contemporary heroes from popular culture.

In addition to the connections we made across content units of the course, or between the past and the present, we also made connections between the stories and the human conditions they have faced in their own lives, or will face in their futures. A main focus of the class, for example, is to determine how our choices influence our fate. Luke Skywalker and Harry Potter both share a remarkable set of circumstances and traits with their arch-nemeses, Darth Vader and Lord Voldemort. What makes one turn out a hero for the ages and the other become a super villain? This question fostered a great deal of reflection on the everyday choices first-year students find themselves making in their new campus environment.

Finally, we made frequent connections between the course texts and our current historical moment. We talked about the racism depicted in Shakespeare's *Othello*. Years ago, when teaching this play, I drew parallels with the Rodney King riots of 1992. These days I don't have to look back so far. Not only do my students typically not know who Rodney King was, but there are far-too-frequent events sparked by racial tensions in much more recent history.

Some teachers might view all of these connections to the lives of students as superfluous to student mastery of the content. They should know the texts, those critics might suggest, and not worry about all of that outside stuff. But we now have plenty of research that suggests that if we want students to master the texts – or course content of any kind – those kinds of connections between the course material and their lives outside of the course are one of the best tools we have available to us.

IN THEORY

For students to learn something deeply, they must make the kinds of connections described above, both internal (across the course content) and external (from the course content to the students' experiences). Doing so has at least two positive benefits for learning, one cognitive and one motivational.

The cognitive benefits are reviewed pretty thoroughly in the original *Small Teaching*. The short version of that explanation is that new learners within a discipline (and usually we are working with new learners, at least in comparison to ourselves) have trouble seeing how all of the different elements of a field of knowledge hang together. They tend to focus on isolated facts, easily-mastered skills, or quick formulas instead of gaining the big picture. As an expert in your field, you have a much clearer view of that picture. You see how everything connects, and you see the structures that create those connections.

One of the most important effects of your wider view is that it helps you process new, incoming knowledge. When you have a rich network of knowledge in place within a particular field, you can extend your knowledge in productive and coherent ways. Multiple studies have found, for example, that "when students are provided with an organizational structure in which to fit new knowledge, they learn more effectively and efficiently than when they are left to deduce this conceptual structure for themselves" (Ambrose, Bridges, DiPietro, Lovett, and Norman, 2010). Of course, everything we know about the power of active learning would tell us that the *most* effective way to provide that conceptual structure would be to co-create it with your students. You provide frameworks, seed in some connections, and then guide the students as they begin making connections between the course material and their own experiences and aspirations.

Providing them the opportunity to participate in this process would help spur the second important benefit of connected learning: increasing student motivation. The University of California at Irvine has a Connected Learning Lab that has been actively pursuing and promoting research in this area, including the link between student interest in a topic and their ability to see how it connects to their lives. One of their studies discovered by exploring their resources – something that we highly encourage readers to undertake as well – describes a very simple experiment with high school students that demonstrates how motivation and performance can both be enhanced through facilitating connections for students.

As they describe it in an overview of the experiment in *Science* (Hulleman and Harackiewicz, 2009), the researchers worked with a group of more than 250 high school students in three different science courses. In the control condition, the students wrote summaries of the material they were learning; in the experimental condition, the students wrote short essays about how the material they were learning was useful or relevant to their lives. The students in the experimental condition not only received higher grades at the end of the term but also reported increases in their interest in science.

This was true in general, but broken down a little more finely, the results get more interesting. For stronger-performing students who already reported high interest in science, this experiment didn't do much for them. The results were primarily observed in the students who came into the course without much interest in science, and without much expectation of success in the course. As the authors explain,

> Our results demonstrate that encouraging students to make connections between science course material and their lives promoted both interest and performance for students with low success expectancies. The effect on performance was particularly striking, because students with low-success expectancies improved nearly two thirds of a letter grade in the relevance condition compared with the control condition.

This makes a kind of intuitive sense. Students who come into a course with a preexisting interest likely already see how it connects to their lives, and how it might be useful to them in the future. The students who can't see these things benefit when they are made visible.

If you are teaching all of your online courses to students who are completely confident in their abilities, have a preexisting interest in your subject matter, and are excellent all-around learners, then creating these kinds of connections might not be all that important for you. (Also, Flower and Jim would like to trade jobs with you.) If, on the other hand, you are teaching courses to students who need all the help they can get, and who don't always see the relevance of your course material to their lives outside of the course, then the connection-making strategies described in this chapter will help both inspire your students and improve their learning.

MODELS

Helping online students form connections between class material and their existing knowledge and experience is vitally important. Without such connections, new concepts and information are discrete "islets" of the kind Jim describes in *Small Teaching*. As novice learners of our subject matter, our students don't have the organizing framework that helps them make sense of new information. Without this framework, learners don't experience the full meaning of what they are learning. Without finding meaning in their work, students are not as motivated as they might be otherwise. Help students develop a better understanding of the meaning and purpose of what they are doing in your class. Pekrun's control-value theory suggests that increased motivation to learn will result.

The following models, some of which parallel those Jim presents in the original *Small Teaching*, offer ways for students to interact with content so that they create their own connections – ones that will be far more meaningful to them than ones we might create for them.

Activate Prior Knowledge

This strategy comes directly out of *Small Teaching*. It is highly effective and quite easy to implement online. In his book, Jim describes ways of helping students articulate their existing knowledge about your subject. He explains that asking your students what they already know "fertilizes the intellectual soil for the knowledge and skills that you will help them build over the coming days and weeks" (Lang, 2016, p. 101). Such fertilization can occur at the beginning of the semester as well as throughout the course to connect new concepts across topics and modules. Modules are a ubiquitous feature of online courses, and they help us organize course material, but they may also create a false separation between course concepts. Activating prior knowledge can help students see how new information relates to what they already know.

For example, at the end of your Start Here or Orientation module, students might take a quiz or submit an assignment that represents what they already know about the topic in order to open the remainder of the course content. Whether you create a pretest or an assignment will likely depend on your discipline as well as how many students are enrolled. For example, if you are teaching a class with upwards of 70 or 80 students, a machine-graded pretest might be the most sensible option. Be sure to set an early deadline for this activity, such as Days 1–3. Get students engaged with course content and tasks as soon as possible, which will communicate your expectation that students will be active frequently throughout each week of the course.

Once students complete the task, the rest of the course content automatically opens up. This way, students are not waiting on your feedback before they can proceed with coursework.

Although students are not waiting on you, your response should be timely. When you set the pre-assessment deadline, evaluate your availability to create and share a response. Don't make the pre-test due on Tuesday evening if you know you won't be able to analyze and respond to the results until Friday morning. Coordinate their deadline to submit with your own schedule to ensure timely feedback.

Once you've analyzed the pre-assessment data (this may be possible through increasingly available analytics dashboards), write or record your reactions and share with your students. Generally, I prefer to capture an informal video announcement as described in Chapter 3. Students in online courses welcome hearing your voice and seeing your face. They gain better understanding when they can experience nonverbal cues such as vocal intonations and emphasis, and facial expressions that communicate your interest in their success. Just as you wouldn't give instruction in the classroom via a handout that students read silently to themselves, move away from written guidance and instruction in the online class. Let your students see and hear you as often as possible.

In this message, share your reactions to what they said they know. Point out areas of strength in the collective understanding of the class. Identify one or two common misunderstandings. Let students know that you'll come back to these points for additional information or clarification as the semester progresses.

Make sure you follow up on that promise. Periodically throughout the course, remind students of what they indicated they knew about the subject matter. When you come to these topics in the course, highlight areas where they demonstrated good prior knowledge. Direct students to devote extra attention in modules where the preassessment indicated gaps in understanding. Weave these references into discussion replies, announcements, and individual or group feedback. Help students see how what they are learning this week connects to their thinking during the first week of class. In so doing, help students form those connections between and among course concepts for themselves.

Provide the Framework

In *Small Teaching*, Jim describes the benefits of providing a partial outline or other organizing structure for students to complete while consuming content – that is, reading text or watching a video. He refers to research in which students who were given partial notes prior to a lecture performed better on the final exam than did students who received full notes (Cornelius and Owen-DeSchryver, 2008, p. 8) and suggests "giving students an organizing framework with hierarchies and key concepts in advance of the lecture." Doing so can "help them build accurate connections without simply handing them an already completed network and without leaving them to devise the organizational principles of the material on their own (which, as novice learners, they will have trouble doing)" (Lang, 2016, p. 103). Scaffolding the student note-taking process in this way can make a big impact in online classes. Giving the students something to do while watching a mini-lecture video, for example, encourages active listening and attentive processing of new information.

One way you might implement this approach is to post a partially complete PDF file of lecture notes or presentation slides placed just before the mini-lecture video in the module. Encourage (or require) students to print the file and take hand-written notes while they watch. The first time they do this in your class, point students to the research on how writing notes by hand leads to better retention of material than typing notes on a keyboard. Explain that although they may be surprised to have to print a document, you would like them to try it to see if it proves helpful to their learning.

If you decide to require that students complete a partial outline, you can still collect their work. Ask students to take a picture of their completed notes, upload it to the Learning Management System (LMS), and submit it as an assignment. Award nominal points for submission, or set the assignment to show as Complete/Incomplete in the LMS gradebook. Either way, it should be a quick check-off task to ensure that students made a good-faith effort to take notes on the mini-lecture.

Mini-lecture videos are great for making an otherwise text-heavy course more interesting and dynamic. But students tend to stop watching after a short amount of time, sometimes only a few seconds into the video. Or if they play the entire recording, chances are they are also cooking dinner, doing dishes, folding laundry, or carrying out a host of other on- or offline activities. Help students actively engage with your content by providing partial outlines or slides to complete and submit.

Hate the thought of all that printing? Want to save your students money? You could have students copy and paste the partial outline into a Google Doc, complete it there, and submit the link as an assignment. Or suggest that instead of printing your file, they copy the headings into a spiral notebook, fill in the additional points, and submit a photo of their work in that form. With only a little effort and creativity, you can provide students with just enough of an organizing framework to help them form connections between and among concepts for themselves.

Embed Concept Maps

One more idea from *Small Teaching* is to take advantage of the power of concept maps. "A rich literature exists on the use of concept maps (also sometimes called mind maps)," Jim writes, "which present a fast and easy method to help students visualize the organization of key ideas in your course" (Lang, 2016, p. 104). He recommends asking students to create concept maps at various points in your online class or modules to help them create and demonstrate the connections that are forming in their own minds as they learn and process new information. According to the Eberly Center of Teaching Excellence and Instructional Innovation at Carnegie Mellon University,

> Having students create concept maps can provide you with insights into how they organize and represent knowledge. This can be a useful strategy for assessing both the knowledge students have coming into a program or course and their developing knowledge of course material. (Eberly Center, Carnegie Mellon University, n.d.)

This visual representation of students' understanding can clearly show gaps as well as creative associations.

In Chapter 1, I recommended starting the class with an activity related to the final project. Let me connect that strategy with this one (see what I did there?) by suggesting that you ask students to create a concept map with ideas for a major research paper or presentation in Week 1. Students can create their map with free concept mapping software (my favorite is Bubbl.us) and submit a link to it or a PDF of it. Or they could hand-write their concept map on paper and submit a photo of it. They might use colorful Post-it Notes to create a concept map on a whiteboard or poster board and then submit a picture of that artifact. Better yet, let students choose what format they want to create their map. Allowing students to choose their preferred medium builds agency and encourages creativity. Since we want them to form and identify new connections, we should do everything we can to foster the creative process.

Getting students to generate ideas and possible topics to explore for a research project in Week 1 is an excellent way of helping them to see the overall design, or outcome, of your course (for more on that, see Chapter 1). Allowing students to submit their early thinking in this format is likely to be far more interesting to them than requiring some kind of formal proposal. You may assign a written proposal later, but as a first step in idea generation, concept maps have a lot going for them.

This is just one example of small online teaching with concept maps. I could create an entire concept map of other ways to incorporate these in your online class. Sometimes I take a picture of my class-related whiteboard- or notepaper-scribbled maps and post those online. Making my thinking visible in this way can help my students see how I as an expert connect and organize concepts.

You can also have students create a concept map as the concluding activity in a module to demonstrate their new understanding of key ideas. A biology professor I know provides a partial concept map for processes such as membrane transport. She provides some of the organizing structure and information to students. As they work through the topic, they fill in missing elements and blank ovals and boxes on the map. My colleague provides the complete and accurate map to her students just before the exam so that they can check their work. This is a great way to help students construct their own understanding while simultaneously making sure they have the correct information to study before taking the module test.

The more you think about how to include concept maps in your online class, the more potential you will see for these valuable small teaching tools. Harness the power of student-generated connections to help your online learners see how key themes and concepts relate within your course.

Relate Learning to Personal Experience, Outside Interests, and Goals

This strategy is a great way to help students find relevance in classwork and therefore be more motivated to engage. Saundra McGuire, in *Teach Students How to Learn* (McGuire and McGuire, 2015), describes the importance of getting students to make connections for themselves in order to make meaning of new information:

> We don't have to make the connections for them; in fact it is much better if we don't. We can just throw a concept out there, like a ball, and ask, "What does this remind you of that you've encountered in your everyday life?" When students hit the ball back, they come up with the most wonderful examples and ideas that give them not only an efficient path to learning and mastery, but also *the most efficient path for them.* (p. 26)

As McGuire points out, this approach allows each student to relate new information to existing knowledge and personal interests. The result is an individualized ability to process and master our content.

One of the affordances of online learning is student access to internet resources and tools. Students are already online when they're in class. Encourage them to explore the web, to create new connections and artifacts that extend beyond the confines of your course into their personal and future professional lives.

Earlier, I described the connections we make in my First-Year Seminar between themes in films and literature and current campus, local, national and global events. I also encourage students to apply what we are learning to their own personal context. For example, I ask them to consider the similarities between their current experience as a freshman at university, away from home and family for the first time, and that of Harry Potter as a First Year at Hogwarts. What can we learn from his feelings of uncertainty? From his sense of belonging, or lack thereof? From his interactions with friends, enemies, or professors? When will we need to summon courage as Harry does, and how can we do that?

Online courses provide a great deal of potential for helping students see that what they learn in your class is not restricted to the walled garden of your LMS. Using the rich set of resources available on the internet, empower students to discover that class content applies to the real world, their own life, other courses, and long-term academic and career goals. Here are some ways to do this.

- Students in my online graduate-level technology fluency class contribute two current resources each week that relate to that week's topics. Online news stories, blog posts, informative videos, and infographics all qualify. They post these in a Google Doc with a sentence or two about why the content is interesting and relevant for them as they develop their technical savvy. This strategy could work in almost any discipline. What is happening in the world that relates to your subject matter? Ask students to locate relevant news stories or other content and share in discussion posts, a blog or journal. Have them describe why this particularly resonates with them as they apply key ideas to their interests and activities.
- Using their own technology, have students engage in activities that capitalize on the affordances of learning anytime, anywhere. What can they do when not restricted to the walls of a physical classroom? Students in my tech fluency class video a leader in their chosen career path, someone who has found success at work and who uses technology well. You would likely not bring all of these experts into your classroom, but when there are no walls, opportunities are limitless.

- A physical therapy professor I know asks his doctoral students to follow leading experts in the field of PT on Twitter. This way they take in the most up-to-date information and developments in their future profession. If they choose to interact with these leaders, they're potentially forming the basis of a future personal learning network (PLN).

Once you begin to see the possibilities of putting the internet and the wider world to work for your class, you will find endless ways of helping students connect class concepts with real life.

Assign Personal Learning Networks

We all use our PLN for much of our ongoing learning and growth even though we might not use that exact label for it. For example, when you are curious about the newest developments in the smartphone world, who do you talk to? If you are unsure what to do about a pest problem in your house, who do you ask? If you're considering a smart home assistant, where do you go to inform yourself? To find out about the latest innovations in educational technology, are there people or organizations you follow on Twitter or LinkedIn? If you engage in any of these activities, you're working within your PLN.

I see the value of helping students create connections beyond the confines of my class, so we actively attend to developing PLNs in my technology fluency class. We all know that technology is changing rapidly. There's a constant learning curve if we want to stay current with the tech that we use at work and at home. We formalize this idea in my online course, first reading a bit about what PLNs are and why they are important for the life-long learning that is so necessary for thriving in the twenty-first century. Then, over a few weeks' time, my students actively seek out colleagues, experts, and friends and family to become part of their learning network.

Higher education thought leader Bernard Bull articulates the value of PLNs in a 2013 blog post, "Helping Students Develop Personal Learning Networks." He recommends taking "the idea of a personal learning network, combining it with the promise and possibility of self-directed learning and starting to think more about how we might empower and encourage students to cultivate their own personal learning networks" (Bull, 2013). Bull's take on engaging students with their PLNs to help them develop the ability to direct their own learning is of particular interest, since it emphasizes the value of helping students develop into lifelong learners.

Indeed, this is the very name of the PLN assignment in my class. Students write Lifelong Learning Log (journal) entries each week to describe actions they've taken to formalize and expand their PLN. They tell me about connecting with people on LinkedIn, about setting up a structured mentorship with a supervisor at work, about attending local politicians' campaign rallies in order to explore public service. As they find increased connections between the course and the world beyond the LMS, they engage with class material in striking new ways.

You can find more ideas for getting students engaged with their PLNs in Bull's blog. For example, consider a few of his suggestions:

· Create a concept map of your own PLN and share it with your students.
· Ask students to depict their PLNs in their own concept maps.
· Assign tasks that require students to build new contacts in their PLN or ask existing ones for help.

Any of these ideas would be an effective yet small way of helping students develop and see the value of their PLNs, and in so doing, fostering their growth as lifelong learners.

PRINCIPLES

As Jim writes in *Small Teaching*, "Connection exercises provide a bridge between your expert comprehension of your subject matter and the novice understanding of your students" (Lang, 2016, p. 109). I would add that connecting course material and their daily experience can also foster increased value, deep processing, and rich understanding. Enable students to develop a bigger perspective regarding key ideas, and they'll form the neural networks that will help them move toward expertise in your discipline.

Tap into Prior Experience

To prepare students for a new course or a new topic, get them thinking about what they know about the subject and what they think they know. Identify collective areas of fairly well developed understanding. Point out concepts about which the class has little knowledge or active misunderstanding. Show students how their current knowledge about the topic can prime the pump for learning new information. Then, weave references to your students' input throughout the module or course. Adjust your instruction. Remind students to pay extra attention to topics where there was a gap in collective understanding. Contextualize content within your students' frame of reference to help them see the value of their learning.

Provide Organizing Structure

As we have seen, novice learners lack the framework to understand how concepts relate to one another. Giving students an organizing structure helps them sort and connect new information with previously acquired knowledge. Scaffold the ability to organize and store key ideas to help them identify how this week's concepts relate to those learned the week before and the week before that. Make these connections explicit for your students while they learn to make them for themselves.

Foster (Unlooked-for) Connections

Helping students recognize how course material relates to lots of other things (especially surprising things) inspires and engages students in a unique way. We should absolutely help the students connect new information to content from preceding modules. But if that's all we do, we miss an important opportunity to help students situate new learning in their existing set of experiences. What better way to develop the critical and creative thinkers we need in today's society than by helping students relate concepts to things they're learning in other courses, what they experience at work, events that unfold in the news? Guide students to discover how class content extends beyond your class. You'll contribute to their lifelong ability to analyze, synthesize, create.

SMALL TEACHING ONLINE QUICK TIPS: MAKING CONNECTIONS

Because your students lack expertise in your discipline, they will not naturally see how concepts relate and fit together. Because they may be used to thinking about classes as silos of information, they may not realize that what they learn in your class can inform what they're experiencing elsewhere. When we help students form these connections, we help them find increased meaning and worth in what they're learning. Motivated to engage, students will process, organize, and work with new information in powerful new ways.

· *Activate prior knowledge by asking students to take a short pre-test to describe what they know about your subject matter.* Submitting this quiz or assignment releases the rest of the course or module content.

- *Provide a partial outline or slides for students to print and fill in the missing information.* They can upload a photo of their completed notes and submit as an assignment.
- *Assign concept maps to help students see the connections between ideas.* Let them decide whether to create their map online or on paper. Students submit a link to an online map or a photo of a physical one.
- *Take advantage of the affordances of online learning to extend learning beyond the confines of your course.* Assign students to curate online articles or blog posts, for example, to explore how class concepts relate to what's happening in the world outside of class. They can post these in a Google Doc, discussion forum, or journal as a repository of their learning.
- *Assign PLNs.* Help students see the importance of cultivating a web of people and sources of knowledge to direct and expand their own learning moving forward.

CONCLUSION

A biology professor friend of mine, the one who assigns partially complete concept maps, tried something new on her first day of class this past fall. Students in her general education course often struggle to see the relevance of topics like the structure and function of the cell nucleus. They're not interested and not engaged. But last August, my friend conducted an activity to introduce major course topics and explain how each one keeps us alive. She calls this first-day activity Ways to Die. "This is how you would die if this function didn't happen," she told me, as we discussed her planned activity, "and this is why you would die without this other process working correctly." For instance, she told me that people die of hyponatremia at the Grand Canyon, though they have plenty of water, because they don't eat enough. Electrolytes lost through sweat are not replenished. Membrane transport doesn't function without salt.

My friend suspected that relating seemingly boring biological processes to a general morbid fascination with death would capture the interest and attention of her students. And she was right. I observed her first day of class; I saw for myself the tangible shock that her first-year students experienced when she instructed them to get into groups so they could discuss Ways to Die. They couldn't believe this was an actual class assignment. What I found especially interesting is that not one student in the large enrollment class googled the answers to the matching activity, though she hadn't told them they couldn't. Instead, they dove right in to the task with their neighbors, complete strangers a moment before, now motivated partners investigating the life-and-death importance of various cell functions. The activity set the tone for a whole semester of interesting and engaging learner-centered pedagogy. It was a phenomenal success.

Helping learners connect our content – our *passion* – with topics that interest *them*, with their prior experience, with things they have already learned, is sure to enhance student motivation as they find increased value and worth in what they are studying. The result? Richer and more engaged learning for all.

Chapter 9

Developing as an Online Instructor

INTRODUCTION

My entry into college teaching was through the back door. I earned a bachelor of arts in English literature, then did the typical liberal arts thing of not knowing what to do with the degree. I had no desire to teach when I first declared my English major as a first-year college student. I knew there would be too much grading.

Immediately after graduation, my husband's student worker job developed into a full-time staff position. We weren't going anywhere any time soon. His new position afforded excellent tuition benefits. I applied for the master's program in English literature, deciding it couldn't hurt.

One of my undergraduate faculty mentors, on learning that I intended to pursue a master's degree, encouraged me to apply for a graduate teaching assistantship. I did so on a whim. It seemed like that's what all the good students were doing, those who were serious about their studies. That was about all the thought I put into it. I decided to apply because all the cool kids were doing it.

Though I never intended to teach, I discovered a passion for it. I had declared an English major in the first place because

I figured that no matter what profession I ended up in, the ability to read, think, and write would only serve me well. As it happened, this became a guiding principle in my English teaching. Strong reading, critical thinking, and effective communication skills are essential no matter where life takes you. These overarching values shaped my course design, my interactions with my students, my very teaching persona.

Like many of you, I love teaching in the classroom. I am so energized by teaching that it's the best part of my day. However, about 10 years ago I was offered an online English course. I thought I might not like teaching online, but on another whim I decided to give it a try. It seemed like online learning was only going to grow. I figured I might want to be ahead of the curve, so I decided to teach one section and see how it went.

To my amazement, I found that I really enjoyed teaching online. Just like you, I appreciated the flexibility: being able to teach from home, the local coffee shop, or from overseas. I eventually moved to teaching exclusively online, which allowed me to stay home with my young daughters. This was certainly rewarding and worthwhile – not to mention that I enjoyed my online interactions with students far more than I expected.

Eventually, after 17 years of in-person and online teaching, I was ready for a change. I'd honed my online teaching practice to a fine art, but it was still the case that there was too much grading, just as I had suspected as an undergrad. On yet another whim (it seems like I make a lot of life-changing decisions on a sudden fancy. Huh. Call me adventurous), I attended a faculty professional development workshop on the topics of instructional design and quality online teaching. During the course of those two days, I discovered my new passion: effective learning design and teaching practice.

My discovery spurred a career change. Six months later, I found myself supporting faculty across the disciplines in their online and in-person teaching. One day, when I was only a few weeks into my new role of instructional designer, I was consulting with a faculty member from the College of Education. She was new to our campus and not particularly excited about the class she'd been assigned to teach, because it didn't align with her research focus and area of expertise. "You should really be teaching this course," my colleague told me. "You're way more qualified than I am for this."

Although I was quite new in the role, my faculty colleague didn't know that. The class under discussion was Educational Technology in the College Classroom. My colleague felt neither qualified nor enthusiastic about the topic. Me, though? She thought I could bring valuable professional experience to the class, based solely on my title. The idea of teaching in a new-to-me discipline appealed to my sense of adventure. I was intrigued.

I was offered the class and asked to update it. I accepted without really knowing what I was signing on to do. I was English faculty. I taught literature, writing, critical thinking, argumentation. What did I know about educational technology in the college classroom?

As it happened, quite a lot.

It was, however, a lot of work to winkle it out of the hidden recesses of my brain. Developing and teaching this class proved one of the biggest challenges of my career. But I was deeply engaged. I worked hard. I thought hard. I stretched myself to create an exemplary online course that modeled best practice in design and delivery.

I had lots of help. The resulting course showcased the best thinking from several of my colleagues, seminal research in the area, and purposeful yet innovative use of technology tools. I had become bored with teaching online composition courses. I wasn't bored anymore.

Elsewhere in this book, I've described the evolution of my educational technology course. To meet the needs of a newly defined student population, it became what is now called Technological Fluency and Leadership. This was yet another stretching process that helped me stay deeply engaged in my teaching. I'm proud of the new course, again developed with valuable input from my colleagues.

As online instructors, we can easily disengage from our teaching. Without that physical energy we feel in the classroom, we can slip into neutral. Not bring our best selves to our online teaching responsibility. So what can we do? How can we actively remind ourselves of the value in what we are doing? How do we make sure we are not losing sight of what our students are experiencing? How do we make sure that we are doing what we ask our students to do: being self-aware, analyzing our performance, and trying to get better?

IN THEORY

The models that follow are recommendations for how to grow and improve as an online instructor, and we hope you are motivated enough that you don't need much theoretical justification for that. Most faculty are driven by a passion for their work – we're certainly not in it for the big salaries. But we still want to make two cases for why you should work deliberately at your own practice as an online instructor.

The first of those is a hazard for teachers everywhere, at every level, in every format: burnout. While you might have entered academica as a result of your passion for your discipline, and then become a teacher because of your desire to share that passion with others, you might have wandered less directly into online teaching and learning, as described above. You may have found yourself drawn into it by your own curiosity or experiences, nudged into it by financial need, or you might have been dragooned into it by your institution. In every case, chances are good that you did not envision online education as your life's work, at least initially.

Teaching is also an incredibly challenging profession, and online teaching has its own particular ways of being difficult. So the combination of your potentially accidental entry into this work and the challenges you will face within it can be a potent force for creating burnout. Burned-out teachers don't do well for their students, as one can certainly imagine intuitively, but as research has also demonstrated (Klusmann et al., 2016). Burnout negatively impacts our own well-being, and that seems to have ripple effects into our courses and with our students.

In an article specifically dedicated to helping online instructors avoid burnout, Edna Murugan and Noura Badawi point to "instructional vitality" as one of the core strategies that can push back burnout and keep you engaged and committed to your work as an online teacher. In a variation of one of our recommendations below, for example, they suggest that online faculty "call a fellow online instructor to discuss curriculum/teaching strategies" (2018). Faculty teaching within the same institution, living in the same hallway, can pick up a great teaching idea from a neighbor and feel instantly revitalized and excited to get back into the classroom and try it out. As an online instructor, you have to work more deliberately to create those moments of excitement and renewed energy for your teaching. Talking to other teachers, exploring new resources, creating a personal learning network—all of these tactics will work toward that end.

Our second and more fundamental argument for continuing to grow and explore as an online teacher is that this field of teaching and research is young and growing fast. Almost every aspect of face-to-face teaching has been studied and analyzed by dozens or hundreds or even thousands of researchers. Prior to the rise of such experimental research, we still had two thousand years of smart thinkers and educators thinking and talking to one another about how to educate other human beings, such as Aristotle, who wrote about the necessity of learning by doing – as in, active learning – in his *Ethics*. We've been talking about active learning ever since. For most of those two thousand years, however, that talk has been focused on face-to-face education.

We just haven't had much time to study how our existing educational methods can translate into online teaching and learning, or to develop new methods that we can analyze and debate. We view this as a cause for interest and excitement, and we hope you will as well: much about online teaching and learning still remains to be discovered, and you might even contribute something to that field of knowledge. In any case, some of those potential discoveries will have implications for your specific teaching context. Taking some modest steps to keep abreast of new developments in online teaching and learning will help ensure that you are using the most effective learning strategies for your students.

MODELS

It's truly important to continue growing as an online instructor in order to avoid stagnating in the role. Perhaps because we don't experience the communal energy of the physical classroom, it's easy to withdraw or do the minimum. Without intending to do so, we may experience a tempering of our teaching enthusiasm. Online teaching can remain fresh, however. We can continue finding ways to make our online teaching stimulating and enjoyable. The following simple strategies can help keep us challenged, stay inspired, and find satisfaction in our work.

Take an Online Class

This strategy, like some others in this book, is so simple that it might not occur to you. Yet it is probably the most impactful action you can take in order to improve your online teaching: Take an online class. See how it feels to be a student in an online learning environment. You'll learn more about online learning in general, and online teaching changes you want to make in particular, than you will about the content itself.

Recently, I had an opportunity to live the student experience in a class setting that was completely foreign to me: the large lecture hall. For a major active learning redesign project, I attended BIO 181 with 240 freshmen during the first week of the fall semester. I was fascinated. All of my in-person teaching experience has been in seminar-style classes capped at 25 students. Being in a lecture hall with such a large number of apprehensive students proved a new and uncomfortable situation. Though I was there to do a class observation, I paid attention to my own experience sitting among the 18- and 19-year-olds in the back of the room.

Through some kind of energy osmosis, I tuned in to their anxiety. It was the first day of class, indeed the first day of the fall semester. We didn't know exactly what to expect. We couldn't quite hear the instructor at the front of the hall. The projection screens were hard to read. We weren't sure we had what it took to be successful in this challenging course in our first semester in college. We didn't know if we belonged there. Most of us in the room were nervous. Anxious. Scared.

It didn't take much imagination for me to recognize how those same emotions might occur for my online students. When we create our online classes, we know exactly where everything is in the course site. The organization, navigation, and instructions make perfect sense to us. We know when we intend to communicate with students or grade their work, so we're not worried about it. But when we put the shoe on the other foot, when we are the student in an online environment that we did not design, we have rather a different experience.

Suddenly we may be confused about the layout of the class. We may not understand the scoring system. It may not be clear where to submit an assignment or when the test will be open. We might be waiting for an answer from our instructor, with no sense of when or whether we'll hear back. We can experience a million little anxieties when we take a class online. Doing so motivates us to improve our own approach to online teaching.

There are lots of ways to take on online class. Find one for personal or professional development. I don't recommend a massive open online course (MOOC) for this purpose unless that is actually the format in which you teach. Instead, take an online foreign language or a photography course offered at your institution. Take a class in Adobe Photoshop or web design. Or, enroll in one of the many faculty professional development offerings from the Online Learning Consortium, Quality Matters, Magna Publications, or Educause, among others. You will see some great examples of new things to try, and you'll also learn what not to do.

A few months ago, my husband took an online graduate course. He did not enjoy his experience very much, as the instructor was not very engaged in the class. But he learned an important lesson from that lack of instructor presence. This semester, he's teaching online for a local community college, and he's much more present and responsive than he was before taking that course. He checks in more often. He is more patient with students who have questions. He is more encouraging. In sum, he has more empathy for his online learners, and it has transformed him as an online instructor.

Ideally, you won't have a poor experience when you take an online class. But I bet it will be eye-opening in some regard. You might find inspiration for things you want to try, things you want to improve. You'll certainly grow as an online instructor.

Seek Exemplars

The 1989 film *Dead Poets Society* has inspired countless instructors to strive for the teaching excellence portrayed by Robin Williams in the role of John Keating. Who among us can forget the moving scene in which his students stand on their desktops to declare their loyalty as Keating departs? Which of us has never dreamed of hearing "O captain, my captain" from the lips of a transformed pupil?

Until we have a Hollywood movie depicting an inspiring online professor, however, we have to look closer to home. Fortunately, this is quite doable, with a little investment of time and effort.

As already noted, learning about the methods used by excellent online faculty requires intentionality. You are less likely to bump into your colleague in the hallway and strike up a conversation about online approaches than you might be to compare notes about what happened in class that day. Yet there are many small actions you can take to discover exemplary online teaching approaches to emulate. Consider one or more of the following:

· Make time to attend faculty professional development workshops, book discussions, or learning communities at your institution. Many schools offer remote opportunities such as webinars or participation via videoconference. As a seasoned presenter of such opportunities, I can tell you that the conversations you have with your colleagues from other disciplines, who are with you in the online teaching trenches, are just as valuable as the topic of the event itself.

· Ask your department chair if you may observe the online class of a great instructor in your unit. Notice details such as the organization of the course, how the instructor interacts with students, how often they are present in the class. Determine what to copy in your own approach.

· Visit your Center for Teaching and Learning. Ask if there are examples of online courses you can explore. Many institutions showcase courses from a range of disciplines to help you see different approaches that work in different subject areas.

· Seek online sources of inspiration. One example is the Teaching Online Pedagogical Repository offered by the University of Central Florida. This rich resource presents evidence-based practical strategies with examples of how to do them from real courses.

With a bit of effort, you can find numerous ways to expand your online teaching approach. Prevent stagnation by seeking inspiration. Fortunately, there are numerous ways of doing this – even without the influence of Hollywood.

Build Self-Efficacy

The premise of this book is that you can make small, incremental changes to your online teaching that have an outsized impact on student learning and success. I'd like to slow down and reinforce this idea here. I have had innumerable conversations with new online faculty who think they have to do it all right out of the gate. Such an approach almost guarantees significant problems in your online class.

I intentionally labeled this model with the same name as one in Chapter 6. There, we consider how to help students gain confidence with simpler tasks before tackling more complex ones. We can structure our own learning and development in the same way.

As we wrap up this book, let's remind ourselves to take our online teaching growth one small step at a time. Identify one challenge you have in your online class. Think carefully about when you want to address that challenge: next week? Next semester? Then select an approach in one of the preceding chapters that will help you address your issue in a way that *you* – not your colleague down the hall, not your instructional designer, but *you* – can manage.

Years ago, a friend told me that she'd successfully lost weight following the Change One diet. The premise is simple: pick one thing about your nutritional habits to change, something you can sustain. Make that change for one week. Maybe it's substituting carrots for potato chips with your sandwich. Maybe it's having a banana instead of a brownie for an afternoon snack. Whatever the change is, maintain it for a week, then change something else.

We can do the same thing in our online teaching. Change one thing. Develop a new practice you can sustain. Get good at it. Next semester, change something else.

As you consider which new strategy to adopt, be careful not to bite off more than you can chew. If a strategy overwhelms you, it's not a good strategy. If you aren't confident using a technology tool, don't use it. You'll only cause yourself stress and harm your credibility with your online students if you do.

Instead, choose one manageable action that you feel confident about. Want to increase your presence in your online class? You don't have to be in class 8 hours a day, 5 days per week. Rather, make a weekly schedule of 30-minute blocks when you will post in the discussion board.

Want to learn to use video to make your class more engaging? Don't set out to record mini-lectures for each week. Start with a short video welcome message. If that goes well, try a handful of video announcements as your course progresses. You'll work up to creating a comprehensive set of video lectures, but first practice recording yourself giving two-minute casual messages. Build your confidence before tackling the bigger task.

We know from the literature that learners get frustrated and want to give up when an undertaking is too challenging. Breaking down a complex task into manageable chunks makes it more feasible. Yet many faculty members neglect to apply this thinking to their own development as an online teacher. Don't set out to scale Mount Everest in your next online class. It'll only make you want to quit. Surmount a small hill. Then set your sights on the next one, slightly higher than the last. Keep climbing.

Certify Your Course Design and Teaching for Quality

The concept of online course quality has gained a lot of momentum in recent years. My personal theory is that the field of online learning expanded so rapidly that, initially at least, little attention was paid to how to create effective online classes in which real learning takes place. This is also why online learning suffers from a bad reputation, and why employers have considered fully online degrees with skepticism as not being equivalent to traditional degrees earned in person. That perception is changing, but slowly (Etherington, 2018).

But online learning is changing. Now there are various course quality rubrics, based squarely in the research, to help course developers and faculty authors design and teach effective, rigorous online classes. As a next step in your growth as an online teacher, get your course certified for quality.

Two of the current leading rubrics are the Quality Matters (QM) Higher Education Rubric and OSCQR, affectionately known as "Oscar," the Open SUNY (State University of New York) Course Quality Review Rubric. Your institution may subscribe to one of these approaches. Some schools have developed internal quality checklists or standards. You can also use the QM or OSCQR rubric as an individual if your school isn't pursuing this idea at this time.

Seeking quality certification enhances your online teaching in many ways. You will likely undergo some professional development to equip you to successfully meet the standards. As I said earlier in this chapter, simply having time and space during a course design quality workshop to talk with other online instructors will improve your practice. But these rubrics or checklists also provide a systematic structure for considering design elements that you may not have critically examined before.

As I noted earlier in this book, our online class often makes perfect sense to us. We understand the logic, the design thinking, behind every component. A quality rubric helps us take a big step back and consider the course from a student's perspective. This change in vantage point identifies gaps or areas for improvement in the course design that we may never have seen otherwise.

Even if you don't seek the actual course quality certification, both the QM and the OSCQR rubric can be used for a focused self-review. Simply work through the quality standards as you honestly assess your own online course for areas where you can strengthen the learner experience. Make (small) improvements where you can.

To be clear, most of these rubrics are centered on the quality of design, not how well you teach the class. There's a difference. The course design consists of everything you do to create and prepare the class before Day 1. The delivery of it, or teaching, is what takes place as you interact with students while the course is in session. Many online course quality rubrics only address the planning of the class, not the teaching of it. Still, with deliberate attention to the design of your online class, you set the stage for better teaching of it. Working toward quality certification demonstrates your commitment to student success in your online class. This commitment is sure to come out in the way you teach the online class as well.

That said, you may want to critically examine your online teaching practice as well. Your institution might have a process in place to evaluate online teaching, but many do not. To address this gap, Thomas J. Tobin, B. Jean Mandernach, and Ann H. Taylor present arguments for developing such processes – and practical suggestions for how to do so – in *Evaluating Online Teaching: Implementing Best Practices* (2015). These authors share various reasons why online teaching evaluation might be somewhat neglected at many schools. For example, "the private, behind-a-password nature of online teaching" (p. 76) does not lend itself to another faculty member dropping in to class the way they might visit your in-person classroom.

Tobin and his colleagues identify another challenge that is unique to online teaching evaluation, namely, that we don't have as many norms for this process as we do for peer evaluations in the classroom. Typically, when colleagues observe our classroom, they attend one class session, then complete an evaluation form or provide feedback using some other mechanism. "What is the online equivalent," ask the authors, "to visiting a colleague's classroom for 90 minutes?" (p. 15). Here, Tobin and his colleagues propose that an observer might think about "how much content to observe, (e.g. one week or unit worth of materials and interactions)" since "*class period* is not a meaningful term within an online course" (p. 16). Clearly, peer evaluations of online teaching require some creative approaches, especially if we're more accustomed to observing teaching in person.

However, we can always conduct self-evaluations, and *Evaluating Online Teaching* provides useful suggestions for doing so. Formative evaluations, that is, gathering feedback from students while the course is in session, so that you have an opportunity to adjust your approach, can be particularly useful. Consider these suggestions:

> For formative evaluation to be effective, it must be goal-directed with a clear purpose, provide feedback that enables actionable revisions, and be implemented in a timely manner to enable revisions within the active teaching-learning cycle. Formative evaluations are most effective when they are focused on a specific instructional strategy or concern.... For example, rather than ask a general question such as "How can the instructor be more effective in the online classroom?" one might ask about a specific aspect of the online classroom, such as "What can the instructor do in the asynchronous discussion threads to foster more engaged dialogue?" (Tobin, Mandernach, and Taylor, 2015, p. 78)

Do you want to know how you can be a better online teacher? Ask your students. I have a feeling they'll let you know. In response, make minor adjustments to your teaching practices. Your students will appreciate that you asked, and made changes, in time for them to enjoy an improved learning experience in your class.

One final note: some institutions are moving toward certifying effective online teaching as well. Northern Arizona University is currently engaging in numerous initiatives in the teaching success movement. Some schools are developing internal certification programs of teaching excellence. Others are partnering with organizations such as The Association of College and University Educators (ACUE) to certify exemplary instructors through their Course in Effective Teaching Practices. Either way, a focus on excellent teaching for student success is emerging nationwide. Growing as an online instructor, motivating yourself to continuously improve, falls right in line with this movement. And you'll likely experience increased personal and professional satisfaction as well.

Pursue These Resources (or Others)

Prioritizing your professional development is key to continuing your online teaching journey with any degree of personal and professional satisfaction. I've provided many small approaches already in this chapter, but I want to leave you with a list of additional resources to help you take those crucial next steps as you grow in this area. Compared to in-person teaching, which has been happening informally since the beginning of time, and formally for millennia, online teaching is in its infancy. Yet we know it's not going away – and that there is much to be done to improve this new realm of teaching and learning. Establish yourself as a leader in this field by pursuing some of the resources below (some of which I've mentioned elsewhere in this book). You may find this will set you on course for a new, stimulating, and personally and professionally rewarding journey of online teaching excellence.

Read Books on Relevant Topics

As Jim noted in *Small Teaching*, recently we have seen tremendous growth in the field of higher education teaching and learning. You can find many new books on relevant topics that have the potential to improve your day-to-day teaching practice. Here are a few that I think will make a big impact on the quality of online educational experiences.

- *Online Teaching at Its Best: Merging Instructional Design with Teaching and Learning Research* (Nilson and Goodson, 2018). Linda Nilson and Ludwika Goodson identify a real gap in conversations about teaching and learning in online courses: that the instructional design literature and teaching and learning research are often not in dialogue with each other. Read this book, which is solid in both theory and practice, to remedy that lack.
- *Thrive Online: A New Approach for College Educators* (Riggs, forthcoming in 2019). What I love about this book is Shannon Riggs's enthusiastic vision for all that online teaching can be – not as inferior to teaching in person, but rather, joy-giving in its own right. Get inspired and discover practical ways to "hit your stride" as an online instructor.
- *The Online Teaching Survival Guide: Simple and Practical Pedagogical Tips*, 2nd ed. (Boettcher and Conrad, 2016). If you like a handbook approach, this is the book for you. Judith Boettcher and Rita-Marie Conrad offer extremely practical suggestions for faculty who want to improve their online teaching practice, helpfully organized by what to do when as you prepare, teach, and conclude an online class.
- *Reach Everyone, Teach Everyone: Universal Design for Learning in Higher Education* (Tobin and Behling, 2018). Thomas Tobin and Kirsten Behling provide convincing arguments for applying UDL to every college learning experience as well as student services and interactions to help all students in higher education succeed. Even better, they recommend feasible strategies for doing so. This book is a must-read for anyone who wants to increase access to higher ed.
- *Minds Online: Teaching Effectively with Technology* (Miller, 2014). Cognitive psychologist Michelle Miller explains how to take

advantage of the affordances of technology to maximize what we know from learning science. Full of solid research and pragmatic suggestions for applying it, this book deserves pride of place on any online instructor's bookshelf.

Access Other Resources for Ongoing Development

I love to read the latest book on excellent evidence-based teaching, but it's difficult to find the time to read more than one or two each year. These resources allow you to keep learning and growing in the midst of all of your other commitments.

· *Faculty Focus*: https://www.facultyfocus.com This is my go-to website for practical teaching advice and easily digestible summaries of new research. Sign up for the free eNewsletter to keep up with the latest developments and find inspiration for excellent in-person and online teaching.
· *Teaching in Higher Ed podcast*: https://teachinginhighered.com/episodes/ A recent discovery for me, I wish I'd known about this invaluable resource for professional growth a lot sooner. Enjoy weekly episodes featuring interviews with educators who are passionate about their vocation. At 40 minutes or less, these are perfect for your commute to campus, your walk across campus, or your time on the elliptical trainer.
· *Your local teaching and learning support professionals*. Get to know your colleagues in your center for teaching excellence or equivalent. Often underutilized, these experts on teaching and learning research and practice can help you successfully implement small changes in your online, blended and in-person course design and teaching. Educational developers, instructional designers, educational technologists, media specialists and Learning Management System (LMS) help desk heroes are all uniquely situated to support your success.

- *The Teaching Professor Conference hosted by Magna Publications*. Put this annual event on your calendar. You'll find hundreds of like-minded new friends, professionals who care about their teaching as much as you do. After you experience stimulating and invigorating conference sessions and informal networking opportunities, you'll leave with renewed energy and practical approaches, based on research and experience, to reinvigorate your online and onsite teaching practice.

- *The ACUE Course in Effective Teaching Practices*: https://acue.org/ This practical professional development course from ACUE offers a wealth of evidence-based strategies in a comprehensive curriculum that addresses everything from syllabus design to engaging underprepared students, from embracing diversity to facilitating great discussions. This course is great for both online and in-person teaching, but currently it's only available for institutional cohorts. Take advantage of this rich learning experience if your school offers the course; if it doesn't, talk to your academic leadership about the possibility of doing so.

PRINCIPLES

The overarching principle for this chapter is to put deliberate effort into challenging yourself to keep growing in your online teaching abilities. Find ways of impassioning yourself so that you don't become stale in your online classes.

Critically Examine Your Online Teaching Practice

Many of us accidentally fell into online teaching, or were pressed into it against our will. I suspect many faculty members view their online classes as somehow not as valid as their in-person ones. I fear some instructors put forth minimal effort, viewing their online classes as a burden to be borne or merely a source of supplemental income. We do our students a great disservice with this attitude. Embrace the challenge of becoming an excellent online instructor. Reflect on the moral obligation to help these learners succeed, earn a degree, and enjoy multiple benefits related to their well-being. Think critically about how you can get better at teaching online. Experience increased engagement and satisfaction as a result.

Make Time to Grow

It's hard to bump into a fellow online instructor in a virtual hallway somewhere and begin conversing about your online teaching challenges and solutions. It just doesn't happen as naturally as the parallel experience might in the physical world. Given the very newness of online learning, however, it's even more vital to seek to learn from others who are engaged in the same pursuit. Since this won't likely happen serendipitously, create the time to invest in your own development. Attend workshops and programs offered by your faculty development center. Request access to exemplary instructors and courses—then take the time to look around in the online class to see what's so effective. Knowing that learning doesn't just happen by accident, create time and space to cultivate your online teaching practice.

Seek to Energize Yourself

Our students struggle to feel the person-to-person energy in an online class. If we're honest, so do we. There's a call-and-response kind of energy in the physical classroom, a tangible feeling of (hopefully) positive synergy between ourselves and our students. This energy doesn't build as naturally in the online classroom.

But it's still possible to create – you might just have to bring it yourself. So find ways of keeping yourself challenged, inspired, motivated. Seek new opportunities. Strive to always be improving. Invest active energy into improving your online teaching skills. Bring that renewed energy into your online class. You can positively impact the atmosphere in your online class as tangibly as you can in the classroom. It just takes a little more proactive effort.

SMALL TEACHING ONLINE QUICK TIPS: DEVELOPING AS AN ONLINE INSTRUCTOR

Online learning has become an integral part of higher education. If you haven't tried teaching online already, you might be doing so sooner than you imagine. Embrace the unique opportunity we have not only to improve this new modality but to improve equity and access for a newly diverse population of learners. These small strategies can help.

· *Take an online class, be it credit-bearing, personal interest, or professional development.* There's no better way to improve your online teaching practice than to become an online learner.
· *Look for models and examples of best practice.* Observe an excellent online class, or request access to showcase online course designs.
· *Add complexity after you build confidence with simple techniques.* To avoid burning out in your online teaching, play the long game. Make one small change, master it, try something more adventurous next semester.
· *Seek quality certification for your online course design, and if possible, your online teaching.* Commit to your personal continuous improvement by striving to meet quality standards in your online course.

CONCLUSION

I worked closely with a colleague and friend for several months to help her prepare to teach her first online class. As seasoned, tenured faculty in social work, she was confident in her in-person teaching skills. But teaching online would be entirely new.

We spent several weeks altering the content she was given to make it her own. Along the way I had many opportunities to coach her in online teaching methods and best practices. Indeed, most of the suggestions I made in these sessions found their way into this book.

My colleague was very receptive to my guidance as she prepared for her first online class. She listened with an open ear and a teachable attitude. She told me that because she was coordinating the department's new online master's program, she wanted to learn as much as she could about online teaching best practices.

However, my friend also told me numerous times that she only planned to teach this online class one time. After this, she asserted, she would find someone else to teach the class. As I write, she is only one week into teaching online. I'd like to think she'll discover a sense of professional satisfaction in this new challenge. That she'll change her mind. Continue to teach online, learning and improving with every subsequent class. Time will tell, I suppose, but I remain hopeful that she will rise to the challenge.

Whether in our first semester teaching online or our fifteenth, we should challenge ourselves to keep getting better. We should seek inspiration to keep seeing the value, the purpose in this worthwhile pursuit. Doing so will contribute to this growing field, your students' success, and your own personal satisfaction in a job well done.

Conclusion: Finding Inspiration

Most of the examples and stories about college teaching in this book come from my experience at NAU. Just like many online instructors, however, I also adjunct at a nearby two-year institution, Estrella Mountain Community College. Teaching in this context has convinced me of the importance of investing in these learners – hard-working individuals who will constitute tomorrow's workforce, who want a better life and are willing to work for it. To inspire us to keep moving forward in our pursuit of online teaching excellence, I want to share two final stories that come out of the community college setting.

The first one has large implications for my motivation to write this book in the first place. As we know, online learning has grown exponentially in the last decade. It's on track to continue to do so. Many online learners only have access to college classes because they can go to school online. In the past, a percentage of our current online students may have gone to night school in order to further their education and improve their career prospects. A much larger percentage of the population who can't attend college in a traditional way are now enrolling online.

I believe deeply in the importance of improving online education for all of these students. I'd like to tell you why.

About three years ago, I led an online course review for Quality Matters (QM), a nonprofit quality assurance organization that promotes effective online courses. This particular review was of an English composition course at a rural community college in an economically depressed area. My charge was to lead the review and provide feedback for improvement to the course developer, who in this case was also the instructor. QM highly recommends providing professional development to enable the course creator to design the course up to standard in the first place, prior to review. Due to the desire of enthusiastic college leadership to get courses QM certified, however, this step had been missed.

What I observed was the very best effort of a well-intentioned online professor, undeniably with a heart of gold, to help her students learn. But without adequate preparation for designing and teaching an online class, the course was woefully under par. I was hit hard with the sense that students at this college, seeking personal improvement, would struggle to pass this class. The institution and instructor simply hadn't provided the support required to help them succeed. I imagined that other online classes at this college would be similarly challenging. It seemed likely that defeated students would drop out. They might give up on their dream of earning a college degree, and of using that degree to make a better life.

I have no wish to criticize one school in particular. I commend any institution that seeks to improve its online course offerings, because that work is essential. Instructors who diligently apply themselves to getting better at teaching online deserve our highest respect. The task can feel isolating and unrewarding. But when I think of our underrepresented students, perhaps underprepared for success in college, who only wish to improve their situation, I find renewed energy for the challenge. We have to focus on helping these learners, for whom online learning may be their only option, achieve success.

The other story from which I draw inspiration, like many others in this book, is not explicitly related to online learning. But it is about helping our learners, *all* of our learners, attain their goals.

Several months ago, my brother told me about a bright young guy who had recently joined his network engineering team. A few years earlier, this young man came to a realization that his aimless life of bordering-on-criminal pursuits would only lead him into trouble. He enrolled at the local community college.

Instinctively recognizing his need for extra support, this student went to the Computer Commons where my good friend, then the department chair of Instructional Computing, was providing tutoring. My friend helped to turn this man's life around. He was there when he was needed. He showed personal interest. He contributed to the successful reorientation of this young man's life. My brother wanted me to pass on the thanks of his new co-worker to the community college faculty member who cared enough to invest in him as a person, who helped him transform himself and the path he was taking.

Although this student's interactions took place on campus, we can have the same impact on our online students' success.

At the end of Chapter 3, I briefly mentioned a report published in 2017 by the American Academy of Arts and Sciences, titled *The Future of Undergraduate Education, The Future of America*. I want to slow down and consider in just a bit more depth the report's argument that we are in "a critical moment in our nation's history, when so many long-standing assumptions about who we are as a people, and where we are headed, have been called into question." The authors proceed to summarize the aim of the commission's work:

> This report offers practical and actionable recommendations to improve the undergraduate experience. But in its practicality, it is motivated by the highest ideals: faith that every person, from every background, can succeed in America when given the proper training and preparation; confidence that our existing institutions of higher

education can and will evolve to meet the needs of today's and future students; and an unwavering commitment to the free exchange of ideas as the basis of a creative, productive, and democratic society. (2017, p. v)

This pursuit is the ultimate in social justice. We have the ability to empower our students to succeed. We know that online classes may be the only option for learners juggling full-time work and family obligations.

We also know that college graduates enjoy benefits ranging from improved health to more rewarding work to more time with family to increased community engagement – not to mention increased earning potential (American Academy of Arts and Sciences, 2017, p. 3).

I hope you will join me in the effort to improve online teaching and learning in higher education in order to help as many people as possible achieve these benefits in their lives. But I also want to make sure you won't get overwhelmed. So think about your online class this week, and your online students right now. What can you do tomorrow to help them succeed?

Maybe you'll post a two-minute video announcement encouraging your learners about how far they've come in the course. You may decide to email select students and suggest a short phone call to provide additional support. Perhaps you'll schedule a bit of extra time this week to interact with students in discussion, to ask questions, praise contributions, and highlight overarching themes or important concepts. If you carve out an extra 30 minutes this week to implement these or any other of the suggestions presented in this book, you can impact your students' ability to learn new concepts.

Then consider the online class you're teaching next semester. What small modifications will you make to your course design, instructional activities, or communication strategy to help your students learn? What small adjustments are warranted based on the research presented in this book?

You could decide to activate prior knowledge by adding a conditional-release pre-test that opens remaining module content upon submission. You may choose to implement a new technology tool such as video mini-lectures or Hypothesis to engage students in their learning. Perhaps you will increase learner autonomy and your application of UDL principles by weaving in choice in assignment topics and formats.

Finally, think critically about how to promote your own growth and development in this area. How will you keep yourself motivated? How do you plan to assess the impact of your efforts? How can you contribute to the development of online teaching excellence, both at your institution and more broadly? Maybe you gather a group of colleagues to meet regularly and discuss small improvements in online teaching. Maybe you write. Publish. Present. The time is right to develop ourselves and help others do the same. For the sake of our increasingly diverse online student population, prioritize your professional learning. Share your discoveries with the rest of us.

But let's bring it back home. Let's focus on the here and now. Your online class is taking place today. You have students who, this very moment, want and need your guidance and expertise.

As you put down this book and log in to class, consider: How will you begin?

References

Agarwal, A. (2019, January 02). Three education trends that will revolutionize the workplace in 2019. Retrieved from https://www.forbes.com/sites/anantagarwal/2019/01/02/three-education-trends-that-will-revolutionize-the-workplace-in-2019/#5c7f19eb6363

Ambrose, S. A., Bridges, M. W., DiPietro, M., Lovett, M. C., & Norman, M. K. (2010). *How learning works: Seven research-based principles for smart teaching*. San Francisco: Jossey-Bass.

American Academy of Arts and Sciences (2017). *The future of undergraduate education, the future of America*. Cambridge, MA: American Academy of Arts and Sciences.

Bandura, A. (1977). Self-efficacy: Toward a unifying theory of behavioral change. *Psychological Review, 84*(2), 191–215. https://doi.org/10.1037//0033-295x.84.2.191

Bawa, P. (2016). Retention in online courses: Exploring issues and solutions – a literature review. *SAGE Open, 6*(1), 215824401562177. doi:https://doi.org/10.1177/2158244015621777

Belcher, A., Hall, B. M., Kelley, K., & Pressey, K. L. (2015). An analysis of faculty promotion of critical thinking and peer interaction within threaded discussions. *Online Learning, 19*(4). https://doi.org/10.24059/olj.v19i4.544

Blake, C. (2017, November 13). How online teachers can improve discussion boards [blog post]. Retrieved from https://education.cu-portland.edu/blog/classroom-resources/online-instructor-discussion-boards/.

Boettcher, J. V., & Conrad, R. (2016). *The online teaching survival guide: Simple and practical pedagogical tips* (2nd ed.). San Francisco: Jossey-Bass.

Bolliger, D. U., & Inan, F. A. (2012). Development and validation of the Online Student Connectedness Survey (OSCS). *The International Review of Research in Open and Distributed Learning, 13*(3), 41. https://doi.org/10.19173/irrodl.v13i3.1171

Bowen, J. (2018, Nov.) Nudges, the learning economy and a new 3Rs: Redesigning for student relationships, resilience, and reflection. Conference keynote presented at the annual meeting of the POD Network.

Brame, C. J. (2015) Effective educational videos. Retrieved from http://cft.vanderbilt.edu/guides-sub-pages/effective-educational-videos/

Brown, P. C., Roediger, H. L., & McDaniel, M. A. (2014). *Make it stick: The science of successful learning*. Cambridge, MA: Harvard University Press.

Bruff, D. (in press). *Intentional Tech: Principles to Guide the Use of Educational Technology in College Teaching*. Morgantown, WV: West Virginia University Press.

Bull, B. (2013, November 22). Helping students develop personal learning networks. [web log comment]. Retrieved from http://etale.org/main/2013/11/22/helping-students-develop-personal-learning-networks/.

Carrell, S. C., Kurlaender, M. and Bhatt, M. B. (2016). Experimental evidence of professor engagement on student outcomes. Working Paper.

Cavanagh, S. R. (2016). *The spark of learning: Energizing the college classroom with the science of emotion*. Morgantown, WV: West Virginia University Press.

Cavanaugh, A. J., & Song, L. (2014). Audio feedback versus written feedback: Instructors' and students' perspectives. *Journal of Online Learning and Teaching, 10*(1), 122–138.

Chickering, A. W., & Gamson, Z. F. (1987). *Seven principles for good practice in undergraduate education* (pp. 3–7). American Association for Higher Education.

Cohen, Z. (2018, July 17). *Small changes, large rewards: How individualized emails increase classroom performance* The evoLLLution. Retrieved from https://evolllution.com/attracting-students/retention/small-changes-large-rewards-how-individualized-emails-increase-class room-performance/?elqTrackId=2245bda9a1ce490e8e79dccb469 4a108andelq=a5fe401af251426997e169442f230414andelqaid=20 066andelqat=1andelqCampaignId=9348

Cornelius, T. L., & Owen-DeSchryver, J. (2008). Differential effects of full and partial notes on learning outcomes and attendance. *Teaching of Psychology, 35,* 6–12.

Covey, S. R. (1989). *The 7 habits of highly effective people: Powerful lessons in personal change.* New York, NY: Free Press.

Deacon, A. (2012). Creating a context of care in the online classroom. *Journal of Faculty Development, 26*(1), 5–12.

Dimeo, J. (2017). *Take my advice.* Inside Higher Ed. Retrieved from https://www.insidehighered.com/digital-learning/article/2017/ 11/15/peer-advice-instructors-teaching-online-first-time

Doyle, T. (2011). *Learner-centered teaching: Putting the research on learning into practice.* Sterling, VA: Stylus Publishing.

Dweck, C. S. (2007). *Mindset: The new psychology of success.* New York, NY: Ballantine.

Dweck, C. S. (2015). *Carol Dweck revisits the 'growth mindset.'* Education Week. Retrieved from https://www.edweek.org/ew/articles/2015/ 09/23/carol-dweck-revisits-the-growth-mindset.html

Eberly Center, Carnegie Mellon University (n.d.) Using concept maps. Retrieved from https://www.cmu.edu/teaching/assessment/ assesslearning/conceptmaps.html

Eodice, M., Geller, A. E., & Lerner, N. (2016). *The meaningful writing project: Learning, teaching, and writing in higher education.* Logan, UT: Utah State University Press.

Etherington, C. (2018). *Have online degrees and credentials finally lost their stigma?* eLearning Inside. Retrieved from https://news .elearninginside.com/have-online-degrees-and-credentials-finally-lost-their-stigma/

Eyler, J. R. (2018). *How humans learn: The science and stories behind effective college teaching.* Morgantown, WV: West Virginia University Press.

Field, T., & Kasdan, J. (2017). *Jumanji: Welcome to the jungle*. [Motion picture]. United States of America: Columbia Pictures.

Fink, L. D. (2013). *Creating significant learning experiences: An integrated approach to designing college courses* (2nd ed.). San Francisco, CA: Jossey-Bass.

Fisher, L., Brinthaupt, T. M., Gardner, J., & Raffo, D. (2015). The effects of conditional release of course materials on student performance. *Journal of Student Success and Retention, 2*(1), 1–14.

Gannon, K. (2018a, June 25). Some thoughts on pedagogy and the problem of "empathy." [web log comment]. Retrieved from http://www .thetattooedprof.com/2018/06/25/some-thoughts-on-pedagogy- and-the-problem-of-empathy/

Gannon, K. (2018b). How to create a syllabus. *The Chronicle of Higher Education*. Retrieved from https://www.chronicle.com/interactives/ advice-syllabus

Garrison, D. R., Anderson, T., & Archer, W. (1999). Critical inquiry in a text-based environment: Computer conferencing in higher education. *The Internet and Higher Education, 2*(2–3), 87–105. https://doi .org/10.1016/s1096-7516(00)00016-6

Gernsbacher, M. A. (2016, October 31). Five tips for improving online discussion boards. *Observer, 29*(8). Retrieved from https://www .psychologicalscience.org/observer/five-tips-for-improving-online- discussion-boards

Gilliard-Cook, T. and West, B. (2015). Authentic learning: Rethinking quizzes and exams for greater impact. The evoLLLution. Retrieved from https://evolllution.com/opinions/authentic- learning-rethinking-quizzes-exams-greater-impact/.

Girante, M. J. (2015, September 14). Faculty showcase: Short introductory video announcements. Retrieved from https://teachonline.asu .edu/2015/09/short-introductory-video-announcements/.

Goldrick-Rab, S. (2016). *Paying the price: College costs, financial aid, and the betrayal of the American dream*. Chicago, IL: The University of Chicago Press.

Gorski, P. C. (n.d.) *Critical Multicultural Pavilion–an EdChange project.* Retrieved from http://www.edchange.org/multicultural/index .html.

Guo, P. J. (2013, November 13). Optimal video length for student engagement. Retrieved from https://blog.edx.org/optimal-video-length-student-engagement.

Guo, P. J., Kim, J., and Rubin, R. How video production affects student engagement: An empirical study of MOOC videos. (2014). Proceedings from *ACM Conference on Learning at Scale*, (L@S 2014). Atlanta, GA.

Hanover Research (2018). *Best practices in online faculty development.* Arlington, VA: Hanover.

Haras, C., Ginsberg, M., Férnandez, E., & Magruder, E. D. (2017). Future goals and actions of faculty development. In C. Haras, S. C. Taylor, M. D. Sorcinelli, & L. von Hoene (Eds.), *Institutional commitment to teaching excellence: Assessing the impacts and outcomes of faculty development* (pp. 55–67). Washington, DC: American Council on Education, October 30, 2017. Reprinted in CUNY Academic Works.

Henderson, M., & Phillips, M. (2015). Video-based feedback on student assessment: Scarily personal. *Australasian Journal of Educational Technology, 31*(1). https://doi.org/10.14742/ajet.1878

Herman, J. H., & Nilson, L. B. (2018). *Creating engaging discussions: Strategies for "avoiding crickets" in any size classroom and online.* Sterling, VA: Stylus Publishing.

Howard, J. R. (2015). *Discussion in the college classroom: Getting your students engaged and participating in person and online.* San Francisco, CA: Jossey-Bass.

Hulleman, C. S., & Harackiewicz, J. M. (2009). Promoting interest and performance in high school science classes. *Science, 326*(5958), 1410–1412. https://doi.org/10.1126/science.1177067

Kalir, R. (2018, August 13). And because the annotated syllabus is available to students throughout the semester, this record of Q&A is a persistent resource. This shifts classic "It's in the syllabus, did you read?" to constructive "We discussed this when annotating our syllabus [Tweet]. Retrieved from http://remikalir.com/courses/annotate-your-syllabus/.

Kalir, R. (n.d.-a) Annotate your syllabus. [web log comment]. Retrieved from http://remikalir.com/courses/annotate-your-syllabus/.

Kalir, R. (n.d.-b) Annotate your syllabus 2.0. [web log comment]. Retrieved from http://remikalir.com/courses/annotate-your-syllabus-2-0/.

Kauffman, H. (2015). A review of predictive factors of student success in and satisfaction with online learning. *Research in Learning Technology, 23*. https://doi.org/10.3402/rlt.v23.26507

Klusmann, U., Richter, D., & Lüdtke, O. (2016). Teachers' emotional exhaustion is negatively related to students' achievement: Evidence from a large-scale assessment study. *Journal of Educational Psychology, 108*(8), 1193–1203.

Kuh, G. D. (2008). *High-impact education practices: What are they, who has access to them, and why they matter.* Washington, DC: Association of American Colleges and Universities.

Kulik, J. A., & Kulik, C. C. (1988). Timing of feedback and verbal learning. *Review of Educational Research, 58*(1), 79–97. https://doi.org/10.2307/1170349

Ladyshewsky, R. K. (2013). Instructor presence in online courses and student satisfaction. *International Journal for the Scholarship of Teaching and Learning, 7*(1). https://doi.org/10.20429/ijsotl.2013.070113

Lang, J. M. (2016). *Small teaching: Everyday lessons from the science of learning.* San Francisco, CA: Jossey-Bass.

Lang, J. (2019, Jan. 4). How to teach a good first day of class. *The Chronicle of Higher Education.* Retrieved from: https://www.chronicle.com/interactives/advice-firstday.

Lehman, R. M., & Conceição, S. C. (2010). *Creating a sense of presence in online teaching: How to "be there" for distance learners.* San Francisco, CA: Jossey-Bass.

LeVan, K. S., & King, M. E. (2016, April 15). Audio reflection assignments help students develop metacognitive skills. *Faculty Focus.* Retrieved from https://www.facultyfocus.com/articles/effective-teaching-strategies/audio-reflection-assignments-help-students-develop-metacognitive-skills/

Lieberman, M. (2018, April 11). What online teachers have learned from teaching online. *Inside Higher Ed.* Retrieved from https://www.insidehighered.com/digital-learning/article/2018/04/11/veteran-online-instructors-share-tips-improving-their-practices

Lortie, D. C. (2002). *Schoolteacher: A sociological study.* Chicago, IL: University of Chicago Press.

Lowenthal, P. R., Dunlap, J. C., & Snelson, C. (2017). Live synchronous web meetings in asynchronous online courses: Reconceptualizing virtual office hours. *Online Learning, 21*(4). https://doi.org/10.24059/olj.v21i4.1285

Mayer, R. E. (2009). *Multimedia learning* (2nd ed.). New York: Cambridge University Press.

McGuire, S. Y., & McGuire, S. (2015). *Teach students how to learn: Strategies you can incorporate into any course to improve student metacognition, study skills, and motivation.* Sterling, VA: Stylus Publishing.

Milheim, K. (2017). A fundamental look at cultural diversity and the online classroom. *eLearn Magazine.* Retrieved from https://elearnmag.acm.org/archive.cfm?aid=3041614.

Miller, M. D. (2014). *Minds online: Teaching effectively with technology.* Cambridge, MA: Harvard University Press.

Morris, C., & Chikwa, G. (2016). Audio versus written feedback: Exploring learners' preference and the impact of feedback format on students' academic performance. *Active Learning in Higher Education, 17*(2), 125–137. https://doi.org/10.1177/1469787416637482

Murugan, E., & Badawi, N. (2017, December 18). What online faculty can do to avoid burnout. *Faculty Focus.* Retrieved from https://www.facultyfocus.com/articles/online-education/online-faculty-can-avoid-burnout/

Nadworny, E., & Depenbrock, J. (2018, September 4). Today's college students aren't who you think they are. *National Public Radio.* Retrieved from https://www.facultyfocus.com/articles/effective-teaching-strategies/audio-reflection-assignments-help-students-develop-metacognitive-skills/https://www.npr.org/sections/ed/2018/09/04/638561407/todays-college-students-arent-who-you-think-they-are

National Academy of Sciences (2018). *How people learn II: Learners, contexts and cultures*. Washington, DC: The National Academies Press.

Netsanity, Are messaging apps and texting ruining real relationships? (2017, July 22). Retrieved from https://netsanity.net/messaging-apps-texting-ruining-real-relationships/.

Nilson, L. B. (2013). *Creating self-regulated learners: Strategies to strengthen students' self-awareness and learning skills*. Sterling, VA: Stylus Publishing.

Nilson, L. B. (2015). *Specifications grading: Restoring rigor, motivating students, and saving faculty time*. Sterling, VA: Stylus Publishing.

Nilson, L. B., & Goodson, L. A. (2018). *Online teaching at its best*. San Francisco, CA: Jossey-Bass.

Orlando, J. (2017, March 16). What research tells us about online discussion. *Faculty Focus*. Retrieved from https://www.facultyfocus.com/articles/online-education/research-tells-us-online-discussion/

Patterson, B., & McFadden, C. (2009). Attrition in online and campus degree programs. *Online Journal of Distance Learning Administration*, *12*(2), 1–8.

Pomerantz, J., & Brooks, C. D. (2017). *ECAR study of faculty and information technology, 2017*. Research report. Louisville, CO: Educause Center for Analysis and Research.

Riggs, S. (2019). *Thrive online: A new approach for college educators*. Sterling, VA: Stylus Publishing.

Robertson, R. J., & Riggs, S. (2018). Collaborative assignments and projects. In K. E. Linder & C. M. Hayes (Eds.), *High-impact practices in online education* (pp. 71–84). Sterling, VA: Stylus Publishing.

Schmidt, S. W., Tschida, C. M., & Hodge, E. M. (2016). How faculty learn to teach online: What administrators need to know. *Online Journal of Distance Learning Administration*, *19*(1), 1–10.

Seaman, J. E., Allen, I. E., & Seaman, J. (2018). *Grade increase: Tracking distance education in the United States.* Research report. Babson Park, MA: Babson Survey Research Group.

Sneed, O. (2016, January 12). Fostering an inclusive environment when developing online courses. Retrieved from https://teachonline .asu.edu/2016/01/fostering-inclusive-environment-developing-online-courses/.

Stanford University Libraries. (n.d.) Copyright and fair use: Copyright overview. Retrieved from https://fairuse.stanford.edu/overview/.

Stevens, D. D., & Levi, A. J. (2012). *Introduction to rubrics: An assessment tool to save grading time, convey effective feedback, and promote student learning* (2nd ed.). Sterling, VA: Stylus Publishing.

Thaler, R. H., & Sunstein, C. R. (2008). *Nudge: Improving decisions about health, wealth, and happiness.* New York, NY: Penguin Books.

TILT higher ed. *Transparency in learning and teaching.* (n.d.) Retrieved from https://tilthighered.com/

Tobin, T. J., & Behling, K. (2018). *Reach everyone, teach everyone: Universal design for learning in higher education.* Morgantown, WV: West Virginia University Press.

Tobin, T. J., Mandernach, B. J., & Taylor, A. H. (2015). *Evaluating online teaching: Implementing best practices.* San Francisco, CA: Jossey-Bass.

University of Waterloo Centre for Teaching Excellence. (n.d.) Self-directed learning: Learning contracts. Retrieved from https:// uwaterloo.ca/centre-for-teaching-excellence/teaching-resources/ teaching-tips/tips-students/self-directed-learning/self-directed-learning-learning-contracts.

Vann, L. S. (2017). Demonstrating empathy: A phenomenological study of instructional designers making instructional strategy decisions for adult learners. *International Journal of Teaching and Learning in Higher Education, 29*(2), 233–244.

Voelkel, S., & Mello, L. V. (2014). Audio feedback – better feedback? *Bioscience Education, 22*(1), 16–30. https://doi.org/10.11120/beej.2014 .00022

Vygotsky, L. S. (1978). *Mind in society: The development of higher psychological processes*. Cambridge, MA: Harvard University Press.

Walvoord, B. E., & Anderson, V. J. (2010). *Effective grading: A tool for learning and assessment in college* (2nd ed.). San Francisco, CA: Jossey-Bass.

Warner, J. (2019). *The writer's practice: Building confidence in your nonfiction writing*. New York, NY: Penguin Books.

Wiggins, G., & McTighe, J. (2005). *Understanding by design* (2nd ed.). Alexandria, VA: Association for Supervision and Curriculum Development.

Zhou, H. (2015). A systematic review of empirical studies on participants' interactions in internet-mediated discussion boards as a course component in formal higher education settings. *Online Learning, 19*(3). https://doi.org/10.24059/olj.v19i3.495

Zull, J. (2002). *The art of changing the brain: Enriching the practices of teaching by exploring the biology of learning*. Sterling, VA: Stylus Publishing.

Index

A

Accountability: assessments and, 12; building-in and expecting, 56–57, 69, 176; group work encouraging, 168; scheduling and, xxvii, 9; Specs Grading and, 99, 169–170

Activities. *See* Assignments and activities

ACUE. *See* Association of College and University Educators

Adaptive courseware, xxviii

Adaptive release. *See* Conditional release

Agency. *See* Autonomy and control, student

American Academy of Arts and Sciences, 70, 223–224

Anderson, T., 79

Anderson, Virginia Johnson, 110–112

Anxiety: for faculty in creating change, xxii; with feedback time, 114; with instructor video making, 59; for new students, xv–xvi; for nontraditional students, xvi; for online students, xvi–xvii;

with student video making, 146–147

Apprenticeship of observation, xix

Archer, W., 79

Aristotle, 204

The Art of Changing the Brain (Zull), 160

Assessments: accountability and, 12; clarity in objective of, 34–35; in course design, role of, 2–3; course learning objectives alignment to, 6, 9; of course learning objectives understanding, 11, 18–19; CR use with and prior to, 36–37; first week, 11–13, 24; low-stakes, feedback from, 110–111, 142–143; mastery quizzes as, 142–144, 150; mini-assignments as cumulative, 45; preassessment, 22, 24, 185–187; prior knowledge, 185–187, 189, 196–197; student engagement with, approaches to, 12, 30–32, 57–58; on syllabus understanding, 11, 18–19; with

Assessments: accountability and (*continued*)
videos for student engagement, 57–58, 69. *See also* Feedback; Final assessments; Formative assessments; Grades/scores; Summative assessments

Assignments and activities, xxx; for beginning and end of course connection, 23–24; course learning objectives alignment with, 15; CR approach to, 35–38, 45; for cultural inclusion and awareness, 95, 104; cumulative assessment with mini, 45; first week, 12–13, 20; incremental and manageable steps for, 27–28, 32–35, 43–44; Oops Token for, 98–99, 104, 168–169, 171; PLN, 193–194, 197; prior knowledge, 185–187, 189, 196–197; prompt template for, 16–17; rationale transparency for, 15–17, 24; reflection fostered by, 24; reflection on goal of, 33; reflection on meaningfulness of, 30–32; reminders about, 22–23; scaffolding of, 145–148, 150; for student accountability, 12; Three Takeaways, 20–21; for writing instruction, 16

Association of College and University Educators (ACUE): certification, 214; Course in Effective Teaching Practices, 41, 217

Attention span, 53, 60

Attrition rates, xxvi, 136, 150

Autonomy and control, student: *agency* contrasted with, 160; choice relation to, 162–164, 175–176, 177, 189; course design considering, 159; in forums/online discussions choice, 162–164, 177; in group work enrollment, 164–168, 177; increasing, approaches to, 155; models for encouraging, 161–175; motivation relation to, 154–155, 158, 159–160, 184; principles for developing, 175–176; Specs Grading for, 168–172, 177; support and guidance fostering, 161, 176, 177–178; syllabus co-creation and, 172–175, 177; theories and research on, 154, 159–161, 184; tips overview for creating, 177

B

Backward design, xxv–xxvi; alignment of elements as priority in, 10–11, 14, 25; course learning objectives primacy in, 3, 7, 8–9; course materials selection in, 9; course schedule in, 9; for final assessments, 11–13, 22, 23, 24; intentionality with, 3; models for, 10–21; principles of, 22–25; questions/decisions in starting, 8–9; theory of, 7–10; tips overview for, 24–25; transparency for students, 10, 11, 13–15

Badawi, Noura, 203

Bandura, Albert, 145

Behling, Kirsten, xxiv–xxv, 215

Best Practices in Online Faculty Development (Hanover Research), xx
Blake, Caitrin, 42
Bloom's Taxonomy, 64–65
Boettcher, Judith V., 63–64, 65–66, 215
Books, recommended. *See* Resources and books
Bowen, José, 37–38
Brown, P. C., xxiii, 13, 17–18
Bruff, Derek, 48–49
Bull, Bernard, 194

C

Canvas, 53, 125
Captioning, video, 15, 54–55, 68, 92
Caring/empathy (for students): in community building, 95–101; in feedback, 127–128; flexibility relation to, 98–99, 104, 168–169; for marginalized/underserved populations, 223; phone/video conference calls impact in, 99–100, 118–119; in student support and guidance, 95–101, 118–119, 131–132, 149, 151
CASEPS. *See* Council for At Risk Student Education and Professional Standards
Cavanagh, Sarah, 154, 162
Certification, quality, 210–214, 219, 221–222
Chat function, 114
Chickering, Arthur, 111
The Chronicle of Higher Education (Gannon), 172
Classroom response system (clickers), 48

Cognitive presence, 79–80, 88
Cohen, Zoë, 137–138, 139
Collaboration: in learning process, research on, 77–78; on syllabus creation, 172–175, 177. *See also* Group work
Communication: clarity, cues indicating, 34, 45; of course learning objectives, 3, 10–11, 13–15, 24; in group work, 167; nonverbal, challenges with lack of, xxx–xxxi; nonverbal, in instructor videos, 61, 69, 186; in video announcements, styles of, 58–61, 91–92; in video lectures, styles of, 54. *See also* Forums; Transparency
Community building, xxvi, 72; with care and support for student, 95–101; cognitive presence in, 79–80, 88; cultural inclusion and awareness in, 92–95; debates role in, 75–76; instructor sharing personality for, 90–92, 103–104; intentionality in, 77; models of, 81–101; principles of, 101–103; social presence in, 79, 80–87, 92, 102–104; student interaction structuring for, 81–86, 101, 103; teaching presence in, 79–81, 86–92, 101–102, 103–104; theories and research behind, 77–81; tips overview for, 103–104; zones of proximal development and, 77–78, 101, 104
Community of Inquiry framework, 79–81, 86, 104
Conceição, Simone, 90

Concept maps, 188–190, 194, 197
Conditional release (CR):
assessments and, 36–37; for
feedback, 37–38; student
engagement aided with, 35–38,
45
Conferences, teaching
development, 217
Confidence, student:
assignments/activities in
increments for, 27–28, 32–35,
43–44; scaffolding impact for,
146–147
Connections, making, xxiii, 155;
between beginning and end of
course, 23–24; cognitive
benefits in, 181–183; concept
maps for, 188–190, 194, 197;
film and literature used in, 62,
179–181, 191–192; framework
for, providing, 187–188,
195–196, 197; historical
parallels in, 181; models of,
184–194; PLN assignment for,
193–194, 197; principles of,
195–196; prior knowledge
activation in, 185–187, 195,
196–197; with student goals
and interests, 183–184,
191–193, 196, 197–198;
technology and media tools
for, 191–192, 197; theories and
research on, 181–184; tips
overview for, 196–197; for
value/relevance, 183–184,
191–193
Conrad, Rita-Marie, 63–64,
65–66, 215
Content release, 35–38, 45
Control. *See* Autonomy and
control, student

Control-value theory, 154, 184
Copyright permissions, 62, 63
Council for At Risk Student
Education and Professional
Standards (CASEPS), 93
Course design: assessments in,
role of, 2–3; change in
increments, 209–210, 219,
224–225; Community of
Inquiry established in, 80–81,
104; core challenges of, xxvi;
cultural inclusion in, 92–95,
104; "enduring
understanding" in, 8;
fundamentals of, xxv–xxvi;
intentionality in, 2–3, 22, 71,
104; modifications from
session to session, xxx; patience
and persistence required in,
xxxiii; peer relationships
considered in, 80, 103; quality
certification and rubrics for,
210–214, 219; recommended
reading on, 7–8; student
autonomy considerations in,
159; UDL principles in,
xxiv–xxv, 14, 37, 164, 215. *See
also* Backward design
Course evaluations: rubrics and
organizations for online,
210–214; teaching presence
relation to student, 86–87
Course learning objectives:
assessments alignment with, 6,
9; assessments on
understanding of, 11, 18–19;
assignments and activities
alignment with, 15; backward
design focus on, 3, 7, 8–9;
communicating, 3, 10–11,
13–15, 24; end-of-course

reflection on, 20–21, 25; of "enduring understanding," 8; feedback aiding in, 9; GTAs training and, 6; module goals alignment with, 14, 23; reminders about, 22–23; student goals alignment with, 20–21; student reflection on, 17–21, 24–25; student supported for and informed of, 3; in syllabus, 9; teaching development/training on, 6; technology and media tools alignment with, 51, 63–66, 67; transparency of, 11, 13–15, 24

Course materials, selection of, 9

Course plan: for new instructors, 5–7; for online compared to physical courses, 71

Courses/classrooms, physical: communication differences between online and, xxx–xxxi; course plan for online compared to, 71; CR impact for online compared to, 36; furniture significance in, 49; for GTA, 5–6; new student anxiety in, xv–xvi; norms and routines of online compared to, xvii–xviii; online hybrid with, xxix; relationships online compared with, 71–72; student motivation online compared to, 153, 156; student support challenges online compared to, xvi–xviii, 3, 10, 11; techniques/ principles of, applied online, xxi–xxii, xxvii

Covey, Stephen, xxiii

CR. *See* Conditional release

Creating a Sense of Presence in Online Teaching (Lehman and Conceição), 90

Creating Engaging Discussions (Herman and Nilson), 83

Creating Significant Learning Experiences (Fink), 8

Creativity, fostering, 84, 189–190, 196

Critical Multicultural Pavilion Ed Change project, 95

Cultural inclusion and awareness: activities and resources for, 94, 95, 104; for community building, 92–95, 104; monitoring forums for, 94–95

D

Dance instruction, 27–28, 133

Deacon, Andrea, 96–97

Deadlines: allowances with, 97–99, 104, 168–169, 171; for forums/online discussions, 83; setting, 113–115, 128

Debates, community building with, 75–76

Discussion in the College Classroom (Howard), xvii–xviii

Diversity. *See* Cultural inclusion and awareness; Universal Design for Learning principles

Doyle, Terry, 169

Dweck, Carol, 134, 135

E

Effective Grading (Walvoord and Anderson, V.), 110–111

Email nudges, 137–139, 150

Empathy. *See* Caring/empathy

Enrollment rates, xviii–xix

Eodice, M., 30–33, 159–160, 161

Evaluating Online Teaching (Tobin, Mandernach, and Taylor), 212–213
Eyler, Joshua, 81–82, 85

F

Faculty. *See* Instructors/faculty
Faculty Focus (website), 216
Faculty training. *See* Teaching development/training
FAQs. *See* Frequently asked questions
Feedback: course learning objectives aided with, 9; CR for nonevaluative, 37–38; deadlines relation to, 113–115, 128; empathy in giving, 127–128; grading rubrics for, 121–123, 127, 129, 172; on incremental tasks, 34, 44; intentionality with, 115, 126; lack of, examples and impacts of, 107, 108–109, 129; from low-stakes assessments, 110–111, 142–143; models for, 112–126; phone/video conference, 114, 117–119, 128; principles of, 126–128; prior to final assessment, 33, 34–35; rationale for, 111–112; real-time, 114, 115–119, 128; for student engagement, significance of, 31, 44–45, 46, 103, 110–111; on student satisfaction relation to teaching presence, 86–87; in student support, significance of, 9, 72–73; on syllabus from students, 172–175, 177; in teaching development/ training, 109; theories and research on, 110–112, 124–125; time factors and management with, 88–89, 103, 107–108, 111, 113–121, 127; tips overview for, 128–129; video and/or audio, considerations, 123–126, 127, 129; virtual office hours for, 116, 119–121, 128

Films and literature, connection-making with, 62, 179–181, 191–192

Final assessments: backward design for, 11–13, 22, 23, 24; clarity in objective of, 34; feedback opportunities prior to, 33, 34–35; first week work on, 11–13, 23, 24; preparation for, lack of, 28–29

Fink, Dee, 8, 10

Fixed mindset, 134–135

Flexibility: considerations of, xxi, 73; downfalls with, 73; in grading and deadlines, 98–99, 104, 168–169, 171; in teaching online, 200

Formative assessments: course schedule inclusion of, 9; defining, 110; examples of, 9; summative assessments impact compared to, 29

Forums/online discussions: autonomy in choosing, 162–164, 177; creativity and authenticity fostering for, 84; deadlines for, 83; discussion highlights from, 41–42, 45; grading, 83–84, 170–171; instructor interaction in, 40–41, 42–43, 44, 88; key points and questions outlined in, 42–43; monitoring for cultural sensitivity, 94–95; monitoring for student engagement opportunities, 40–41, 42–43, 44, 88; question-and-answer, 39, 64; small groups creation benefits for, 84–85, 101; Specs Grading for, 170–171; student interactions fostered with, 82, 103; student-made videos for, 164; tips for structuring, 83–84; UDL principles in designing, 164

Frequently asked questions (FAQs), inclusion of, 39

Furniture, classroom, 49

The Future of Undergraduate Education, The Future of America (American Academy of Arts and Sciences), 70, 223–224

G

Gamson, Zelda, 111

Gannon, Kevin, 96, 172

Garrison, D. R., 79

Geller, A. E., 30–33, 159–160, 161

Gender diversity, 93

Gernsbacher, Morton Ann, 84–85

Gilliard-Cook, Theresa, 142

Girante, Joana, 60–61

Goals. *See* Course learning objectives; Module goals; Student goals

Goals contract, 139–142, 150

Goodson, Ludwika, 90–91, 143, 215

Google Docs and Slides, 51, 65, 117, 163, 175, 188, 192

Gorski, Paul C., 95

Grades/scores: CR impact on, 36; feedback rationale beyond, 111–112; flexibility and allowances for, 98–99, 104, 168–169, 171; for forums/online discussions, 83–84, 170–171; rubrics for, 121–123, 127, 129, 172; time factor considerations in posting, 89, 108. *See also* Specifications Grading

Graduate teaching assistant (GTA): classroom experience for, 5–6; inspiration from experience as, 199

Group work: accountability encouraged in, 168; assignments in incremental steps for, 33; autonomy in enrollment in, 164–168, 177; example of structuring, 167–168; Google Docs for, 51, 65; practice, 166; scaffolding, 165–166; transparency in communication in, 167; value/relevance in designing, 166

Growth mindset, 134, 149

GTA. *See* Graduate teaching assistant

Guo, Philip, 53, 60

H

Habits, change relation to, xxiii

Hanover Research, xx

Herman, Jennifer, 83

High-Impact Practices in Online Education (Robertson and Riggs), 165–166

How Humans Learn (Eyler), 81–82

How People Learn II (National Academy of Sciences), 93
Howard, Jay, xvii–xviii
Hybrid courses, xxix
Hypothesis, 65, 172–175, 177, 225

I

Improvisation: course planning balanced with, 6–7; in physical classrooms, 71
Instructors/faculty: anxiety in creating change, xxii; biographies, creating, 91; course plan for new, 5–7; first online course experience for, 28–29; forums/online discussions participation of, 40–41, 42–43, 44, 88; personal sharing of, impacts of, 90–92, 103–104; self-efficacy of, building, 208–210; student satisfaction relation to participation of, 86–87; technology and media tools comfort of, 65–66; video introductions/announcements from, 14–15, 58–61, 68, 87–88, 91, 102, 186; video lectures tools and tips for, 52–56, 69. *See also* Motivation and growth, instructor; Teaching development/training; Teaching presence
Intentional Tech (Bruff), 49
Intentionality: with backward design, 3; in community building, 77; in content release, 35–37; in course design, 2–3, 22, 71, 104; with feedback, 115, 126; in technology and media

tools selection, 3–4, 48, 62–63, 69
Isolation, student, 3, 44, 72, 76

J

Joyner, David, 55–56

K

Kalir, Remi, 173–175
Kauffman, Heather, xxi
Kuh, George, 165–166

L

Ladyshewsky, R. K., 86–87, 88
Large-enrollment classes, 48, 84–85, 117
Learning Management System (LMS): challenges with, xvii; class interactions monitored through, 39; CR function in, 35–38; grading rubrics, 121–123, 127, 129, 172; group projects with, 33; for hybrid courses, xxix; instructor video announcements in, 15, 87–88; mastery quizzes set-up in, 144; new instructor benefit in using, 65–66; note-taking framework in, 187–188; one-directional uses of, xxix; platform/tools outside of, considerations with, xxviii, 66; small discussion groups creation in, 84–85; video tools in, 53, 55
Learning science principles: Community of Inquiry framework relation to, 79–81, 86, 104; major divisions of, xxv–xxvii; peer relationships relation to, 77–78, 81, 104; in small teaching approach,

primary, xxiii–xxiv; on task attempt before readiness, 12–13; UDL relation with, xxv
Lecture-capture systems, 52–53
Lehman, Rosemary, 90
Lerner, N., 30–33, 159–160, 161
LGBTQ students, 93
Literature. *See* Films and literature, connection-making with
LMS. *See* Learning Management System
Lortie, Dan, xix
Lowenthal, Patrick, 119–121

M

Magna Publications, 206, 217
Make It Stick (Brown, Roediger, and McDaniel), xxiii, 13, 17–18
Mandernach, B. Jean, 212–213
Marginalized/underserved populations, 166, 221; care and empathy for, 223; inclusion in course design, 92–95; teaching presence importance for, 89
Maris, Mindy, 49–50
Massive open online course (MOOC), xxxii, 206
Mastery quizzes, 142–144, 150
Math instruction, 36
Mayer, Richard, 62
Mazur, Eric, 49
McDaniel, M. A., xxiii, 13, 17–18
McGuire, Saundra, 191
McTighe, Jay, 7–8, 10
The Meaningful Writing Project (Eodice, Geller, and Lerner), 30–33, 159–160, 161
Media tools. *See* Technology and media tools
Milheim, Karen, 94

Miller, Michelle, 49–50, 54, 62–63, 215–216
Mind in Society (Vygotsky), 78
Minds Online (Miller), 62–63, 215–216
Mindset, xxiv; fixed, 134–135; growth, 134, 149; theory, 134–136
Module goals: course learning objectives alignment with, 14, 23; student reflection on, 19, 23
MOOC. *See* Massive open online course
Motivation, student, xxiv; approaches for increasing, overview of, xxvi–xxvii; interest relation to, 160–161; in online compared to physical classrooms, 153, 156; student control relation to, 154–155, 158, 159–160, 184; theories and research on, 154, 184; value/relevance of content impact on, 154, 184–185. *See also* Autonomy and control, student; Connections, making
Motivation and growth, instructor, xviii, xxvi, 155; burnout role in, 202–203; challenge and change increasing, 201–202; critical examination of teaching for, 217–218, 225; exemplars for, Seeking out, 207–208, 219; incremental and manageable, 209–210, 219; models for, 204–217; passion relation to, 199–200, 223–224; principles for, 217–219; proactive effort for, 218–219, 220, 224–225;

Motivation and growth, instructor (*continued*)
quality certification and rubrics for, 210–214, 219; resources and books for, 214–217; self-efficacy for, building, 208–210; taking an online class for, 205–207, 219; theories and research on, 202–204; tips overview for, 219
Multimedia theory, 62
Murugan, Edna, 203

N
"Name Stories" activity, 95, 104
National Academy of Sciences, 93
National Survey of Student Engagement, 31
Nilson, Linda, 83, 90–91, 98, 143, 168–171, 215
Nontraditional students, xvii, 221. *See also* Marginalized/underserved populations
Norms and routines, xvii–xviii
Note-taking framework, 187–188, 197
Nudge (Thaler and Sunstein), 138
Nudges, 137–139, 150

O
Office hours, virtual, 116, 119–121, 128
Online discussions. *See* Forums/online discussions
Online Teaching at Its Best (Nilson and Goodson), 90–91, 215
The Online Teaching Survival Guide (Boettcher and Conrad), 63–64, 215

Oops Token, 98–99, 104, 168–169, 171
Orlando, John, 84

P
Pacansky-Brock, Michelle, 89
Peer instruction, 49
Peer relationships, 71; course design consideration of, 80, 103; debates and, 75–76; in learning, research on, 77–78, 81, 104. *See also* Student interactions
Pekrun, Reinhard, 154, 184
Personal learning network (PLN), 193–194, 197
Personalized learning, xxviii
Phone/video conference calls: care shown through, 99–100, 118–119; feedback through, 114, 117–119, 128
Pilates instruction, 132–133
PLN. *See* Personal learning network
Plotts, Courtney, 93–94
Plus-One design model, xxv
Podcast, teaching development, 216
Practice: group work, 166; for instructor video making, 54, 56, 59, 60, 61, 210; learning skills relation to, xxiii, 27–28; preassessment, 22, 24; for student video making, 147–148
Preassessments: practice with, 22, 24; of prior knowledge, 185–187
Prediction, xxiii
Presence, areas of, 79–81

Prior knowledge: assessments, 185–187, 189, 196–197; concept maps for assessing, 189; connection-making and, 185–187, 195, 196–197
Purpose. *See* Course learning objectives

Q

QM. *See* Quality Matters
Quality certification and rubrics, 210–214, 219
Quality Matters (QM), 211, 221–222
Question-and-answer forums/tools, 39, 64
Quizlet, 64

R

Radford, Alexandria Walton, xvii
Reach Everyone, Teach Everyone (Tobin and Behling), xxiv–xxv, 215
Redundancy effect, 50
Reflection, student: on assignment meaningfulness, 30–32; assignments fostering, 24; on assignments/activities goals, 33; cognitive benefits of, 17–18; on course learning objectives, 17–21, 24–25; end-of-course, 20–21, 23–24, 25; on module goals, 19, 23; private compared to public, considerations, 21; self-discipline/regulation benefits of, 18; student support aided with, 148; Three Takeaways assignment and, 20–21; videos for, 18

Relationships: attention to, 71–72; learning fostered in, 76, 81–82, 89; online compared to physical classroom, 71–72; on social media, 105; teaching development, 216. *See also* Community building; Peer relationships; Student interactions
Reminders, 22–23
Research. *See* Theories and research
Research universities, teaching development at, 1
Resources and books: on course design, 7–8; cultural inclusion and awareness, 94, 95, 104; teaching development, 206, 214–217
Retrieval, xxiii, 17, 37
Riggs, Shannon, xx, 165–166, 215
Robertson, Robert John, 165–166
Roediger, H. L., xxiii, 13, 17–18
Rubrics: course-quality, 210–214, 219; grading, 121–123, 127, 129, 172

S

Scaffolding: of assignments, 145–148, 150; confidence impacted by, 146–147; with connection-making strategies, 187, 195–196; CR function for, 35–36; group work, 165–166; in student video creation, 146–148; theory behind, 29–30
Scheduling: accountability and, xxvii, 9; of formative assessments, 9; tools, 117, 118, 120. *See also* Deadlines; Time factors and management

Schoolteacher (Lortie), xix

Self-discipline/regulation, xxi, 151; flexibility impact on, 73; goals contract aiding, 140; reflection aiding, 18; Specs Grading impact on, 99, 169–170; student support and guidance impact on, 73

Self-efficacy: instructor, building, 208–210; student, building, 145–148, 150; theory, 145–146

Self-explanation, xxiii

The 7 Habits of Highly Effective People (Covey), xxiii

Sexual orientation, 93

Small teaching approach: overview of, xxiii–xxiv; structure and categories of, xxix–xxxii. *See also specific topics*

Social justice, 223–224

Social media: relationships and engagement on, 105; tools, 66, 126

Social presence: challenges with, in online courses, 80–81, 102; establishing, 79, 80–86, 102–103; with instructor personal sharing, 92, 103–104; student satisfaction relation to, 86–87; teaching presence relation to, 80–81

The Spark of Learning (Cavanagh), 154

Specifications Grading (Nilson), 98, 171

Specifications (Specs) Grading: application overview for, 169–170; for autonomy and control, student, 168–172, 177; for forums/online discussions, 170–171; self-regulation and

accountability impact of, 99, 169–170

Sports instruction, 28

Student engagement: with assessments, approaches to, 12, 30–32, 57–58; assignments broken into increments for, 32–35, 43–44; CR of content and, 35–38, 45; experience of lack of, 28–29; FAQs aiding in, 39; feedback significance for, 31, 44–45, 46, 103, 110–111; forum discussions highlights for, 41–42, 45; forum monitoring and interaction for, 40–41, 42–43, 44, 88; instructor personal sharing impact on, 90; models for, 32–43; principles of, 43–44; reflections from students on, 30–32; reminders for, 23; scaffolding for, 29–30; student interactions as opportunities for, 38–41, 44; technology and media tools to spur, 56–58; theories and research on, 29–32; time factors and management in, 34–35, 40–41, 58; tips overview for, 44–45; video announcements impact for, 14–15; during video lectures, 55

Student goals and interests: content connection with, 157–158, 183–184, 191–193, 196, 197–198; content misalignment with, 157–158; course learning objectives alignment with, 20–21; in goals contract, 141–142; motivation relation to, 160–161

Student interactions, xxx; debates impact for, 75-76; forums role in, 82, 103; identification of online, 38-41; monitoring for cultural sensitivity, 94-95; monitoring for student engagement opportunities in, 38-41, 44; structuring for feedback, 116-117; structuring in community building, 81-86, 101, 103; technology use considerations for, 85-86; video introductions by students for fostering, 82-83, 103. *See also* Forums/online discussions

Student support and guidance: accountability expectations in, 176; assignments scaffolding for, 145-148, 150; attrition rates relation to, xxvi; autonomy and independence fostered in, 161, 176, 177-178; care and empathy shown in, 95-101, 118-119, 131-132, 149, 151; on course learning objectives, 3; creativity fostering with, 84, 189-190, 196; encouragement importance in, 132-134, 148-149; feedback significance for, 9, 72-73; goals contract for, 139-142, 150; lack of, xv-xvi; mastery quizzes for, 142-144, 150; models of, 136-148; nudges for, 137-139, 150; online compared to physical classrooms, xvii-xviii, 3, 10, 11; principles for, xxiii-xxiv, 148-149; scope of, 131-132; self-reflection role in,

148; structure significance for, 149; theories and research on, 134-136; tips overview for, 150; UDL principles role in, xxiv-xxv

Students, online: anxiety for, xvi-xvii; attrition rates for, xxvi, 136, 150; backward design transparency for, 10, 11, 13-15; characteristics of successful, xxi; isolation for, 3, 44, 72, 76; motivation challenges for, 153-154; relationships for, 71-72; self-discipline skills for, xxi, 151; statistics of, xvii; support and guidance challenges for, xvii-xviii, 3, 10, 11

Summative assessments: course learning objectives and, 9; defining and examples of, 9, 110; formative assessments impact compared to, 29

Sunstein, C. R., 138

Syllabus: annotating, benefits of and tools for, 172-175, 177; assessments on understanding of, 11, 18-19; learning objectives in, 9; student autonomy and co-creation of, 172-175, 177

Synchronous live web meetings, 119-121

T

Taylor, Ann H., 212-213

Teach Students How to Learn (McGuire), 191

Teaching development/training: "apprenticeship of observation" role in, xix;

Teaching development/training: "apprenticeship of observation" role in (*continued*)
  commitment to, 204, 218; course learning objectives discussions in, 6; on cultural inclusion, 94; feedback in, 109; forum discussion highlights impact in, 41–42; lack of, impacts of, 222; for new instructors, xix, 2–3, 6–7; opportunities and requirements for, xx, 1–2, 222; passion and career in, 200–201; patience and persistence required in, xxxiii; relationships for, 216; resources and books for, 206, 214–217; on technology in classrooms, 201–202. *See also* Motivation and growth, instructor
Teaching in Higher Ed (podcast), 216
Teaching presence: establishing, 79–80, 86–92, 101–102, 103; personality revealed in, 90–92, 103–104; social presence relation to, 80–81; student course evaluations relation to, 86–87; for underserved populations, importance of, 89; video introductions/announcements to build, 87–88, 102
The Teaching Professor Conference, 217
Technology and media tools: access to, considerations of, 68, 92; alternatives to use of, 49, 68; Bloom's Taxonomy and

selection of, 64–65; challenges with, xvii, xviii; connection-making using online, 191–192, 197; copyright considerations for, 62, 63; course learning objectives alignment with, 51, 63–66, 67; downfalls with, 50; for feedback, 125–126, 127, 129; Google Docs and Slides, 51, 65, 117, 163, 175, 188, 192; grading rubrics and, 121–123, 127, 129, 172; Hypothesis, 65, 172–175, 177, 225; instructor comfort with, importance of, 65–66; intentionality in selection of, 3–4, 48, 62–63, 69; for lecture videos, 52–56, 69; models for using, 51–66; outside of LMS, xxviii, 66; personalized learning, xxviii; pervasiveness of, 47–48, 70; principles of incorporating, 67–68; problem-solving with, examples of, 51–52; scheduling, 117, 118, 120; sourcing existing, 61–63, 69; student barriers with, awareness of, 66, 67–68; student engagement creation with, 56–58; student interaction consideration with, 85–86; for syllabus annotations and co-creation, 172–175, 177; task/objective-targeted, examples of, 64–65; tasks and objectives alignment with, 51, 63–66, 67; teaching development/training on, 201–202; theories and research on, 48–51, 61; tips overview for using, 68–69; for video conferencing, 117–118; for video creation, 52–56, 69, 91, 125–126, 127, 129, 147

Thaler, R. H., 138

Theories and research, xxiii; of backward design, 7–10; on collaboration in learning process, 77–78; on community building, 77–81; on connection-making, 181–184; on feedback, 110–112, 124–125; on instructor motivation and growth, 202–204; mindset, 134–136; multimedia, 63; on peer relationships in learning, 77–78, 81, 104; scaffolding, 29–30; self-efficacy, 145–146; on student autonomy and control, 154, 159–161, 184; on student engagement, 29–32; on student motivation, 154, 184; on student support and guidance, 134–136; on technology and media tools, 48–51, 61. See also Learning science principles

Three Takeaways assignment, 20–21

Thrive Online (Riggs), xx, 215

Time factors and management: balance for personal, 109; in deadline setting, 113–115, 128; in feedback, importance of, 88–89, 103, 107–108, 111, 113–121, 127; in posting grades/scores, 89, 108; in student engagement, 34–35, 40–41, 58

Tobin, Thomas, xxiv–xxv, 212–213, 215

Transcripts, video, 15, 54–55, 68, 92

Transparency: in assignments and activities rationale, 15–17, 24; backward design, 10, 11, 13–15; of course learning objectives, 11, 13–15, 24; creating, examples of, 14–15; in group work communication, 167; resources for increasing, 16

Transparency in Learning and Teaching in Higher Ed project, 16

Trial and error approach: in course design, xxxiii; experience of, 27; structured learning compared with, 45–46

U

UDL principles. *See* Universal Design for Learning principles

Underserved populations. *See* Marginalized/underserved populations

Understanding by Design (Wiggins and McTighe), 7–8

Universal Design for Learning (UDL) principles: aligning with, 37; benefits and resources on, xxiv–xxv, 215; forums design and, 164; video introductions consideration of, 14

V

Value/relevance: connection-making strategies for, 183–184, 191–193; in group

Value/relevance: connection-making strategies for (*continued*)
work design, 166; maximizing, approaches to, 162; motivation for student and, 154, 184–185; student goals and content, 157–158

Video conferencing. *See* Phone/video conference calls

Videos/video making: assessments in tandem with, 57–58, 69; attention span considerations for, 53, 60; communication styles for, 54, 58–61, 91–92; connecting elements between, downfalls in, 55–56; copyright considerations for, 62, 63; feedback with, 123–126, 129; instructor introductions/announcements, 14–15, 58–61, 68, 87–88, 91, 102, 186; lecture, 52–56, 69, 210; polished and scripted instructor, 60–61; practice for instructor, importance of, 54, 56, 59, 60, 61, 210; practice for student, importance of, 147–148; real-time and real-life, response to, 59–60; sourcing existing media, 61–63, 69; student engagement tips for lecture, 55; for student reflections, 18; student-made, scaffolding for, 146–148; student-made forum, 164; student-made introduction, 82–83, 146–147; synchronous live web meetings, 119–121; text transcript and/or captioning for, 15, 54–55, 68, 92; tools for creating, 52–56, 69, 91, 125–126, 127, 129, 147; with YouTube, 68

Virtual office hours, 116, 119–121, 128

Vygotsky, Lev, 77–78

W

Walvoord, Barbara E., 110–112

Warner, John, 16

West, Brandon, 142

Wiggins, Grant, 7–8, 10

Winkelmes, Mary-Ann, 16

The Writer's Practice (Warner), 16

Writing instruction: assignments for, 16; instructor experience for first online course on, 28–29; interactive writing processes for, 31; survey on assignment meaningfulness in, 30–32

Y

YouTube: feedback using, 126; video announcements with, 68

Z

Zone of proximal development, 77–78, 101, 104

Zoom, 54, 64, 117

Zull, James, 160